GW00537012

PLANETARY
SPELLS & RITUALS

ABOUT THE AUTHOR

Raven Digitalis (Missoula, MT) is the author of *Shadow Magick Compendium* and *Goth Craft*. He is a Neopagan Priest and cofounder of the "disciplined eclectic" shadow magick tradition and training coven Opus Aima Obscuræ, and is a radio and club DJ of Gothic and industrial music. Also trained in Georgian Witchcraft and Buddhist philosophy, Raven has been a Witch since 1999 and a Priest since 2003, and has been an Empath all of his life. Raven holds a degree in anthropology from the University of Montana and is also an animal rights activist, black-and-white photographic artist, Tarot reader, and co-owner of Twigs & Brews Herbs, specializing in bath salts, herbal blends, essential oils, and incenses. He has appeared on the cover of *newWitch* and *Spellcraft* magazines, is a regular contributor to *The Ninth Gate* magazine, and has been featured on MTV *News* and the 'X' *Zone Radio* show.

TO WRITE TO THE AUTHOR

If you wish to contact the author or would like more information about this book, please write to the author in care of Llewellyn Worldwide and we will forward your request. Both the author and publisher appreciate hearing from you and learning of your enjoyment of this book and how it has helped you. Llewellyn Worldwide cannot guarantee that every letter written to the author can be answered, but all will be forwarded. Please write to:

Raven Digitalis
℅ Llewellyn Worldwide
2143 Wooddale Drive, Dept. 978-0-7387-1971-9
Woodbury, MN 55125-2989, U.S.A.
Please enclose a self-addressed stamped envelope for reply,
or $1.00 to cover costs. If outside the U.S.A., enclose
an international postal reply coupon.

Many of Llewellyn's authors have websites with additional information and resources. For more information, please visit our website at http://www.llewellyn.com.

RAVEN DIGITALIS

— · —

PLANETARY
SPELLS & RITUALS

— · —

Practicing Dark & Light Magick
Aligned with the Cosmic Bodies

Llewellyn Publications
Woodbury, Minnesota

First Edition
First Printing, 2010

Book design by Donna Burch
Cover design by Kevin R. Brown
Editing by Nicole Edman
Interior illustrations by Llewellyn Art Department

Llewellyn is a registered trademark of Llewellyn Worldwide, Ltd.

Library of Congress Cataloging-in-Publication Data

Digitalis, Raven.
  Planetary spells & rituals : practicing dark & light magick aligned with the cosmic bodies / Raven Digitalis. — 1st ed.
     p.   cm.
  Includes bibliographical references and index.
  ISBN 978-0-7387-1971-9
  1. Magic. 2. Astrology. I. Title. II. Title: Planetary spells and rituals.
  BF1729.M33D64 2010
  133.4'3—dc22

                                                                    2009040757

Llewellyn Worldwide does not participate in, endorse, or have any authority or responsibility concerning private business transactions between our authors and the public.

All mail addressed to the author is forwarded but the publisher cannot, unless specifically instructed by the author, give out an address or phone number.

Any Internet references contained in this work are current at publication time, but the publisher cannot guarantee that a specific location will continue to be maintained. Please refer to the publisher's website for links to authors' websites and other sources.

Llewellyn Publications
A Division of Llewellyn Worldwide, Ltd.
2143 Wooddale Drive
Woodbury, MN 55125-2989, U.S.A.
www.llewellyn.com

Printed in the United States of America

OTHER BOOKS BY THIS AUTHOR

Goth Craft: The Magickal Side of Dark Culture

Shadow Magick Compendium:
Exploring Darker Aspects of Magickal Spirituality

FORTHCOMING BOOKS BY THIS AUTHOR

Black Magick: 13 Tales of Darkness, Horror & the Occult (fiction)

Zodiacal Spells & Rituals

Empathy

CONTENTS

ACKNOWLEDGMENTS

Thank you, Estha McNevin, for insisting that I continue to deepen my knowledge of astrology and utilize its magick to transform even the darkest times. The annual tide through the planetary spheres summarizes reality; its cyclical nature seeks perfection. Astrology has, over the years, served to make the world become so much more alive for me, and to make its lessons and intricacies better perceived. Thanks for guiding my path, Estha, and for being the supreme spiritual being that you are!

Huge thanks and cosmic hugs to my spiritual sister MoonCat, whose astrological services and brilliant Astro Missive e-newsletters have long served to make me more aware of the planets and stars. Long live Cat Over the Moon Astrology!

Love and blessings to Lisa (Calantirniel), whose astrological insight has helped make the workings of reality clearer more times than I can count. Thanks for the continued advice and limitless friendship. Special thanks to Cathy Crane, Lucy-Myrtle, and Suzanne DeMarinis for giving me that "life in death, death in life" aspect. Blessed be.

Eternal blessings to my Coven, my family (both spiritual and biological), my friends, fans, and comrades. I'm blessed to know every single one of you!

Who is the Goddess?

The Goddess is the unifying force of kinship between all women, all females of all species. She is the Birth Mother, Nurturer, Lover—the very bonds of love that hold a family together through all hardship. She enhances joy, and helps us to bear our sorrows. The Goddess can be seen as that mischievous, girlish twinkle in an aged grandmother's eye. She is the ancient wisdom a young child exhibits with frightening clarity when even adults are overwhelmed by circumstances or unaware of events transpiring around them. She is the Grand Dame who lends us dignity and courage in times of great crisis and change; the strength of Character, the indomitable Will to survive, our spiritual spine, so to speak. She is, too, that natural fury that blazes in the breast of a mother who perceives a threat to her young. The Goddess is the Evolutional Director for all Her children. She strengthens all that is worthy in us; She disassembles, re-evaluates, renews, and reuses the genetic or spiritual material that has worn thin. She is the Ultimate Recycler on all levels. She is you, I, everyone; the World being *and* the great feminine principle of the Cosmos . . . The Goddess we speak of here is All That Is. All is contained within Her vast love—everything is a part of a working Whole. We need only to look within to see the light, love, and beauty of Spirit that has always been with us. We look to the Goddess of the past for strength in the present and growth in the future. For from the roots of the past we nourish the seeds of the future.

—Zanoni Silverknife, First Priestess of Georgian Witchcraft

Who is the God?

His is the common denominator that unites all men, all males of all species. He is the Hunter, Protector, Warrior, All-Father, and Bringer of Joy. He is the husband who is strong, yet tender. He enhances drive and ambition, gives us the strength to persevere. He is clever, inventive, and at times lazy. The God can be seen as the Puckish little boy; the young lad who protects his younger siblings against all odds. He is a charming lover, a steadfast man of business. He is the Mage and the King who complements the Lady Goddess in all Her aspects. As the Lady represents the fallow field, the Lord represents the farmer who tills and sows that field. His is the spirit of the explorer, the pioneer—He urges us ever onward to new horizons. His, too, is the primal force of rage, of volcanic fury, Pan: the instiller of fear and awe. He renews our love of life and reinforces our lustiness and joys in things simple and complex; the joyous child, the innovative scientist. The God is Patrix, the penetrator, and the impregnator of the receptive Matrix with the active force of His being. The two forces combine as Materials and animation to make life viable. The balance of the two forces causes the Wheel of Life to continue to turn. Without both, the Wheel is broken.

—Zanoni Silverknife, First Priestess of Georgian Witchcraft

SPELLING
IT OUT

THE PLACE OF SPELLCRAFT

Witchcraft is a living, vibrant spiritual path that filters into our every experience, interaction, emotion, and perception. There is nothing in reality that is not spiritual. Even though many non-Pagans like to believe that Witchcraft is "all about spells," this is far from true. Though I've compiled this book of spells and rituals for a number of reasons (the first being that many readers of my previous books—*Goth Craft* and *Shadow Magick Compendium*—requested more practical magick!), I must first emphasize that magickal and esoteric rituals such as these are only *extensions* of one's ever-present spirituality.

Spells are only a small aspect of Witchcraft as an art and spiritual path. I personally feel that spells are frequently overemphasized in the Craft, and people can easily come to the conclusion that magickal spirituality = spellcraft. Magick is not about *doing*, but about *being*. Spells are not the cornerstone of the Craft; instead, they are but an aspect of expressing the Mysteries of the land and the self. Simply put, spells are ceremonies designed to project a person's intention into reality.

I always like to say that the biggest ritual a person does is the cycle of their life itself, and that the grandest of all magicks is Perfect Love. We exist in this temporary physical plane for innumerable spiritual reasons, and we all have a destiny. This destiny goes hand-in-hand with what occultists, many Witches included, refer to as spiritual Will. The Will is the alignment to one's proper path in life—one's destined and higher purpose. This can easily be misunderstood. A person's Will is not one single grand achievement or revelation; the Will is something meant to be lived every moment of every day. Reality and spirituality are *not* separate entities. If a person is following their Will, everything falls into place. Truly realizing and fully aligning to one's Will is a rare thing; most of us fluctuate between spiritual alignment and imbalance.

——— • ———

Spells, prayers, rituals, and other acts of intention are significant in the process of aligning to Will because they help rebalance us. Spells affect the caster's inner psyche and external reality—two equal-opposites that go hand-in-hand in the process of existing. The Hermetic axiom As Above/So Below necessarily encompasses As Within/So Without.

Within the Craft, formal spells such as these are often seen as a route secondary to causing change via much more mundane and everyday methods. Formal spells are also usually secondary to simple, informal charms, prayers, meditations, and candle lightings.

Everyone, whether they realize it or not, is constantly using the force we call "magick" every day. Our realities are constructed by our thoughts, both conscious and otherwise, and our experiences are those that are meant to convey spiritual life lessons. Though we are constantly creating our experiences with our minds, actually ritualizing these conscious intentions—through spellcraft, prayer, visualization, or another method—attunes us even more to the process of creation and reminds us of the immense power we hold as human beings.

HOW SPELLS WORK

Witches and magicians often use a "layer cake" structure for describing the levels on which "active" or "operative" magick and spellcraft work. One example is as follows, and is a simple way of viewing the various composite forces at work. Keep in mind that this is not a definitive list of the mechanisms of magick or the cosmos. One can only truly realize how and why magick works through experience and contemplation. This list is only a brief glimpse of magickal components, and can (and probably *should*) be deconstructed, dissected, and reconstructed in a million ways!

Physical Plane

Physically gathering the components of a working and performing the working on the mundane or manifest plane. The physical plane is strictly the material used in the spell. This material comprises any and every physical factor, including the color of robes one is wearing, the gestures being used, the incense being burned, the words being said, or the current phase of the Moon. Again, these are merely physical; the magick and metaphysical properties behind the correspondences are nonphysical. The physical plane also represents the magician's work associated with the magick *within* the physical plane (be it physically ritualizing the intention or following it up in physical reality—for example, submitting résumés to employers after casting a spell for a new job) and represents the potential—or likelihood—for it to spring into existence. In other words, the goal must *not* be impossible or highly unattainable.

Mental Plane

Using thoughtforms, visualizations, and other mentally constructed components. Thoughts create reality, and accurately projecting intention through the mind encourages other planes to follow suit. Visualization is hugely important in spellcraft because the mind is the force that thinks things into existence. Shifting one's mind prompts the other planes to manifest accordingly. Magick follows intention.

Emotional Plane

Utilizing one's emotional body to send forth a spell's energy. Truly desiring change helps it naturally manifest and gives a working both spiritual and creative power. This is the bridge between thoughts and unseen energy, and it is the spark of the Divine within us. Emotions dictate our actions, thoughts, and perceptions, and casting spells aligned to the emotional body bridges the gap between the higher and lower spheres.

Etheric Plane

Working with the web of near-manifest energy that links all things in existence. The ether exists in all things physical, yet is nonphysical itself (such as the aura of the human body). I view planetary energies as etheric in nature, whereas the planets' actual placements are physical (astronomical), much like the elements themselves (earth, air, fire, and water) are physical items that also carry an etheric essence.

Astral Plane

Working with the abstract. The astral plane is greatly symbolic in nature, and tapping into humankind's wellspring of associations draws upon cosmic energy. These associations can be seen in the Qabalistic Tree of Life, among other units of association. Gods exist and "come to life" on the astral plane, seeing as they are created constructs of human experience. Abstract symbolism and associations draw upon the astral plane, or the unconscious "group mind."

Spiritual Plane

The ultimate plane of unity; the source of all things. Terms such as *destiny, karma, Gnosis, Kether, Spirit, Oneness,* and *Godhood* are all used to describe this. The spiritual plane is the ultimate paradox, as it is everything and nothing simultaneously. The spiritual plane encompasses our individual karma as well as cosmic destiny. This plane affirms that *all is God.* Spellcraft taps into this force of creation and destiny to encourage manifestation and change on all levels.

When casting, one must suspend strict rationality and disbelief to some extent but also mustn't view the process as something based purely in fantasy and imagination. If a person casts a spell with a heavy amount of uncertainty, fear, anxiety, moral dilemma, or is unfocused while doing so, they will get the same in return. In all ways, you get what you give, and this holds true for spellcraft. If one knows, beyond the shadow of a doubt, that their magick "works," it will do just that. Magick greatly revolves around intention and the knowledge of a working's success. Spellcraft does not, of course, depend on the "recipe" alone.

Though successful spellcraft boils down to intention, intention is not the only factor that deserves attention in the process. For example, let's say that Billy wanted to perform a spell for money. For the spell, he is to light a green candle, put herbs associated with money at its base, and write the desired outcome on parchment with dragon's blood ink. However, let's say Billy only had a black candle, belladonna, and bat's blood ink available as tools. If he were to substitute the black candle for the green one, belladonna for the abundance herbs, and bat's blood ink for dragon's blood ink, the spell would be likely to fail simply because the ingredients were not aligned to the purpose. However, if he were to observe the necessity of aligning *tools* to *purpose*, he could modify the spell by using the black candle to banish debt and the belladonna to absorb the sadness associated with not having enough. He could then write the name of the lack (and its associated woes) with the bat's blood, and finish the spell by burning the paper and throwing the herbs and candle stub off the side of a bridge. (Certainly, it would be advisable for him to also perform manifestation magick to fill the energetic hole of the things that were banished.)

In the above example of a simple spell, we helped Billy use what he had to modify the spell for his purposes. It's essential to have a realization of correspondences and to project one's intention through those correspondences to magnify and amplify the magick. If everything you are using is aligned to the purpose at hand—including the spell's herbs, stones, colors, spirits, guides, gods, or guardians being summoned, the current astrological configuration, the stage of the Moon, and so on— the only missing ingredients are intention, focus, and willpower.

Again, one must follow up magick with real-life action. Spells, no matter how involved and complex, are not a substitute for mundane action. The mundane plane is where our physical bodies operate and where we can best assist in the manifestation of magickal intention. As they say, one cannot cast a spell for a new job without filling out applications.

DARK & LIGHT?

As the subtitle of this book implies, spells of both a "light" and a "dark" nature are explored here. But what does this mean? Such terms are relative, and are loaded with all sorts of connotations, both personal and cultural. It would be redundant of me to rehash descriptions and explorations of "light" and "dark" energies, as I've done so extensively in my first two books (particularly *Shadow Magick Compendium*). Let it suffice to say that neither term has a strict definition, and that both forces work together to create successful magick and a spiritual life.

Reality cannot exist with either shadow or light alone. Neither force is "evil," and neither is better or worse than the other. Duality is greatly an illusion; both light and darkness are in everything. When thinking of these forces, keep in mind the symbolism of the Taoist Yin and Yang.

Life itself is a constant balancing act between opposing yet complementary forces.

Some spiritual practitioners—namely those with *extreme* "New Age" leanings—tend to view darkness as destruction, pain, and spiritual blindness. While these things are certainly aspects of darkness, there's much more to them. I see darkness as the blank slate from which all things manifest. I see the force of darkness as beautiful, mysterious, and Otherworldly . . . as the subconscious mind, the night sky, and the world of spirits and dreaming. At the same time, darkness can represent negative and destructive things.

Similarly, some practitioners view light as a supreme spiritual force, an ultimate force of healing and consciousness. While that is true, light can also be blinding and illusory. Personally, most of my work stems from darkness, in a shamanic sense. I find it much more healing to journey into the dark recesses of the psyche than to compensate imbalance with light. Still, I realize that everyone's method of spiritual alignment and healing is different, and that each of us is on our own individual path to awareness and connection to the Divine. It's only when one gets caught in any extreme that misalignment follows.

In terms of the spells in this book, ones that I would term "dark" include those that are focused on working through trauma, through suicidal impulses, those for cursing, and so on. "Light" spells include things like spells for study, love, divination, and other such subjects. However, as I said, such terms are relative and rely greatly on personal definition. Labels should only be used as easy references, not as terminologies to cling to or become reliant upon.

Spells can be serious and dire, or they can be lighthearted and fun. They can be healing and theurgic, or destructive and difficult. This book presents a combination of these things, and I leave it up to each reader to come to his or her own conclusions about utilizing the magick for one's own purposes and according to one's own code of ethics.

PLANNING
& PROCEDURE

RITUAL PREP

When preparing to do a ritual of any sort, many things need to be considered. It's extremely beneficial to plot a procedure accordingly, ensuring that everything is in alignment to the intention at hand. I'm certainly one to advocate proper, and even in-depth, occult correspondences in magick, but I am not one to endorse becoming paranoid about everything being exactly, perfectly "right."

Magick is both an art and a science, and spellcraft blends intellect and intuition. Erring too much to one side of the spectrum can inhibit the success of any working. For instance, if you believe yourself to be of a more intellectual and scientific mind, try pushing yourself to bring out your creative and spontaneous side in ritual.

——— • ———

"Emergency magick" should also be mentioned: if something comes up that requires you to perform magick, prayer, or spellcraft as immediately as possible, it would be wise to simply perform the magick in the moment rather than stressing about the zodiacal configuration of the day or all of the spell's ideal ingredients. When you don't have much time to prepare, you must work with what you have. Remember that all the components are only tools that amplify the intention being woven into reality. *You* are the magick, and sometimes rituals need to be performed quickly, regardless of planetary and material alignments.

If, however, you have ample time to prepare for a ritual procedure, be very precise when calculating the best time. For example, a spell for success in communication would be best performed when the Sun or Moon is in an air sign (air ruling communication and the intellect). One could be more precise and hone this air sign to an additional alignment: because Gemini, Libra, and Aquarius are all ruled by air, examine them further. Gemini is governed by Mercury, Libra by Venus, and Aquarius by Uranus (or Saturn in classical astrology). Because this spell is to be concerned with communication, it would be most ideal to select Gemini because of its Mercurial alignments. Or, if the spell was for communication in a romantic partnership, for example, one would best choose to utilize Libra because it is ruled by Venus, the planet of love.

One could wait until the Moon and/or Sun is in Gemini to perform this communication spell. If you feel the need to perform this spell before the Sun shifts into Gemini (which, of course, only happens once a year and only for four weeks), you may instead choose to wait until the Moon is in Gemini, which occurs much more frequently. If, however, there is a deadline and this spell should be performed as soon as possible, the caster may choose an astrological *hour* of Gemini. The caster could also wait until Wednesday (governed by Mercury) and/or perform the spell at sunrise (to represent new beginnings) or during the waxing Moon (to represent "increasing" energies). In any example, the caster should be mindful of the *additional* astrological configurations occurring at the time. What sign is the Moon in? The Sun? What day of the week is it? Is there a planet in retrograde? If there is a particular time frame in which the spell must be cast, the caster should incorporate and utilize the current astrological energies rather than just disregarding them. For information on further reading on correspondences, astrology, and occult systems, please see Appendix 1.

The caster of this spell may intuitively feel the desire to further exalt aspects of air, and may decide to summon elemental spirits associated with air (such as sylphs, the eastern wind Eurus, a god of the Sun, etc.) and will face the east during ritual. Because elemental correspondences are virtually endless, there are a multitude of routes the practitioner can take when choosing appropriate spellcasting components, times, tools, and methods. There are also a number of ways the practitioner can hone the energies to precisely fit his or her magickal purpose—the most common way to do this is to utilize planetary energies (schools of esoteric Qabalah, Hermeticism, and alchemy had mastered and continue to master such categorizations through the cataloguing of all aspects of reality). The complexity of spellcraft is up to the individual caster, and everyone must create or modify spells according to what they personally know.

ASTROLOGICAL TIMING

The history of astrology and planetary magick is vast, hearkening back to the beginnings of human civilization. Mythos surrounding the cosmic bodies is interwoven with creation mythology worldwide, and the archetypal alignments of the celestial forces are vast, spanning virtually every culture imaginable, both past and present, to some degree. It's widely accepted that planets influence energy (physical, mental, emotional) beyond simply the Moon and Sun, whose effects are obvious and palpable.

In the West, astrology and astronomy were once indistinguishable, operating simultaneously as a conglomerate science. Astrology is ever-evolving, and this particular book makes use of *modern* astrology as opposed to *classical* astrology. These two Western astro "types," as well as descriptions of Vedic astrology, Chinese astrology, and so on, can be explored in some of the reference books mentioned in Appendix 1. It is assumed that all readers are familiar with basic astrology, including their own natal zodiacal charts, or will familiarize themselves before performing the rituals aligned in this book.

When timing a spell, and in particular when utilizing a spell from this book, the planetary influences present must be given attention. For starters, be sure you have an astrological ephemeris or a calendar that gives, at the very least, the Moon sign transits. Aside from a complex astrological ephemeris, ideal daily planners include *Llewellyn's Witches' Calendar*, *Llewellyn's Astrological Calendar*, and the annual *Witches' Almanac* published by Rhode Island's Witches' Almanac, Ltd. There are also many astrology-centered ephemerides and planners which give complete and precise astrological information that other planners may not. Regardless of calendar, it's important to know what is going on astrologically each day. If you use the Internet, you may wish to subscribe to astrological update forums or newsletters, which give precise information about certain planetary shifts, both simple and complex. (I personally recommend the accurate and eccentric—and free!—Astro Missive email updates from *MoonCat! Astrology*. See www.catoverthemoon.com for more information.) You may also wish to find daily email updates that give you exact astrological information based on your own unique natal chart.

Please note that zodiacal and astrological correspondences are listed in Appendix 2 of this book—just flip to the back for easy reference while reading this section and while determining times to work magick.

Remember that the Sun influences the external or projected, while the Moon influences the internal or receptive. It's important to note which sign the Moon and Sun are in at any given time for spellcraft, as well as any other planetary occurrences going on (such as a planet in retrograde motion, a planetary opposition, and so on). Again, this takes much more time to describe than I have here; astrological sciences are incredibly vast! (I'll explore these things a bit more in my eventual follow-up book *Zodiacal Spells & Rituals*.)

To simplify, let's take an example from the book. Let's say I wanted to perform the spell "Sweeten Up & Chill Out: To Mend Quarrels with Another." Because the spell falls under the Venus chapter, it's correct to assume that the spell is aligned to Venusian energies. Therefore, I'll utilize the planet in my spellwork. First, I'll consider the energy of the situation in my circumstances. Because I'm utilizing the vibes of Venus, I can choose to work with the signs Taurus or Libra, seeing as Venus rules both. Looking at the qualities of the signs (again, see Appendix 2 if necessary), I see that Taurus deals with fruition, strength, fertility, abundance, and is associated with the element of earth (stability, structure). I see that Libra represents balance, diplomacy, art, and other qualities, and is associated with air (the mind, communication). Because, let's say, I've been arguing with a good friend and wish to use the spell to help mend the situation, I decide that Libra would be the most ideal sign to utilize. Had I been arguing with a lover or family member, I might choose to utilize Taurus instead.

Let's say that it also happens to be New Year's Day today. This means, of course, that the Sun is in the sign Capricorn (December 22–January 20). Because of this, I'll wait until the Moon is in Libra to take advantage of Venusian energies. Because the Sun is in Capricorn, which represents structure, work, discipline, and other qualities, and is associated both with earth and Saturn, I decide to draw upon Capricornian energy in the spell as well, and modify the spell to work with its energy. For example, I may incorporate an additional prayer or representation of "working together," which can be seen as Capricornian, and I may add some extra stones to the ritual for earth, or paint the Capricorn and Saturn symbol on the spell's items.

So, in this example, I'm working with the Moon in Libra to assist with inner balance (and draw upon the energy of Venus, since the spell is in the Venus chapter), and I am working with the Sun in Capricorn (simply because it happens to be in Capricorn during the month I want to cast), and I have modified the spell according to these energies. Great!

For some people, this may be enough of an alignment. For those who wish to take it a couple steps further and hone the energy even more, they can follow the daily and hourly alignments. For example, let's say that the conflict I had with the friend was highly emotional in nature. Thus, I would like to perform the spell on a Monday, which is ruled by the Moon. Since I already decided to perform the spell during a day in which the Moon is in Libra, I check my calendar to see if one of those days is a Monday. But let's say that the next Moon in Libra cycle occurs on a Tuesday through Thursday. Drats! Because of this, I look at these daily planetary energies: Tuesday is governed by Mars, Wednesday by Mercury, and Thursday by Jupiter. Okay: no Venus there either (since Venus governs Friday). Looking at the qualities of these three planets, I realize that I don't want to perform the spell on that Tuesday (because Mars has aggressive qualities, the very thing the spell is working *against*). Thursday (Jupiter) might be a good option, but I decide that Wednesday is best, seeing that Mercury oversees communication (and can thus assist in forming better communication between myself and my friend). Cool.

Finally, I'll choose a planetary hour during which to perform the spell. Following the directions given, I calculate the daily increments of time (see the description on page 16) and decide to perform the spell during a daytime (as opposed to nighttime) hour of Libra, because I really want to draw upon and exalt that sign's energy for the spell—not least because the spell is listed in the Venus section, and, again, Libra is governed by Venus. (If I had been arguing with a roommate or family member, I might choose Cancer because of its representing home and family.) If I feel that the element of communication is particularly important in this spell, and since I'm planning on utilizing Mercury's energy within the working anyway,

I might choose an hour of Virgo or Gemini instead—both signs being ruled by Mercury. (And if I was doing this, I would probably lean toward Gemini simply because of its "twins" association, and its alignments with "duality," which would aid in the spell's success.)

Now, I've aligned the spell as follows: Sun in Capricorn, Moon in Libra, during the day of Mercury, and during the daytime hour of Libra.

Capricorn's energy will aid in grounding the situation (earth) and working together. The Sun is in Capricorn, meaning that the greater or external energy of the spell will be Capricornian.

Because the spell is listed in the Venus chapter, I've chosen a time when the Moon is in Libra. This means that the internal energy of the spell will be concerned with reaching balance (Libra) and will utilize the mind (air).

Because I am using Wednesday as a working day, Mercury will aid in communication.

Because I am performing the spell during a daytime hour of Libra, this sign's energy of balance will be emphasized even more.

So, the spell's astrological alignments are Capricorn, Libra, Mercury, and Libra. This can also be translated as Saturn, Venus, Mercury, and Venus. It can also be looked at as earth, air, air, air. As you can see, there is a zodiacal abundance of air energy in this spell, which means that the applicable qualities of air in this spell (which are mostly that of communication) will be particularly accessible. Thus, I may wish to alter the spell to focus more on energies of "healing through communication." Assuming I work each of these zodiacal energies into the spell, even slightly, the working has potential to be extremely successful.

Confused yet? If so, try slowly reading through these last few pages a few times, ensuring first that you have a basic understanding of astrology. If you can follow my descriptions, you'll be able to construct a cosmically aligned spell or ritual almost automatically after a short period of time. (However, my guess is that a majority of readers are already familiar with this sort of ritual planning.)

If this book is your first dose of astrological timing, I recommend *seriously* getting to know the planets and signs—something beneficial to every Witch and magician. Delve deeply into astrology if you wish; there are tons of resources out there, and the topic is supremely fascinating and significant. Again, please see Appendix 1 for further reading on astrology and Appendix 2 for zodiacal and astrological correspondences.

Also, if you're relatively new to astrology, don't feel too intimidated by all this zodiacal and planetary stuff. It takes time and dedication to learn, and there is always more to learn on top of that (such is the nature of occultism and spirituality!). Spells can be as complex or simple as you wish. For the purpose of this book, however, I recommend *at the very least* you make sure that, when you perform a spell, either the Moon sign or Sun sign is one that is ruled by the planet under which the spell you're performing is listed. If you perform a spell at any ol' time, it won't go *wrong*; it will simply not be as honed as it could be. Keep in mind that simple charms, prayers, meditations, candle lightings, and so on, probably require very little astrological timing, if any. Again, coding your spell astrologically by use of the Sun sign, Moon sign, planetary day, and planetary hour are ways to deeply hone and intend your magick: they are, like anything else, tools. *You* are the magick.

These astrological hours, used in a variety of magickal systems, are aligned to daily increments of time. The increments of time during which each planet has daily (or nightly) influence are different each day. Rather than being increments of 60-minute hours, the times take a little calculation.

I'll give an example. Grabbing the newspaper (or looking on an online weather site), I see that sunrise today is at 7:55 am and sunset is at 5:46 pm. From here, I must determine exactly how many minutes exist between sunrise and sunset, and between sunset and sunrise. Using my calculator, I discover that between 7:55 am and 5:46 pm there are 591 minutes. Because there are 1,440 minutes in a 24-hour period, I take the above minutes of sunset and subtract them from 1,440. This gives me 849. So, my daytime minutes are 591 and my nighttime minutes are 849.

Because the "hours" are in divisions of 12, I divide each number by 12. Doing so, this makes my daytime increments 49.25 minutes and my nighttime increments 70.75 minutes. These are the figures I'll be using to calculate today's daytime and nighttime hours.

Let's say that today is Thursday and that I wish to work my magick during a daytime hour of Venus. The first thing I do is look on the chart of planetary hours found in Appendix 2. For Thursday-daytime-Venus, I will use the fourth planetary hour. Because my daytime increment is approximately 49 minutes, I calculate when the fourth hour will begin. I know the first hour lasts 49 minutes and begins at sunrise (7:55 am). This means the second hour will begin at 8:44 am, the third at 9:33, the fourth at 10:22, the fifth at 11:11, and so on. Because I'm using Venus, the fourth hour, I will perform my spell between 10:22 am and 11:11 am. The same type of calculation, using the approximately 71-minute figure in this case, can be done for nighttime hours.

ALTERING CONSCIOUSNESS

Because this book is centered on personal ritualism, I can't do without a mention of the importance of consciousness alteration. The physical act of casting a spell is but a metaphor. Spells operate on a number of planes, and the caster's state of being is of utmost importance. Witches and magicians must be aware of their minds at *all times*, both inside and outside of ritual. If, during spellcraft, one's mind is wandering away from the intention at hand, the flow of energy becomes interrupted. One way of stopping this from happening is to enter a ritual state of consciousness, wherein the practitioner is entirely and undividedly focused on the intention at hand.

Without the practitioner engaging in meditation and the altering of consciousness, it's likely that a spell will not work. In ritual, we have the option of either controlling or surrendering to the forces at hand. One's approach to this option depends on the purpose of the ritual. To control is to externalize, whereas surrender is internalization. Most rituals should contain a blending of the internal and external. Celebratory rituals like Sabbats are generally more external in nature, whereas personally significant spellcastings are oftentimes more internal or shamanic.

Because Witchcraft is, at its core, rooted in shamanism, one must take a serious look at some original and existing shamanic techniques. The altering of consciousness is something that is promoted in any mystically inclined religion, but is also a term that is misunderstood. It's only from experience that we can learn our own methods of expanding and changing "normal" perception. It's also important to decide exactly *how* altered one wishes to make their consciousness. One must alter their perception in the way that works best for them personally.

Ecstatic dance, trance drumming, fasting, sexual magick, pain induction, and deep meditation are all methods of altering consciousness. It's not enough to "do" a spell—one has to set aside daily thoughts and distractions and fully immerse oneself in the energetic current they're tapping into. When doing this during a ritual of any type, it tells the mind and the Universe that you are *intending* to enter a ritualistic atmosphere that is apart from usual waking perception. Entering Gnosis, or a mystical state of consciousness, is not achieved instantly. Realizing exactly how to enter a mystical state of consciousness takes time, practice, and sometimes the pushing of one's own perceived limits.

Some practitioners use drugs, particularly cannabis (marijuana) or alcohol (often wine or ale) to enter altered states of consciousness before a ritual. The moderate and mindful pre-ritual use of substances is suggested in traditional Gardnerian Wicca. Additionally, some Witches and magicians prefer extreme natural-drug experiences when performing an intense, life-altering ritual, such as a rite of passage or rebirthing experience. This draws on shamanic techniques, though everybody's responses to natural substances vary, which is why this method of consciousness alteration must be carefully planned and intelligently utilized.

Many people abstain from drug use before ritual, feeling as though it has potential to change the working too much. Some practitioners prefer to use substances only when performing alone or during certain celebrations. Again, everybody's response is different, and one should utilize the mind-changing techniques that not only legitimately work, but work best for one's own constitution.

SO MOTE IT BE

PERSONALIZING THE MAGICK

Please don't do these workings exactly as they are written. Yep, I said it. While these spells and rituals are specifically planned and formulated, I would be foolish to ask that they all be followed to the letter. Frankly, I would rather encourage readers to *not* practice any of the spells "by the book," but to experiment, add, subtract, and personally modify each procedure. If the working doesn't carry a large amount of personal significance, its results (both within and without the ritual itself) will be incomplete. Without personalizing the magick and imbuing them with the very essence of the practitioner, the workings remain empty. We must enliven our crafts and allow them to inspire and instigate significant life changes for ourselves and the world!

Spells should be individualized and independently significant to the practitioner. If they're not, they're only other people's operations. Magick is personal, and every act should be personal*ized*. In movies, we see people following spells (usually supposedly ancient, *eeevil* spells) to the letter, for fear of saying the wrong syllable or accidentally adding a raccoon's nose to the cauldron instead of his toes. While it can be said that adding a tablespoon of salt has a different outcome than a tablespoon of sugar for cooking, baking, and alchemy, magick doesn't always work that way. If I get the intuition to add mugwort instead of thyme, I'm gonna do it (that is, assuming that the correspondences are similar for the spell's purpose).

If I don't know the meaning of *Ablanathanalba* and cannot find a definition in any of my books, from any of my teachers or peers, or on a reliable Internet page, I'm probably not going to say it, even if the spell tells me to. If a spell tells me to blend fifteen particular herbs, but I can only acquire eight of them, you betchya I'll do the spell without the other seven (or I'll do some research and find accurate substitutes for them). If a working calls for black cat hair, yet I only have an orange kitty, I'll be using her hair as a substitute (because it is feline, even if the color is different). Or, if I have a black dog and no cat, I might use his hair because of the color (that is, if the spell's focus is on *black animal* hair rather than *feline* hair specifically.) Part of magick's beauty is its versatility!

The main concern of the spells in this book is the *archetypes*, hence the planetary alignments found throughout. The spells found in this book don't follow any particular tradition or pantheon. Instead, they draw from a variety of sources and are open to be tweaked and expanded upon by each practitioner.

There are countless ways to modify spells, but be careful that your modification doesn't interfere with the intended purpose of the spell. As most readers are probably aware, lighting the wrong color candle, mispronouncing a word of power, or using the wrong color altar cloth will *not* mess up a spell . . . unless you believe it will!

—— · ——

Some spells are more specific than others. Some are more "scientific," and others are more "intuitive." Let's say, for example, I'm enchanting an altar to Mercury (or an associated god) and the working calls for some cassia oil. Let's say that I have no cassia (or cinnamon) oil, but I do have peanut oil. Because peanut is not aligned to Mercury, I will refrain from using it. Instead, I may do some research and decide to use flax seed or peppermint essential oil as a substitute, simply because of its alignment to Mercury. If I don't have (and cannot procure) any of these, I may simply use mineral oil or something else that is energetically unfixed.

Let's also say that I must dedicate the altar *this* week, but neither the Moon nor Sun are anywhere close to being in Gemini or Virgo (ruled by Mercury). Instead, I may choose to wait until Wednesday (the day of the week ruled by Mercury) and will choose a Mercurial hour of the day (or night) in which to perform the dedicatory ritual (see page 16).

THINGS TO CONSIDER

For those who are quite experienced in spellcasting, the following list will probably come as second nature. For those who are newer to spellcasting or the magickal path (or who feel they could simply use a refresher), these points are of extreme importance to consider before utilizing spellcraft.

Is the spell's intention destined to occur?

As I mentioned before, a person's spiritual Will is akin to their life's destiny. To align to one's own Will is to come in sync with life's higher, destined, and God-connected cycle; this plays into every moment of one's life. True Will is similar to the *Tao* in Taoism: the Tao is both contained in and constitutes all things in life, and aligning to the Tao is the true path to happiness and destiny. Chaos magick calls this force *Kia*, seeing it as the constant, formless, nonattached foundation of consciousness. Aligning to true Will obliterates the ego-barrier between self and Universe, bringing the magician closer to Kia or the Tao. Complete, absolute, and sustained alignment to one's Will can be called Enlightenment or One-ness, though most magicians and Witches shy away from the terms.

In terms of "active" or "operative" magick, if a manifestation is absolutely not spiritually meant to occur, the greater hand of the Universe—the Fates—will redirect it. In other words, if a spell does not come to light, ask yourself if the spell is aligned to your Will. Like the Wiccan Rede says, "Do as thou Wilt." This *Wilt* refers to Aleister Crowley's definition of *Will*. If you perform magick that is not "meant to be," it simply will not come to pass.

Are you interfering with another person's free will?

A couple of the spells in this book, for example, can potentially be used to harm an undeserving person—hence my mention of free will. Personal accountability and responsibility for one's actions are highly advocated in Neopagan and occult paths. Magick is a neutral force; it can used by anyone for any purpose. However, this doesn't mean that it *should* be. Like everything in life, it's what you *do* with it that matters. Magick is crossculturally intertwined with spirituality for a reason—ethics, belief, and perception are its guiding forces. You get what you give, plain and simple. If someone's magickally harming another who may or may not deserve it, where are their dignity and morals? We all know the difference between right and wrong, and the all-seeing eye of Karma ensures that a person's experience matches the intention they emit. Use cosmic and personal power wisely. One should not have to interfere with another person's free will for personal fulfillment, nor should something as silly as revenge take the place of forgiveness, or harm take the place of health. All styles of magick have their time and place, but it's up to the practitioner to objectively determine the best possible magick to be used for all involved.

Are you casting for the proper thing?

This draws on the point above. Basically, one must get to the root of an issue before casting a spell. As a result, you may be tempted to perform a spell (from this book or elsewhere), but it would be unsuccessful without tackling deeper issues first. For example, say you are casting a spell for happiness in the workplace. A good intention, to be sure! However, before casting the spell, you may think about your workplace and realize that the cause of this desire for change is due to the negativity of your coworkers. Perhaps a spell to fend them off and protect against them would be more appropriate in this case! Additionally, perhaps a spell for peace in the workplace will actually help you get a *different* job where these people won't have to be dealt with. Oftentimes, it's one's own perceptions, rather than the external world, that are in need of transformation. We have to be as straightforward in our perceptions as possible. If we remove our egos, as well as underlying emotions and ulterior motives, spellcraft can be highly successful.

Consider the factors and plan your intention carefully. If you have skeletons in your closet and unrecognized inner torments pertaining to the spell—and the spell is not directly focused on these shadow traits— you're probably doing the wrong sort of working. Additionally, be absolutely certain that you're not casting magick impulsively, and that you've thought about the working for a good amount of time beforehand.

Is the spell realistic and attainable?

The spells listed here are attainable. One of the most important aspects of a spell should be its level of attainability, which is something to consider when structuring your own workings or building from preexisting ones. If something has *potential* to occur in reality, it's likely that the practitioner can make it happen. The further a spell's intention gets from a realistic, attainable outcome, the less likely the spell is to "work," for lack of a better term. Casting a spell to levitate or shoot fireballs, or something equally silly, will not work because it's unrealistic and divorced from the laws of the physical plane. If you add focuses to the spells in this book, be sure the goals are realistic and attainable.

Is there an easier or more practical solution than spellcasting?

Sometimes the most simple solution to a dilemma is the solution to go with. Many practitioners use spellcasting and charmery in conjunction with mundane activities, never relying entirely on either one. So, before you cast, consider whether or not you're pursuing all potential avenues in regular life.

Newbies often come to magick and spellcraft looking for an easy way out. Magick is not a simple solution to complex problems. However, it can serve to project those intentions into the world and start the cosmic ball rolling toward a particular goal. Generally, spells take time and additional effort to manifest. The path to manifestation, whether magickal or otherwise, takes steps and steady action. (It's also worth mentioning that workings of Gnosis, theurgy, and meditation are *magickal* but are not spellcasting by definition. They are *experiential*, which is why they can instantly "work.")

Are you covering all bases in your magick?

A person's spell should precisely match what they're aiming to achieve. When casting, all bases for the outcome should be covered. When casting positive spells, many practitioners like to recite words somewhere in the ritual such as "for the greater good and harm to none," and so on. While it's true that specifying your intention via tools, words, zodiacal configuration, and so on is important for the procedure's intention, it's equally important to pay attention to the details. Be acute, be precise, and be direct. Magick takes the path of least resistance, and it's important to carefully contemplate the spell and its components before actually casting. Spells can go awry if the intention is not specified as much as possible. In other words, a vague ritual can produce a vague outcome!

SOME NOTES

The following bulleted list is a review of some spellcasting details pertinent to the spells included in this book:

- Prior to spellcasting or ritualizing, thoroughly read through the working multiple times (unless you're entirely creating one on your own). Decide how you wish to alter the working to your purposes, and get creative in the process. Only you can decide how simple or complex the working will be.

- Depending on your approach, it may be a good idea to memorize a working before performing. Or, you could record the ritual on an audio device and play it during the spell. If you can avoid glancing at the pages too much while weaving magick, it will help keep the energy of the working constant and unbroken.

- All of these spells are designed for solitary use. However, they can easily be modified for couple or group workings. Just take a pencil to the pages! Indeed, I encourage you to mark up this book and make it your own.

- Many of the components presented in the spells, such as words said, tools used, and so on, are carefully aligned to the planetary energies under which the spells fall. You may not understand all the symbolism or components, and may not choose to use them all as a result, which is perfectly understandable. However, I can assure that they are accurate to the best of my knowledge should you choose to use them. Additionally, don't feel as though you *have* to use every tool I've written. If a mixture lists ten herbs, for example, and you only have five of them, use what you have (or additionally procure the rest if you'd like). Again, the alignments are aplenty so the practitioner can modify the working.

- It's best to perform these rituals skyclad (nude) if the situation permits. If there are too many issues with doing that (either personal or circumstantial), consider wearing particular ritual garb or robes.

It's ideal to wear clothing aligned to the working at hand (in terms of color and appearance), but many practitioners have a single robe or cloak they prefer for all magick. If nothing else, just wear black (Raven writes, in typical Goth manner).

- When spells are complete, dispose of the "remains" properly. Unless otherwise instructed, you may burn, bury, or sink the components of the spell (herbs, stones, candle stubs, etc.), unless your intuition tells you otherwise. Consider the energetic implications of burying (grounding), burning (transforming), and sinking (washing away), and consider any environmental effects (in other words, littering is bad juju). Additionally, my editors reminded me that it's a good idea to call your utility company before digging any significant holes; you don't want to encounter any buried electrical or gas lines!

- When using a candle in a spell, it's best to allow it to burn down fully. Keep an eye on it when you're doing this, and also exercise proper fire safety when working with candles or incense when you're out in nature. If you extend a spell over a series of days, you may wish to relight the candle throughout that period of time, keeping a watchful eye on the fire each time. But don't blow out the flame—it will extinguish the magick! (Just kidding; that's superstitious hogwash.)

- If a spell calls for a black candle, ensure that the candle is *true* black. That is, one should not use, for example, a white or red Halloween candle that simply has a black wax shell on it. Additionally, if you're to be using a yellow or Sun-aligned candle for a spell, a beeswax candle is second to none!

- Spells should be performed uninterrupted in a sacred space. Whether this is a special spot in nature, a temple space, or before an altar in the living room, the location should be consecrated, sacred, inspirational, and spiritually mood-setting.

- Use your own circle-casting method when performing a spell, or modify it to fit the purpose. Instead of reviewing circle-casting methods, elemental calls, the Watchtowers, and directional summonings, I'll assume that every reader is experienced in creating his or her own sacred ceremonial atmosphere. If you are unfamiliar with the ins and outs of Neopagan circle casting, please read introductory Witchcraft books (such as those suggested in Appendix 1) before performing any spells. Through experimentation, one should discover the best way to create their sacred space.

- It's good practice to perform protective and grounding exercises prior to casting a circle. You can do energy work around yourself, smudge with a wand of sage, and/or perform something more formal, such as the Qabalistic Cross, the Lesser Banishing Ritual of the Pentagram (LBRP), the Greater Banishing Ritual of the Pentagram, the Middle Pillar Ritual, and so on.

- Finally, complete all circles with gratitude. The gods and spirits are very much a part of us, yet are still their own sentient and conscious forces. Gratitude is one of the strongest feelings a person can have. Leave appropriate offerings (food, drink, incense, herbs, flowers, or such) at the closing of every spell. Give deep thanks and reverence to those forces of nature without which we would not be.

Happy Casting!

~R~

Chapter 1

— · —

THE
SUN

— · —

THE SUN
Zodiacal rulership: Leo
Color association: Yellow
Sephira: Tiphareth
Number: 6
Day: Sunday
Archetypes: Solar God, the Holy Child
Themes: Power, life, expression, vitality, strength, health, creativity, esteem, joy, manifestation, motivation, confidence, magnanimity, leadership, fatherhood, masculinity

Falling Façades: Removing the Masks You Wear

Throughout our lives, we learn ways to cope with our experience. Sometimes these *modi operandi* are learned from others, but more often than not they are gained through our own successes and failures in life. In terms of daily operation, it would be silly to think that we all don't—even to a slight or subconscious degree—alter our behavior depending on the people we're interacting with in any given circumstance.

As a prime example, and one that certainly makes sense to readers, we naturally alter the words and descriptive depth we use when discussing our esoteric viewpoints with fellow practitioners, as opposed to discussing them with those completely unfamiliar with magick or Earth-based spirituality. For one, those who are unfamiliar with our path, regardless of how open they are, simply won't understand certain terminologies, ritual procedures, and so on. Instead, we communicate with terms and concepts they comprehend. As another example, if a store manager was training an employee, he or she would use different terms, descriptions, and examples than that same person would use at a managerial meeting. The examples are endless, and this communicative adaptation is something we do regularly in varying degrees.

Depending on our routine, we interact with a wide variety of people on a daily basis. Thus, we somewhat change our methods of interaction based on our immediate situation. This is part of life, and it's nothing fake or inauthentic. However, if we become accustomed to acting a certain way, our minds may become accustomed to this behavior and the effects it produces.

Psychologically, this can be considered a reaction to positive reinforcement: if we act a certain way in life, we can be rewarded with praise, respect, or material items. In a sense, this could very easily be a throwback to our primal survival instinct, which tells us that we must remain "on top" to prevent our demise. Hiding certain aspects of our personalities can produce a comfortable illusion of empowerment. If we know ourselves and our minds (and thus our vulnerabilities) more than others possibly could, it gives a sense of protection from the outside world. Knowing oneself is a priority to the humble spiritual seeker.

The false projection of personality is illusory. Aside from instances in extreme situations, putting up a façade in life is dreadfully unhealthy. In an extreme scenario, constantly altering one's personality is outright manipulation—not only of others, but of oneself! On the other end of the spectrum, *never* altering one's personality or communicative methods can lead to misunderstanding and alienation. As with everything in life, striking a balance is the key.

What it boils down to is this: are you being *yourself*? Do you change the way you respond to people based on what works for *them* in the moment, or what works for *you*? What are your motivations behind the changes you make? If you find yourself putting up different social masks and façades, and you recognize this as being unhealthy, dishonest, or deceitful, you may want to consider performing this working.

Stepping Back & Further Application

The primary reason for performing this spell is for releasing social aspects of yourself that are not aligned to your true personality.

What are the roots of your masks, walls, and façades? Where did this behavior originate? How will you function without the aid of these energetic walls? How will your relationships (of all kinds) change if your personality becomes more authentic in any given situation? Will you be able to hold true to your views and emotions, even when it becomes tempting to act differently? These are some things to seriously ponder when preparing for a ritual of this sort.

This spell is a good one to perform multiple times. Additionally, constantly monitoring your daily interaction is key. When, in your daily life, you find yourself putting up one of these masks, bring awareness to the behavior and alter it accordingly. Performing this spell will not remove all these masks instantly. Instead, you must regularly and actively weave the spell's metaphorical work into your life.

Supplies

- a yellow candle
- a stick of cedar, frankincense, or sandalwood incense
- a number of plain plastic masks, either full-face or masquerade masks. These must all be the same size, thin, and should be transparent or white. Additionally, the masks should fit comfortably on top of one another, and should have an elastic cord on the back so that you can wear them all simultaneously.
- a black permanent marker
- a 3×3-foot black veil

Notes

- I don't normally endorse using plastic of any type in ritual work. However, these masks will be reused and are appropriate to the working at hand.
- For this spell, please wear no makeup or decorative jewelry.
- The best time to begin this spell is just before sunrise.

Procedure

Begin by casting a circle, calling the quarters, chanting, or raising energy as you normally would, performing protective exercises, and altering your consciousness. Clear your mind, bring focus to your breath, and meditate for at least a few minutes. When ready, begin the spell.

Light the candle and incense, placing the candle in front of you (elevated if possible). Sit facing the east.

Examine the masks in your hand. See them as representations of your false personality types. Grab the marker and, on the forehead area of the first mask, write a word or short phrase that summarizes a false aspect of your personality. This should be a characteristic that you tend to overemphasize or create for yourself. You may have a habit of portraying these qualities to other people or may trick yourself into believing them to be true about yourself. This could be anything from "yes-man," or "know-it-all" to "perky and chipper" or "unforgiving brute." If you are familiar with sigilry, symbolism, and pictorial communication, you may wish to decorate the mask with these things rather than words alone. Whatever the case, imbue the mask with the energy of the façade.

Repeat the exercise with each mask, assigning one characteristic or term to each. Each mask should be assigned its own individual "face." Take plenty of time to think about your daily life, scrutinizing any possible falsities in personality that you may put up, even unconsciously.

Once finished imbuing each mask, place them atop one another in descending order: the "mask" that you wear most frequently should be on the top, while the one you utilize the least should be on the bottom. Hold these masks up before you, saying:

> *Hail be, guardians of the east and spirits of the Sun! Be with me as I perform this rite. To the great rising Sun of Truth—the All-seeing, All-knowing King—I offer up these masks to you. These represent false aspects of my personality. These are façades I wish to diminish from my life. Blessed be the power of the Holy Rising Sun: you are God, you are Truth! Shine through illusion, shine through fear! Hear my praise, mighty Center of this Universe! Oversee this END to my masquerade.*

Put the masks on your face, stacked on one another as they are. Cover yourself with the veil. Through the masks and veil, you should be able to see the dim light of the candle flame in front of you. Say:

> *The guiding light of the flame before my eyes represents my true self, my pure self: that which I seek to bring to the surface.*

Meditate for a few minutes, thinking about what you wish to accomplish with the spell. In your mind, deconstruct many of the prominent moments in which you allowed various untrue aspects of your personality to emerge. If you cry or feel frustrated, channel that energy into the masks and veil on your face.

When ready, lift the veil and throw it behind you, shouting:

> *With the parting of the veil, I begin my process of transformation!*

Take the outermost mask from your face. Look at it and declare out loud what it represents (e.g., "This mask represents the illusion of superiority I place on myself…"). Throw the mask behind you and, while staring at the candle flame, bellow the word "Sol" six times.

Repeat the process for all masks, one by one.

When finished, gaze at the flame and say:

> *With your infinite light, oh mighty Sun, I ask you now: align my soul to your very essence. With the glory of your radiance, may my true personality shine through illusion.*
>
> ZAHAV! ZAHAV! ZAHAV! ZAHAV! ZAHAV! ZAHAV!
>
> *So mote it be!*

Close the circle as you normally would, saving the masks in a hidden place, wrapped in the black veil. The masks can be reused in the future (individually or altogether) if the need arises.

Saving Face:
Practical Deific Glamoury

Whereas the previous spell was concerned with shedding masks and façades, the following working is designed for those who wish to *construct* a temporary "face" for one reason or another. This face is not designed for daily use and should have a distinct purpose in mind.

In many ways, the magick of glamoury is manipulating and should not be used frequently. The most pertinent reason for using glamoury is for the purpose of *guising*: assuming the qualities and characteristics of a choice deity. This is most applicable before the act of *invocation*, which is an advanced Pagan ritual where a participant (often a Priest or Priestess) assumes the guise of a god or goddess, who then speaks through the practitioner as a human conduit.

Though there are many forms of glamoury, the most successful may be through the use of archetypes. Because the following spell focuses on the melding of one's energy with a particular deity rather than an overarching archetype, the practitioner should be aware of archetypal parallels between traditions and consider common views (both ancient and modern) held by devotees and observers of the god or goddess being worked with.

Every god and goddess in existence embodies a certain set of characteristics and energies, and most have relatively "equal" archetypal representatives across cultures. For example, the Egyptian Ra and Horus are both solar deities, but so are the Greek Apollo and Helios, the Roman Sol, the Hindu Surya, the Norse Balder, the Celtic (Gaulish) Belenus, and so on. Among other things, they all represent the archetype of "Solar God." (Keep in mind that, at the same time, a number of mythological associations attribute goddesses to the Sun and gods to the Moon, so this celestial genderization isn't the same in all pantheons.)

Archetypal alignments occur across all cultures and religions, from ancient indigenous and tribal religions to more well-known paths like Buddhism and Christianity. These forces can be summoned for a number of purposes, including the act of guising, which, in this case, I see as an act of partial invocation. Additionally, it can also be called an act of *enchantment*. Glamoury is a temporary act of illusion in appearance, energy, or general demeanor and can precede a ritualistic act of invocation.

Those readers who are artists, creators, or performers may benefit from the following working. If you have a patron deity, you may wish to choose to work with them directly. Depending on the aspect—or archetype—you wish to draw into yourself, your glamouring may last anywhere from a few minutes to an entire day. If one is a devotee of the god or goddess being summoned, the spell can be practiced more frequently. Still, this can be dangerous if the practitioner does not know themselves first. If one becomes unable to differentiate between one's own, inherent personality and the external force that is invoked, confusion and disorientation can ensue.

Glamour magick is not to be taken lightly, nor should it be performed on a regular basis unless the user has good reason. In medieval times, it was common to believe a Witch deceived others through glamoury. This definition of glamoury is, of course, negative in nature and assumes the practitioner to be deceiving onlookers for evil, scheming purposes. While this sort of dishonesty through glamoury *is* a legitimate practice, I would advise against it unless circumstances are extreme.

Please be aware that other forms of glamoury magick exist. The term *glamoury* represents, in general, an act of deception that can be either beneficial or destructive in nature, and it is widely believed that the term, in reference to magick, originates with Celtic mythology and lore. One form of non-guising glamoury I've heard of is to perform random acts that make others question their reality. For example, I've heard of people working with the faerie realms practicing glamoury in the form of inconspicuously putting food coloring and bath fizzies in public fountains, putting dollar coins in mailboxes, leaving tarot or oracle cards in random locations, and writing intuitive messages on slips of paper for people to find serendipitously. While these things are fun (and certainly make people think twice about their reality, even if for a moment), and I do recommend performing such things when the mood strikes (hey, I do this sort of thing regularly!), the following working is concerned with glamoury in a personal or interpersonal sense.

Stepping Back & Further Application

What are your reasons for wanting to glamour onlookers? Are you avoiding certain aspects of yourself, or is your purpose something of temporary or ritualistic fulfillment? Do you objectively believe the god or goddess you have in mind would like to work with you on altering your appearance and demeanor, or would they find it insulting? These questions and others should be considered before performing glamoury.

It is essential not to constantly practice this form of magick. While it can be tempting to try to align our personalities completely and entirely with a deity or archetypal force, this can lead to internal confusion and even manipulative falsity. One's actual personality should always come before that of a deity; we must work with what we have before merging with forces we idealize.

Before practicing deific glamoury, know yourself and know your mind. If you are going to interact with others, be prepared for any possible scenario, including the need to dismiss the guise. Additionally, and for a more successful glamour, try surrendering to the energies you've called into and onto yourself rather than amplifying aspects of your personality that you feel are aligned to that which has been summoned. The more one allows the magick to work more than the mind or ego, the more successful and accurate the act.

Do not call deities you are unfamiliar with or whose energy may potentially pose a risk if it were to blend with yours. Though glamoury is not full, proper invocation, external energies are still being called somewhat into (or onto, rather) one's person. In other words, be intelligent when choosing a deity to align yourself with, and know all of their symbolism, mythology, and character traits.

Supplies

- 1 yellow candle and 1 purple candle
- items and clothing appropriate to the deity being called (see Notes)
- a small sachet filled with a mixture of catnip, dragon's blood, foxglove, marigold, and poppy, as well as your own hair and fingernail clippings
- an accurate and preferably ancient depiction of the deity being summoned; this could be a statue, painting, print, tapestry, or other image
- appropriate offerings for the deity (research their mythology and common offerings given)

Notes

- In the [bracketed] areas of the spell, fill in the space with the appropriate word or words, depending on the deity you are calling. I suggest only working with deities you are familiar with, have worked with before, or are previously aligned with. Additionally, do not perform glamoury for a long period of time, particularly if it is your first time. If, during the duration of the glamour, you feel intimidated, overwhelmed, or not in control, dismiss and thank the deity earlier than you may have planned.

- Common glamours revolve around changing one's appearance to make it more attractive, honing one's mental or creative focus, gaining compassion, or invoking intimidating aggression. Respectively, one could call forth a deity of beauty, a deity of the arts, a deity of love, or a deity of war. In the spell, use characteristics and other adjectives in the [characteristics] brackets. The possibilities are as endless as the archetypes. All glamours are energetic enchantments, as instantly changing one's physical characteristics is not possible.

- After selecting a deity, choose clothing and other items you can wear or use for the duration of the glamour. This could be makeup and jewelry for a deity of beauty, paints and canvas for a deity of the arts, flowers and gifts for a deity of love, or chainmail and a staff for a deity of war. Be sure your items are deity-specific.

Procedure

Begin by casting a circle, calling the quarters, chanting, or raising energy as you normally would, performing protective exercises, and altering your consciousness. Clear your mind, bring focus to your breath, and meditate for at least a few minutes. When ready, begin the spell.

Facing the east, light the yellow candle and chant six times:

Ascending spirits of the east, enter this space and illuminate my intention. My guise I intend to shift; that I am radiant with the characteristics of [name of deity].

[His/Her] face shall be as my own, that the glory of the Old Ones be ignited into this realm through the Star that is me, but a devoted servant. So shall it be.

Facing the west, light the purple candle and chant six times:

Descending spirits of the west, enter this space and carry forth my intention. My guise I wish to shift; that I am filled with the characteristics of [name of deity]*.*

[His/Her] *face shall be as my own, that the glory of the Old Ones be woven into this realm through the Vessel that is me, but a humble servant. So mote it be.*

Prepare your offerings and dress in the chosen clothing/adornments. Wear the herbal sachet around your neck.

Gaze at the depiction of the deity you are calling forth. Examine their facial features, clothing, and demeanor. Pay particular attention to the symbolism within the depiction: what does the god or goddess's image suggest, including their clothing, stance, expression, and symbolic items depicted with them?

Facing the direction most aligned with the deity, recite:

I *summon you from your abodes, mighty* [name of deity]*!*
I, [your own name], *invoke your assistance in this rite.*
My guise I will to shift, in alignment with your [characteristics]*,*
for the means of [state your goal/intention]*.*
In adoration I have called out to you,
and with honor I shall carry forth your [characteristics]*.*
From your abode to my own, be with me!
For the duration of [state duration of time]*, meld with my person!*
Let us dance with one another; let us work together for but a time.
Come! Ride me! Let me be ridden! Let us be as One!
My appearance and demeanor shall be as yours,
as I simultaneously function within my own paradigm.
As a servant I do now manifest your power within my own.
So mote it be!

After once again gazing at the image of the deity, allow yourself to slip into a light state of trance. Close your eyes and hold the sachet of herbs to your third eye, inhaling deeply a number of times. When ready, release the bag and hold your hands to your face.

With your eyes still closed, "mold" the energy of your face to match that of the deity. Spend a good amount of time doing this. When you feel satisfied with the merging, say the following:

> *Behold! With my appearance and behavior as yours, mighty* [name of deity],
> *I shall bring forth your* [characteristics] *to this plane of operation.*
> *Until this enchantment expires, by my will or yours,*
> *I appear as you, I appear as you, I appear as you.*
> *Connected we are; blended, melded, and seemingly One.*
> *With gratitude and humility, I offer these to you.*

Hold up your offerings and concentrate on the spell. Now that your appearance and, to some extent, your consciousness, have blended with the deity's, think about what you wish to accomplish with this glamour and why you are grateful to the deity.

When ready, place the offerings in an auspicious location and thank the deity once again. Close the circle as you normally would.

When the duration of the glamour has come to a close, "pull" the deity's energy from your face and body, and send it back to the ether until you feel back to normal. Thank the deity once again and reflect on the accomplishments of the glamour.

Witches' Bling: Enchanting a Diurnal or Nocturnal Talisman

The following is a simple spell that one can use to enchant a talisman, pendant, or other jewelry with the energy of the Sun. Because the Sun is a (virtually) limitless center of light—and certainly the center of our Universe—it is an ideal force to draw on when enchanting magickal items intended to carry solar qualities.

Because of the natural Goddess associations with the Moon, many Witches tend to observe their spirituality strictly by the Moon—sometimes neglecting the place of the Sun (aside from Sabbat celebrations)! Because most paths within the Craft hold the forces of God and Goddess in equal regard, it's important to work with both to come to a place of balance.

Because the sign Leo is the only one ruled by the Sun, this spell could be ideally performed while the Sun is in Leo (July 23–August 23). If the Sun is in a different sign, research its qualities to see how it might influence the solar energy being utilized.

Once enchanted, one can use the pendant however they see fit; see the following instructions and ideas for multiple uses of the piece. Be sure the piece you choose to enchant carries some type of solar association. Perhaps it's gold (or golden in appearance), circular like the Sun, represents solar imagery, or is a magickal seal of the Sun.

Stepping Back & Further Application

Before enchanting a talisman, pendant, charm, or jewelry with this method, decide how the item will be used. Will you wear it on a daily basis? Only for certain occasions? Only in ritual?

This spell gives a person the freedom of deciding whether the enchanted piece will be for diurnal or nocturnal use, regardless of whether the piece will be used only in ritual or day to day.

After the piece is enchanted, if you have chosen to enchant it for daytime use, hang it in front of a window where the Sun's rays will reach it as often as possible. In this case, an abundance of sunlight absorbed by the piece will add strength to the enchantment.

If you have chosen to only wear the piece for nighttime use, keep it wrapped in black fabric and tucked in a dark corner or box when not in use. Additionally, if the piece is only to be worn at night, the solar energy it's enchanted with will stay more adhered to the piece if it's never allowed to see the light of the Sun after being charged. In this manner, the piece will energetically act like the Moon, which reflects sunlight at nighttime.

Supplies

- a pendant or talisman of your choice
- prepared Solar Water (see Notes)
- a round incense-burning charcoal disk and sand in a dish or censor
- frankincense resin

- an empty transparent glass bowl
- about a pint of orange juice
- a small amount of olive oil

Notes

- Review the qualities of Sun as a planet. Pay particular attention to the zodiacal sign the Sun is in at the time of the spell; again, Leo is ideal but another can be used for a more specified purpose.

- This spell calls for Solar Water. To create this, fill a jar with purified water, add a citrine stone (the larger the better, and unpolished if possible) and a shot of vodka or another clear liquor. When the Sun is at its peak in the day (between noon and 3 pm), hold the jar to the Sun to "catch" its energy, and focus on the rays entering and charging the water. Let this sit outside or on a windowsill (where it will catch sunlight) for exactly six days before using.

- Even if the piece is only intended to be nocturnally worn, one can still perform the original enchantment spell at night (also with the use of the Solar Water). If the piece is to be worn during the day, it is best to enchant it when the Sun is high in the sky. It is also best to perform this ritual outdoors in a secluded area.

- The *Hasta Uttanasana* (Raised Hands Pose) in Hatha Yoga is a simple pose within a sequence of *Surya Namaskara asanas* (Sun Salutation postures). To get in this position, simply stand and put the palms of your hands together in the *Anjali Mudra* (Prayer Position) high above your head. Bend slightly backwards while looking up at your hands and breathing through your nose.

Procedure

Begin by casting a circle, calling the quarters, chanting, or raising energy as you normally would, performing protective exercises, and altering your consciousness. Clear your mind, bring focus to your breath, and meditate for at least a few minutes. When ready, begin the spell.

First, dip the piece you wish to enchant (pendant, talisman, jewelry) briefly in the Solar Water.

Next, ignite the charcoal, place the frankincense on it, and run the piece through the billowing smoke.

Placing the item in the bowl, pour the orange juice until the piece is completely submerged. Add the olive oil and a splash of Solar Water to the mix.

Cupping your hands over the bowl and staring at the mix, visualize the contents glowing like the Sun. Chant "Sol" repeatedly until you feel that the mix is enchanted. Once finished, take the piece from the mix, ensuring that some of the mix remains on the item.

Facing the east, hold the piece before you and call out to the Sun:

I praise you, Shining Eastern Star!
I draw into this circle your strength and vigor!
Oh he who rises and determines the growth of the land,
stir in your splendor in the sky; rise in your conquering light.
Shine and look down on me now!
With your golden and bountiful light, fill this sacred ornament!
I thank you and praise you. Blessed be!

Envision the Sun's rays filling the piece, seeing the item radiating with light as if it were an emanation of the Sun.

Positioning the item between your palms, perform the Hasta Uttanasana, inhaling through your nose six times while envisioning your hands radiating sunlight. Conclude by bowing to the east and offering the remaining frankincense to the Sun.

Close the circle as you normally would, and store the piece properly (see Stepping Back & Further Application).

Toxic Teatime at Twilight: A Daily Alignment

The following spell is a fun stress-relieving ritual that a person can perform at the end of an overwhelming day. Every day carries a different level of stress and satisfaction. This spell is designed to be performed at the end of those days that are particularly tedious. There's no sense in dwelling on the negative!

The times of dusk and dawn are considered by many to be a "tween" time, a place between the worlds. These beliefs are carryovers of early Celtic and otherwise Pagan worldviews. If, at either dawn or dusk, one pays particular attention to their mind and general energy pattern, they will notice an interesting shift in consciousness and perception. For some people, this shift is barely noticeable. For others, like myself, the Sun's ascent or descent plays an obvious role in the shifting of consciousness.

Our bodies are attuned to the rhythms of the Earth. The foremost rhythm is that of the Sun. Quite naturally, peoples' moods and energies are affected by not only seasonal shifts but by daily changes in sunlight. Physiologically (and thus scientifically), these shifts are recognized as having influence on perception and the psyche (and thus the spirit). While there are a number of ways a person can combat Seasonal Affective Disorder (SAD) and the darker annual turnings of the tide, this spell has one's daily cycles in mind.

When the Sun rises in the east, a new day is born. When it descends in the west, day is concluded and night begins. The "banishing" aspect of the Sun occurs at dusk, preceding twilight. As the Sun descends beyond the horizon, prayers and intentions can be carried along with it. Ancient Egyptians viewed the Sun as a carrier of dead souls: its descent carried deceased daily energies with it, just as its "rebirth" each day would bring forth new life and bounty.

Dawn is the ideal time for a practitioner of any type to summon life-giving, rebirthing energies, and dusk is the time for banishment. Assuming the reader operates on a relatively diurnal schedule, the following spell can be used to help dissipate and put to rest an overabundance of mental, emotional, and psychological stress that has accumulated throughout the day.

Stepping Back & Further Application

Before performing this spell, it's good to ask why such an accumulation of energy has occurred throughout the day. Is this buildup a daily thing? If so, how can a frequent overabundance of stress be navigated, if not conquered?

It's easy for us to feel trapped or bound in a daily cycle, even if it doesn't serve our highest purpose or the greater good of others. Many people become accustomed to staying in high-stress occupations, relationships, parental situations, and a whole slew of other overwhelming factors.

If you find yourself performing this or similar spells on a daily basis, search for the cause of the stress and objectively brainstorm how a constant amount of stress can be dealt with. Contemplate what changes you can make in your daily pattern in order to help you and those around you experience less stress. Additionally, consider the sacrifices and benefits that would come about from a slight or severe shift in your daily cycle.

If the reason for performing this spell is simply due to a bad day (we all have 'em) or isn't something to worry about in a grander scope of life, be sure to analyze the day's ill experiences both in terms of the role others played in the day and the role you yourself played. More often than not, poor situations are the result of two parties' behaviors rather than just one or the other's.

Supplies

- a ballpoint pen
- a square piece of fabric, preferably dark orange, burgundy, or maroon
- the following Major Arcana cards from the Rider-Waite (or similar) tarot: the High Priestess, the Lovers, the Emperor, Death, and Temperance
- a round incense-burning charcoal disk and sand in a dish or censor
- a "tea" made of any of the following baneful herbs: aconite, belladonna, datura, foxglove, henbane, hemlock, or mandrake
- a chalice filled with the prepared (steeped) brew
- a loose incense mixture of equal parts amber, copal, frankincense, and myrrh

Notes

- The "tea" referenced here is *not* designed for human or animal consumption. When preparing or metaphysically using the baneful brew, take all the necessary precautions. I also recommend wearing gloves. Because the herbs used are toxic, lethal, and otherwise poisonous, do not drop loose pieces of the herbs around the house, don't spill it without thoroughly cleaning, wash your hands if you touch the herbs or the tea, wash the cup and tea paraphernalia thoroughly after use, and obviously do *not* drink any of it. Use extreme caution, care, and commonsense when working with these herbs in any spell.

- The layout of the cards in this spell is esoterically significant and has particular meanings for the spell's purposes. If you feel uncomfortable or uncertain about using this spread, try using a more familiar or personally significant layout.

- It is ideal to perform this ritual outdoors, while gazing at the sunset. Look in a local newspaper or online to discover the exact time of the sunset, and plan to begin the spell ten or fifteen minutes beforehand if possible.

- If performing the working outdoors, consider simply purifying the space around you rather than casting a formal circle. Smudge with sage, asperge with saltwater, sweep with a broom, and so on.

Procedure

Begin by purifying the space or casting a circle, calling the quarters, chanting or raising energy as you normally would, performing protective exercises, and altering your consciousness. Clear your mind, bring focus to your breath, and meditate for at least a few minutes. When ready, begin the spell.

Sitting down on the grass or floor, face west. If the ritual is being performed outside, be sure you're in a spot that's receiving sunlight (if it's not overcast). Gaze at the sunset (without injuring your eyes) and feel its light entering your third eye.

With the ballpoint pen, draw symbol 1 on the top of your left hand and symbol 2 on your right.

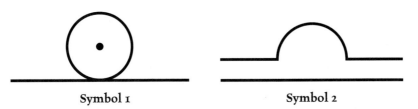

Symbol 1   **Symbol 2**

Situate the following before you: on the square piece of fabric, put the Lovers card in the top left corner, the Emperor card in the top right corner, and the censor in the middle of the fabric. Next, place the High Priestess card on the fabric, just above the censor (slightly lower than the upper two cards), and Temperance beneath the censor. Finally, place the Death card on the lower right corner of the fabric and set the chalice of toxic "tea" on top of it. (Again, this tea is *not* meant to be drunk.)

Ignite the charcoal and place the mix of incense resins on top. Take a few minutes to create a billowing cloud of smoke. While waiting for the charcoal and incense to properly ignite, spend some time looking at the Tarot spread in front of you, contemplating the ascribed and intuitive meanings of each card.

Holding your left hand in the incense smoke, raise your right hand to the Sun. Repeat six times:

Hail unto thee from the Abodes of Day!

Next, cup both hands over the incense smoke, close your eyes, and think of all the stressful thoughts that accumulated throughout the day. Remember the instances that led to your being overwhelmed, rewinding the occurrences—and your reactions—in your mind. Think about other recent stresses and let them evoke feelings of discomfort and frustration. Imagine these ill feelings being pulled from all parts of your body. Push these vibrations through your hands and into the incense smoke. Channel all your distress into the glowing ember and billowing smoke. When a sense of relief and release comes over you, move on to the next step.

Sit calmly and bring your mind to the present moment, separating your mind from the thoughts just raised. Grab the chalice of tea, look toward the sunset, and declare:

As our luminous Sun descends for the night, may he too escort these stresses, sorrows, and pain.

Pouring the tea over the coal, extinguish it fully and affirm:

So mote it be!

Thank the energies at hand and close the circle as you normally would.

Solar Boost: Adding Power to Any Spell

Spells are effective in and of themselves, but sometimes an extra "boost" can add the finishing touch to a spell. This is particularly appropriate in the case of spells meant to send or project energy.

If a spell is performed correctly, there should be a large amount of power risen and sent throughout. Oftentimes, rituals of any type begin with a buildup, a crescendo of power (energy being sent to the land, a person, or a spell), and a subsequent decrease in energy. This is representative of the "cone of power," which is the cast circle of a magician or Witch.

The following are a few suggestions for summoning an increase of power during a ritual. These are by no means the only ways to add a boost of energy; the key is to get creative and follow your intuition.

In Western Mystery traditions, a significant amount of focus is usually given to the timing of a working. Because Wicca and other forms of Neopagan Witchcraft borrowed heavily from Hermeticism and other long-standing ceremonial systems, many Witches pay particular attention to the astrological and planetary influences present during a working (though some choose against it). This book is greatly focused on harnessing planetary and zodiacal influences during spellcraft specifically; aligning one's magick to these forces is one significant key to amplifying and fine-tuning one's magick—at least from my experience.

Though the general planetary influences (such as the current phase of the Sun or Moon, both zodiacally and seasonally/monthly) are very significant in an overarching sense, the Hermetic planetary hours are additionally important if a boost of specific power is the caster's goal. For information on planetary hours, please see page 16 and Appendix 2.

You may use the following information to get creative when deciding to add energy and power to your magick, but be sure to rely as much on your internal reality as you do the external—both are the foundations for balanced living and effective magick.

Stepping Back & Further Application

It is likely that a number of readers turn to this particular spell either because they feel that their spellcasting efforts are relatively ineffective, or that they're somehow "doing it wrong." A key component to ask oneself is, How much power am I drawing from within, and how much am I drawing from outside myself? A number of people, especially when they first discover the "active" or "operative" magickal aspect of Witchcraft and occultism, rely heavily on a spell's components and words. While these things are important, tools, timing, and procedure are always secondary to one's intention. While I talked about this more in the book's beginning, I must again emphasize that true magick is born of one's consciousness—the herbs, the stones, the chants, the incantations, and even the spirits called forth in spellcraft are all secondary to the energy of Will (both intentive free will and one's deeper spiritual Will), which is drawn forth from a practitioner's inner self.

Additionally, one must ask oneself: what is reality's resistance to the magick I'm intending? Oftentimes, the reason for unsuccessful spells is the fact that the flow of Fate—the flow of the Universe—is opposite the working's purpose. There are often other unseen psychological or mundane goals that inhibit a spell's flow into manifestation. For example, one cannot successfully cast a spell for money or love if, deep within, they feel they are undeserving of abundance or partnership. Just the same, one cannot successfully cast a spell for wisdom if they don't study, meditate, or what-have-you. Unfortunately (or perhaps fortunately, depending on how one looks at it), a number of people decide against further pursuing esoteric spirituality when they discover that the perceived "easy way out" of casting a spell doesn't always live up to idealistic expectations. One must objectively examine and step back from the drama of life in order to identify spiritual roadblocks before deciding that a spell needs added "oomph."

Supplies

- 2 portable mirrors capable of standing upright on their own (ideally 1 foot square or larger)
- a drum with a resonant pitch
- any combination of the herbs benzoin, calamus, cinquefoil, dragon's blood, frankincense, High John the Conqueror root, lemon verbena, mandrake, myrrh, rosemary, and vervain
- 1 small stone each of yellow calcite (or optical/clear calcite), citrine, and quartz crystal

Notes

- Once again, this spell is meant as an add-on to other workings and is not a complete spell in and of itself.
- When performing the energy-raising activity described here, it is essential for the practitioner—regardless of how young or new they are to Witchcraft—to not judge themselves as acting "too weird." Unordinary behavior is *very much* a part of the act of ritual, and self-judgment (which is really society's judgment speaking through you) is an extreme hindrance to entering the flow of a solitary ritual act.
- Consider the aforementioned methods for altering one's consciousness (see pages 17–18). This is absolutely vital if one wishes to practice any sort of magick, regardless of whether it's a spell, a pathworking, an inner journey, or a Gnostic connection to a god or the land. If one attempts to perform magick while in a "normal" operative state of mind, both the thoughts of the day and the at-

tention to procedure will detract from the necessary etheric work required for ritualistic success.

Procedure

Begin by casting a circle, calling the quarters, chanting, or raising energy as you normally would, performing protective exercises, and altering your consciousness. Clear your mind, bring focus to your breath, and meditate for at least a few minutes. When ready, begin the spell.

(At this point, we shall assume that the practitioner has physically constructed their spell and has summoned any desired spirits or energies they feel appropriate.)

Currently, the goal should be to send a boost of self-projected energy into the physical spell to empower it with metaphysical intention. For this reason, you now must entirely surrender to the present moment, bringing your mind completely and acutely to the spell's intention. To entirely enter this current of energy, take a number of minutes to gaze at the spell components before you. Do *not* move your eyes away from the physical spell in front of you. As with any meditation, distracting thoughts may arise in the moment—these speak of the mind's desire to escape the present, the Now. Effortlessly dismiss these thoughts as they arise and bring your focus back to the importance of your ritual.

When you feel a sort of "merging" with the energy of the spell—a feeling that many readers are well familiar with—place one of the mirrors behind the items of the spell, ensuring that you can see your own reflection within it. Place the drum either between your legs or in front of you.

With the spell items between you and the mirror, look into your eyes and chant the following *many* times, using only your intuition to tell you when it is a good time to stop. Beat the drum at any pace—slow, fast, or a combination of both—while you chant. Simply flow with the energy and allow yourself to determine the pace of the drumming and the chant while in trance. As long as you are surrendered to the intention of the spell, there is no wrong way to do this. Get as wild, crazy, loud, and selfless as you wish (I encourage practitioners to really push their limits and continue this raising of energy as long as possible). Chant:

Hear my calls and heed them right, piercing through both day and night.
As I wake and as I rest, make this spell come manifest!

When finished, immediately add the mixture of herbs and stones to the spell, either by sprinkling them on or in the spell components, adding them to another mixture, combusting the herbs in incense, or another method. The goal is to affix these "boosting" energies to the spell you've previously created.

Gaze at the now-completed spell for a minute or two, breathing deeply and coming back to the moment. Hold the spell to your third eye and push a surge of built-up energy into it. Take some time to reenter your normal stream of consciousness. When you feel a sense of success, break your eyes away from the spell and perform any other necessary grounding-and-centering exercises (such as holding stones, laying on the ground, breathing deeply, stretching out, eating, etc.).

Place the second mirror precisely opposite the first, ensuring that it reflects both the spell components and the other mirror face-on. When the mirror is situated, whisper ten times:

These mirrors magnify my ambition, amplifying power through transition.

Thank the spirits and close the circle as you normally would.

Chapter 2

——— · · ———

THE
MOON

——— · · ———

THE MOON
Zodiacal rulership: Cancer
Color association: Violet
Sephira: Yesod
Number: 9
Day: Monday
Archetypes: Lunar Goddess, Night Queen, Lady of the Crossroads
Themes: Subtlety, psychic ability, emotions, magick, compassion,
wisdom, intuition, hearth and home, nourishment, security,
imagination, patience, empathy, fertility, motherhood, femininity

Childhood Regression: Healing the Wounds of Youth

Much of our adult behavior is formed during our childhood. It's exceedingly common to have experienced traumatic events in youth that still have emotional effects in the present day. Virtually everyone experiences some level of suffering and trauma in their youth—being young and vulnerable is often difficult. However, the degrees of those experiences vary from person to person.

In this ritual, you will be working with painful experiences from childhood. The Moon is ruled by the element of water, and rules the sign of Cancer—all of which carry emotional energies. In this spell, you may wish to tackle issues of childhood abuse. You may wish to remember injurious words that were said to you, or bring to mind cruel names that you were once called. You may wish to remember accidents, injuries, parental mistreatment, or other emotionally disturbing experiences. If some incidents are too difficult to deal with in a ritual setting, consider other ways that you can work through these imprints, including counseling.

The events that you bring to mind in ritual could be ones that occurred to you at a very young age, or those that happened when you were a bit older. I would recommend only working with pre–high school memories for this particular ritual.

Thankfully, I was never abused as a child. Still, I know many people who were; I don't pretend to empathize with those levels of emotional damage, but I *do* know that they can be worked with and worked through. Though we never fully "get over" deep trauma, we can get to a state of acceptance. Where there's a will, there's a way, and one should truly consider all their options. For deeply traumatic events, let me emphasize: *this ritual is not enough.* Everyone who wishes to heal and come to terms with trauma deserves to discover the best ways of doing this—and everybody is different. My foremost suggestion for working through trauma is therapy. Research various therapists, counselors, and psychologists who specialize in specific areas of trauma. Look in the phone book, spend some time on the Internet, get recommendations from friends and acquaintances, make phone calls, and schedule various introductory meetings with local counselors. Get active, get motivated, and do the work—there are *always* options. Additionally, there exist a number of no-charge counseling services (both over the phone and in person) that could be of benefit. One may also wish to consider working with a reliable spiritual teacher. Therapy and counseling are often the best methods for navigating traumatic occurrences and working to change present behavior and patterned thinking.

Oftentimes, it's difficult to realize how events of the past influence our present circumstances. To use one example from my past, I'll mention that I was sometimes tickled as a child. The adult tickling me seemed not to understand the boundaries I was trying to communicate and would keep tickling until I felt extreme pain. Though this person didn't mean to cause pain, my mind translated the incidents as fear-inducing emotional injury. As a young adult, it wasn't until heavy thinking and regression that I began to understand why I would clench up in fear any time someone touched my belly area. The incidents from the past influenced the unconscious, instinctual behavior to guard myself from even the slightest touch in that area.

Because the pain was psychological and emotional, it was also spiritual. Only after working with the mental and energetic imprints could I change the instinctual behavior, banish the associated fear, and invoke trust and safety. This wasn't accomplished in a day and was not an easy process. For those who have experienced much harsher issues of abuse and damage than my simple example offers, the work will be deeper and greater—as will the rewards. Healing and reworking one's mind takes time and often requires working with—and trusting—other compassionate souls.

This spell is not the answer to healing childhood wounds. However, it can be a step toward greater healing and can accompany other healing methods.

Stepping Back & Further Application

Examine your mental approach to this ritual. It is essential to know your intentions and approach the spell in a balanced state of mind. This is one of those spells that is dualistically fun yet serious, lighthearted yet intense, creative yet pensive. Maintaining this mental and psychological balance is the key for the spell's success. One mustn't get caught up in either the "silly" things being performed in the spell or the incidental pain that may be brought up as a result.

To what extent are you willing to follow up on this ritual? If you come to a realization that your present circumstances and modes of behavior are greatly affected by negative experiences in childhood, will you work on changing your present state of being? If so, in what ways will you work with the behavior? Will you vow to notice your thoughts throughout the day, both pinpointing and changing the negative patterned thinking immediately when it occurs? Will you change restrictive things in your life that have resulted from past experience? Seek cognitive-behavioral therapy? Will you open up about these things with friends? Have conversations with those who have had similar experiences? Perform specific visualizations and meditations? Read self-help books? The possibilities are both endless and available—you are the only one who has the power and ability to seek necessary healing for yourself.

Supplies

- about 1 ounce of powdered valerian root, in a bowl
- a pink candle

- any number of toys and stuffed animals from your childhood (or purchased secondhand items)
- a notebook of sketch paper
- a set of watercolor paints (used or new)
- a pack of crayons (used or new)
- a small crab leg or claw, sitting in a large bowl of warm water (see Notes)
- 1 stone each of rose quartz and pink calcite

Notes

- I recommend that, if possible, you dress in "kid clothing" for this ritual. This can be adult-sized clothing that mimics common clothing you wore in your childhood. Otherwise, I would just recommend wearing loose-fitting clothes or going skyclad.
- The purchased crab leg should ideally have been discarded from a restaurant or store. However, if buying it fresh and unused is the only option, I recommend doing so at the butcher deli of an organic or all-natural food store. Don't forget to smudge the claw and give offerings of gratitude to the spirit of the crab. Put the claw in a large bowl of warm water before starting the ritual.
- It might be a good idea to jot a list of the most damaging childhood experiences—those things you wish to touch on during the ritual—and keep it near you in circle, so as to not forget anything you intend to work with.
- Please note that the crayons and watercolors will not be reused after the ritual, so go nuts.

Procedure

Begin by casting a circle, calling the quarters, chanting, or raising energy as you normally would, performing protective exercises, and altering your consciousness. Clear your mind, bring focus to your breath, and meditate for at least a few minutes. When ready, begin the spell.

With all the spell's items situated in front of you, grab the bowl of powdered valerian root and liberally sprinkle this in the space around you in order to secure its energy in the area.

Light the candle and begin rocking your body back and forth while sitting. Allow your mind to slip into a trancelike state and release inhibitions associated with the ritual. Think about yourself as a child. If your childhood modes of behavior don't easily come back to you, allow yourself to take on the attitudes and perceptions of any child. Slip into a state of mind where you are innocent, curious, creative, risk-taking, and expressive. Allow your "adult" views to slip into the background and your childlike nature to emerge. Invoke the archetype of Child. Take as long as you need to get into this state of mind. Imagine yourself as a very young kid (under five years old), regardless of which memories you've chosen to work with during the ritual.

Opening your eyes, everything should feel a bit different. You're not sure why a candle is lit and you're sitting in a strange place. Explore. Pick up the candle, analyze it, and question how the flame keeps burning. Do you like the color pink? Put the candle down and explore your immediate surrounding environment. Look at items around you as though you're looking through the eyes of a curious child. Examine, explore, and let your curiosity get the best of you. Play with the toys and stuffed animals, going through all the motions and behaviors of a little kid having fun. Curiously analyze items on the altar, on the walls, around the room. If there's something shiny, check it out. If there's something soft and fluffy, lay on it, or pet it!

After a while of exploring, you notice the paper, paints, and crayons in front of you. This gets your creative juices flowing and you decide to make some pictures. Go wild: sketch rainbows, horses, stick figures, sunshine, and anything else you can think of. Be a creative kid, and don't worry about making a mess. Nothing matters except the art you're creating. Dip your watercolor brush in the bowl of water and splash it without thinking. Rip pages out of the sketchpad, especially after you've finished making a picture. Break some crayons so that you can use their "thick" sides. Scribble, clap, laugh, sing, talk to yourself, jump around, throw things across the room, paint your cheeks, and enjoy your artistry.

After you've made some pictures and a decent mess, grab the crab claw from the bowl of water (which should now be colored from the watercolors). Tightly grip the claw in your fist and allow a painful memory from childhood to emerge. Stare at the claw, regressing to the painful experience. Remember how you felt at the time—how long it's taken you to mentally work through the issue. Vividly recall how you were hurt and how you reacted. Think about this for about a minute, and allow yourself to cry if you need to. When the time is right, lift up your shirt (unless you are skyclad) and put the end of the crab claw to your chest. Drag the claw across your chest, applying pressure so that it causes a small amount of pain or discomfort. Shout:

Symbol 3

Stupid dumb pain, I hate you! I am sick and tired of feeling this pain!

Immediately return to your drawing and painting activities, placing the claw back into the bowl of water. Draw a picture that represents the painful experience you just thought of (the image can be as simple or complex as you'd like, and should be from a child's perspective—that is, *you* when you experienced the pain). Immediately after finishing, rip the page from the sketchpad, get a black crayon or watercolor, and put symbol 3 on the back of the piece and a giant black X on the front, covering the image. Crumple the picture into a ball. Declare:

You don't have power over me! Goodbye, stupid hurt! You're just a monster in the closet and you don't exist! Get away from me and leave me alone . . . right now!

Throw the crumpled piece of art across the room and shout:

So there!

Cross your arms across your chest and smile to yourself, knowing that you've banished that particular boogeyman. Repeat this process as many times as you'd like. Cover all the traumatic childhood experiences you feel comfortable reliving at this time. If you experienced extremely traumatic incidents that you feel would be too difficult to work with in this setting, consider approaching them in a different ritual or through professional therapy. There is no shame in getting help from outside sources in order to work through difficult issues.

After having repeated the process as many times as necessary, grasp one of the stones in each fist and gaze at the burning candle. Draw the energies of healing and love into yourself, ground and center your energy, and visualize a soft pink light surrounding your body and entering the scratch marks on your chest. Lie on the floor, meditate, and draw the healing energy from the candle and stones all around you and within yourself. If you've had a particularly difficult time reliving the memories within this ritual, you may want to take a nap in the ritual space before continuing.

Stand and return to your normal state of mind. Think in practical terms: I have a mess to clean up, I better take a shower, I have to get up early in the morning, and so on. When you've returned to your usual state of mind, close the circle as you normally would, clean up the ritual space, let the candle burn down, and throw both the crab claw and the banishing drawings and paintings in the trash.

Mi Casa No Es Su Casa:
Exorcism of the House & Home

When one thinks of the word *exorcism*, they may imagine demonic possession and the process of exorcising an invader. Though rare, a spirit possessing a human body does happen and is a serious occurrence. But more often than not, what appears to be a human body inhabited by an external entity is, in actuality, the manifestation of a psychological imbalance and is better tackled through psychotherapy. (Indeed, we can become "possessed" by certain aspects of our mind if they're not kept at arm's length.) Magick and spirituality are both greatly psychological in nature, making these methods potentially effective as well.

For practical purposes, I'll present an exorcism spell that isn't for demonic or spirit possession of a person, but for the house and home. Rather than focusing on spirits that attach themselves to one's person, this spell is focused on the banishing of unwanted spirits from one's place of occupancy.

——— • ———

There are a number of reasons why a room, house, or plot of land can become invaded by malevolent forces. It's essential to analyze the whys of a haunted house or area of land. To use an example, I once visited an area on the East Coast that seemed to have literally ten times more spirits than human inhabitants—it was unlike anything I had ever seen. The area's brutal, fearful, dense energetic feel contributed to an inevitably scary and unexpected experience throughout my time there. I could perceive ghosts and spirits in nearly every house or building I visited in that area. It was only after I left that I realized the land's history: an epicenter of war, bloodshed, Native American slaughter, palpable curses on the land, and so on. The area's history created not only residual effects for the land, but for any who set foot there. The cause of the area's tainted nature was historical, and each earthbound individual or disincarnate (ghost) had its own story. Some were simply "replaying" their moments of death like a broken record (which can signify that the energy is in a time-loop and may not actually be a sentient being), others seemed to be lost and wandering aimlessly, and still others seemed to have acute awareness and specific intentions.

Because every haunting is dependent on a variety of circumstances, one must first dig for reasons, which requires objectivity. Though you and others may perceive averse forces at work, what is the easiest and most rational explanation behind the events? Taking an objective, skeptical approach can be for the best in this situation, in order to perceive the experience at its clearest.

The following spell assumes that the practitioner genuinely believes that their house is invaded by malevolent, ill-wishing forces—not benign, curious, or generally good-natured entities or beings (which can be dealt with in more subtle ways). It also assumes that the practitioner has both researched the possible reasons for the occurrence and has attempted other methods of spirit banishing, which include compassionate communication, direct orders to "stop and move on," and psychically communicating with said entities. This home-exorcism spell requires a demanding, strict approach to giving the boot to unwanted guests, and it should only be undertaken after all other methods have been exhausted.

Stepping Back & Further Application

There are many things to consider before performing a complete banishing or exorcism on one's house. What is your area's history? How about the history of your house? What have you experienced lately that could contribute to the perception of invading spiritual forces? Are there spirits ghosts, spirit guides, or astral wanderers? Are these actually forces of your own mind, or are they independent and external spirits? Do *they really exist?*

The number of questions required to take an objective approach to such a situation are endless and greatly dependent on each case, certainly including the people experiencing the phenomena. Additionally, one mustn't jump to conclusions about the case without analyzing every piece of evidence. Just as some individuals strictly and wholeheartedly *dis*believe in the paranormal, others tend to believe that nearly *every* occurrence in life carries supernatural associations. Both extremes are unhealthy, and striking a balanced outlook on life is essential for the Witch or magician. This is the benefit of cultivating objectivity.

If you have determined that, yes, your house is indeed haunted by a spirit or spirits, you must next examine the intentions of the beings. Ghosts and other spirit creatures all have their own intentions. Hauntings are not rare, however, as many people simply don't realize they're haunted! Most ghostly experiences are nonthreatening, though their surprising occurrences can make them seem scary. Are you intentionally being frightened, targeted, or attacked? If you've firmly concluded that you are, this spell may be an ideal method of exorcism.

Supplies

- a round incense-burning charcoal disk and sand in a dish or censor
- a fresh book of matches

- Mixture 1: a powdered incense mixture of asafoetida, benzoin, cinnamon, frankincense, mandrake, turmeric, and myrrh
- a fan, feather, or bird's wing (for fanning smoke)
- a very loud and noisy shaker, rattle, or drum
- a small amount of either black sand or black salt ("Witch's salt")
- lemon juice mixed with a small amount of Four Thieves Vinegar (see Notes)
- Mixture 2: a powdered combination of the herbs angelica root, anise, bay leaf, basil, dill, garlic, Low John root, mandrake root, mistletoe, and vervain
- a number of small square pieces of paper
- a purple marker or pen
- a wand of dried sage

Notes

- *Apo pantos kakodaimonos* is Greek, translating as "Away, every evil spirit!" The phrase is greatly used in Thelema and is incorporated in a basic Thelemic ritual called the Star Ruby.
- I recommend having a separate, portable coffee grinder specifically used for powdering herbs. This is the easiest way to create the powders for this spell and others, and ensures that the contents won't be somehow ingested when preparing your morning cuppa'.
- Four Thieves Vinegar, a component of many Hoodoo workings, is said to have gotten its name from the time of the European plague (approximately CE 1334–1350). Many people at the time would rob bodies of their jewelry and other valuables, and legend says that a band of four thieves were able to ward off the plague by rubbing their bodies with a vinegary concoction before robbing the diseased corpses. Four Thieves Vinegar is now used as a strong protection and banishing formula and is available through many occult supply shops. Substitute apple cider vinegar if unavailable.

- The match heads are made of are sulfur (brimstone), thus their use in the spell.

Procedure

Begin by performing protective exercises and altering your consciousness. Clear your mind, bring focus to your breath, and meditate for at least a few minutes. When ready, begin the spell.

With all the tools in front of you (and easily transportable), ignite the incense coal with a match, and wait until it turns into a glowing ember. Stand upright with your arms and legs outstretched. Look ahead and shout:

Apo pantos kakodaimonos!

With your right pointer finger, draw an upright pentagram before you, beginning at the bottom left angle of the star (this is a Banishing Pentagram of Earth). Trace the star in five swoops of the finger, sealing it with a sixth (the sixth stroke should bring your finger to the uppermost point of the pentagram). Envision the star glowing in a blue flame.

Standing in the same position, turn around and face behind you. Shout the phrase once again and trace the pentagram. Turn to your left and do the same, and then to your right. Finish by shouting the phrase while looking at the ceiling, and again while looking at the floor, so that a pentagram is traced in each area.

Light one of the matches, blow it out, and place a small pinch of Mixture 1 on the charcoal. In a widdershins manner, walk around the room, ensuring that the smoke touches every part of the room. Use the fan, feather, or wing to blow the smoke high and low. If necessary, open doors, windows, cupboards, and closets, so that every inch of the area will be touched by smoke.

Next, walk the room in a widdershins manner with the musical instrument in hand. Shake, rattle, and bang loudly so that every inch of the room is touched by the sound vibration.

Complete by once again shouting:

Apo pantos kakodaimonos!

Walking widdershins once again, sprinkle the black sand or salt around the room, ensuring that the grains hit the walls. Do the same with the lemon and vinegar mix, using your fingers to asperge the walls.

Finally, take a bowl of Mixture 2 in your left hand, putting a small pile of the powder in your right hand. With a quick breath, blow the powder in each area of the room. Do this while walking in a deosil manner.

Continue these steps in every room of the house, starting with the igniting of a match. When cleansing hallways, simply treat them as though they are an extension of a room you're exorcising. Additionally, bring all these ingredients around the outside of the house, securing the exorcism "within and without."

When you are completely finished, go to the central area of the house and declare:

> All *cunning, cruel, and crooked spirits of the land,* I *command you back to your terrain!*
> All *ghosts, spooks, and unrest spirits of the past, leave this place and go to the light!*
> All *those who have been created or commanded by the will of another, return now to the original source!*
> All *those energies that wish to injure or feed upon this place,* I *demand your immediate exodus!*
> All *pools of stagnation, vacancy, malady, and vapidity,* I *command you to flee and dissolve!*
> NOW! NOW! NOW!
> *Apo pantos kakodaimonos!*
> ABRAKALA!
> *So mote it be!*

Finally, draw the number 888 in purple marker or pen on the pieces of paper. Do as many as you'd like, and hang them above or on the doors and windows of the house—every single one, if you wish. Otherwise, hang the papers above the doors that see the most foot traffic.

To complete the spell, ignite the wand of sage and walk the entire course of the house (deosil in each room) to get the smoke in every nook and cranny. Finish by walking deosil around the outside of the house with the burning sage.

Honing the Vision: A Divination Bottle

This spell is concerned with the creation of a bottle or vial whose purpose is to aid a person with their divinatory practices. Keeping this bottle next to your tools can add a boost of power to any of your divinations.

Virtually all cultures and religions practice divination in one form or another. Divination reveals the unknown, tapping into mysteries of the self and the world. Divinatory tools allow practitioners to glimpse the unknown, tapping into vibrations of the past and present and lending a certain clarity to present-moment experience. The divinatory tools themselves do not reveal the insights; the reader is the seer, while the tools are just conduits of information.

Divination is connected to psychic phenomena—an ability that all humans possess and can bring forth with proper work. The term *divination* is nearly synonymous with the word *augury*. Augury refers more to divination in preexisting phenomena like bodies of water, trees, and the movement of animals rather than the casting of stones, cards, sticks, and so on. However, many practitioners use the terms interchangeably.

The word *scry* comes from *descry*, meaning "to reveal." These days, scrying refers to the act of gazing, be it in a body of water, crystal ball, black mirror, or anything else. If your intent is strong enough, you can divine in anything. I've gotten visions from the ceiling and scryed in the fish tank and in patterns on wallpaper. There is, in fact, an infinite amount of information around us—Spirit is present in everything, permeating all physical items, just waiting for us to discover the information we need for progressive transformation.

—— · ——

Common divinatory tools include tarot cards, oracle cards, runes, pendulums, crystal balls, scrying mirrors or balls, tea leaves, the Ouija board, and a host of other tools too expansive to list here.

Mugwort seems to be the herb most associated with psychic vision. It's a good idea to cleanse your divination tools with mugwort tea, or smudge them with a bundle of the dried herb. If mugwort isn't immediately available, select another herb that is associated with cultivating psychic powers—those listed in the ingredients for this spell are some of the most potent.

In addition to utilizing mugwort, the tools can also be charged by the light of the Full Moon. It's ideal to let the tools soak up moonlight for at least three days. Another great method is to charge them in a magick circle on the night of the New Moon. They should be allowed to sit outside on the altar, or in a windowsill where moonlight reaches, for one complete Moon cycle (until the next New Moon). At that time they will be fully charged and ready for immediate use. The New Moon is an ideal time to perform divination, as the astral-physical veil is thin, and much of the unseen becomes revealed. It's best to cleanse your divination tools every New Moon, especially if you use them on a regular basis. This, in addition to the following spell, can help boost the power of a psychic, medium, divinator, or any other person wishing to extend their perception beyond our current time, space, and paradigm.

Stepping Back & Further Application

Before performing this spell, question your reasons for wishing to boost your divinatory powers. Do your powers seem to be inaccurate more than not? Are you just starting to hone your abilities? Do you simply wish to add to your accuracy?

If something in your divinatory practices just doesn't seem to be right, try other methods first: perhaps you need to study a different deck of tarot cards or oracle cards. Perhaps you need to experiment with different methods of divination. Maybe your powers are more pronounced in areas like hands-on healing or meditation, thus implying that divination is a skill to revisit later in life.

Whatever your personal experiences, this spell will certainly not ensure complete accuracy in your divinations—such a feat would be impossible, even by the most skilled! I once heard a statistic that roughly 70 percent of legitimate psychic phenomenon tends to be accurate, while

30 percent remains incorrect. This makes sense. Because we are incarnated in this instant of time, it's impossible for us to fully, completely, and accurately immerse ourselves in every detail of the past or future. Along similar lines, this is one reason I personally find divination on one's present moment to be the most successful.

Supplies

- 1 white candle and 1 purple candle
- a stick of sandalwood incense
- a small, transportable glass vial, jar, or bottle
- a small owl feather (gathered, not plucked)
- a freshly picked plant leaf (see Notes)
- any combination of the herbs bay leaf, hemp (or marijuana if it's legal in your area), mugwort, sandalwood, and wormwood, in a bowl
- your own hair and fingernail clippings
- 9 small moonstones (small enough to fit in the bottle)
- a purple permanent marker
- a few drops of bay (laurel) essential oil (*not* "fragrant" oil)
- 9 inches of purple thread
- a small sticky label (small enough to stick on the vial)
- a small piece of transparent tape (to cover the label)

Notes

- When completed, it is best to store this bottle with your divinatory tools; this way, its energy will merge with your tools regularly, and you will have to touch the bottle (linking you to the spell) before divinatory practices.
- The freshly picked plant leaf should ideally come from a plant known to aid with psychic or divinatory work. If one is unavailable, substitute any nontoxic, freshly picked leaf.

- The Greek Gnostic mantra of IAΩ (eye-ay-oh), which is Iota-Alpha-Omega, represents the *Demiurge* (the power of creation) and has numerous correspondences. Its usage here is to tap into worldly energies in order to give the practitioner greater psychic insight.

- The following "knot spell" used for the moonstones is a variation of Doreen Valiente's "Spell of the Cord" (see her *Witchcraft for Tomorrow*) used in traditional Wicca.

Procedure

Begin by casting a circle, calling the quarters, chanting, or raising energy as you normally would, performing protective exercises, and altering your consciousness. Clear your mind, bring focus to your breath, and meditate for at least a few minutes. When ready, begin the spell.

After clearing your mind, ignite the candles and incense and gaze at the tools in front of you. Situate the tools as follows: Place the bowl of herbs at the bottom, the feather resting atop them, the leaf atop the feather, and the bottle on the top. Place the candles on either side.

Pick up the bottle and place your hair and fingernail clippings inside. Next, add the moonstones one by one, saying one line with each stone added:

> By *moonstone one, the spell's begun,*
> By *moonstone two, it cometh true,*
> By *moonstone three, thus shall it be,*
> By *moonstone four, 'tis strengthened more,*
> By *moonstone five, so may it thrive,*
> By *moonstone six, this spell I fix,*
> By *moonstone seven, the stars of heaven,*
> By *moonstone eight, the hand of Fate,*
> By *moonstone nine, these powers are mine!*

On the inner side of the fresh plant leaf, take the marker and write IAΩ. Drizzle the bay oil on top of these letters and roll up the leaf, tying

Symbol 4

it with the purple thread. Place this and the feather inside the bottle and fill it up the rest of the way with the herbal mixture.

Cap the bottle tightly and drip the purple and white wax around the edges to additionally seal it.

On the label for the bottle, draw symbol 4 and adhere it to the glass. Cover this label with the transparent tape to ensure that it doesn't smudge.

Sit the bottle upright and cup your hands above it. Say:

Psychic powers, divination,
I summon the force of all creation.
Empower these items, empower them right,
that I may See through the darkest night.
Bound to me, this creature of Earth and glass,
that I bear witness to the present, future, and past.
With this spell my divination's strong:
to help others in need I mustn't be wrong.
Through Moon and Earth and third eye alight,
this bottle shines magick both day and night.
May I always get vision; may I always See,
as I will, so mote it be.

Press the bottle to your brow (the Ajna chakra) and meditate for a few minutes. Envision the bottle and your third eye being connected by a 3-inch-wide indigo-colored etheric cord. Envision the bottle surrounded with this vibrant color and, when ready, slowly put down the bottle and close the circle as you normally would.

The Crossroads at Midnight: For Indecision & Path-Choosing

When looming decisions rule our thoughts, it can benefit us to utilize magick for the purpose of discovering the best possible course of action. Indecision can be a heavy weight. Not knowing what to do with oneself can lead to all varieties of anxiety. Yet, following through on one path or another can be damaging if the person isn't fully committed or sure of themselves. This spell can help the caster come to learn their destined route and grow secure in the decision.

Spiritually and mythologically, *crossroads* can refer to a number of things. The best way to analyze the term is by understanding the symbolism: two crossing roads, or a fork in the road, signifies two paths. These paths can be spiritually seen as those which intersect "this" with "that." These polarities can represent any two differing ideas, paths, or realms. The most popular idea is the perception of the crossroads being an intersection between this world and the faerie world. Other cultures have long viewed the crossroads as gateways between the realm of the living and that of the dead. Others view the crossroads as the intersection between good and evil forces. Mythologically, the Greek goddess Hekate and god Hermes seem to be those most prevalently associated with the crossroads. Numerous African gods (in Vodoun and other systems) have crossroads associations. In Hoodoo, many practitioners view the crossroads not only as a boundary between worlds, but a place where magickal spells can be placed or buried either for the purpose of fixing/sealing them or destroying an enemy's curse. This may be due to the fact that the crossed roads form an X, or because the roads are assumed to be frequently traveled on (thus carrying forth or "stomping down" energies).

One can utilize the intersection of two paths for a variety of purposes. Because some lunar deities have crossroads associations, and because the crossroads are generally visited for magickal work during the hours of night, the symbolism is frequently aligned with the Moon. Just as the Moon is the illuminated eye in the darkened sky, so may this spell provide the practitioner with the clarity to find their way.

Stepping Back & Further Application

You find yourself at a crossroads in life for a reason. For starters, one must step back from their mental turmoil to see something for what it really is. Is the decision really a big deal, or are you blowing it out of proportion? Is the choice black or white, or is there a balanced middle ground that outweighs the two choices? Are there more options to be considered, and are those options mutually exclusive?

Sometimes the answer to a difficult question is the most simple option. Sometimes the answer is already known, and the seeker is just looking for the confirmation they need; this spell can work in that regard. However, be open to the possibility of receiving messages that contradict your opinions or expectations. Objectivity is a necessity when divining on a situation, whether your own or someone else's.

Supplies

- 5 fresh, organic apples
- chiastolite, saturolite, or another "cross stone"
- an athamé or knife
- your most accurate deck of tarot cards or other divinatory tool

Notes

- This spell is designed to be performed at a crossroads. It is best to find two intersecting dirt roads or paths in nature. I've found the most ideal crossroad locations to be cemeteries, parks, and mountain trails. The spell is best performed at midnight or 3 am while the Moon is full. Finally, be sure that you are alone (as long as safety allows) and undisturbed.
- If you are used to working with deities of the crossroads, you may wish to additionally call on their assistance for this spell. Don't forget to bring proper offerings! For example, if you are working with Hekate, ideal offerings include honey, snake skin, black dog fur, yew, poplar, hazel, cypress, willow, myrrh, almond, lavender, poppy, and aconite.

- The colors red and black are traditionally associated with the cross-roads in Africa. It would be ideal to wear these colors when performing the spell.

Procedure

Begin by casting a circle, calling the quarters, chanting, or raising energy as you normally would, performing protective exercises, and altering your consciousness. While sitting in the middle of the crossroads, clear your mind, bring focus to your breath, and meditate for at least a few minutes. When ready, begin the spell.

Place one apple on each intersecting road. Make sure that the fifth apple is either standing upright on the "cross stone" next to you, or is resting on the stone in your lap. On this fifth apple, use your athamé to carve an X on one side and a Y on the other.

Now that the apples surround you in a square, raise your hands and, either closing your eyes or gazing at the Moon, whisper:

Gods, ancestors, spirits, devas, fae . . . those who guard and protect the crossroads . . . I summon your presence and ask you to bear witness to this divination. Guide me in my way, guard me on my path—may I know the route I am meant to take. Utter the answers I seek. Whisper solutions in my ear. Possess my mind not with glamour, but with solutions.
So mote it be.

At this point, you may call forth any crossroads-associated deities you wish to work with. If you work with any spirit guides or spirit animal helpers, summon their aid. After this, declare:

The question I have is this: [state your dilemma]. *What path shall I take?*

Close your eyes and listen to the sounds around you. Take note of anything applicable that you might hear. After a few moments, say:

If I was to take the road of [state one possibility], *what would be the result?*

Quiet your mind and listen for any answers or signs around you. The wind may pick up, an apple might roll over, a car might blare its horn, and so on. Take note of any synchronicity and determine whether or not it's divine communication. After a few moments, draw a tarot card or divine with the tool of your choice. Take note of any messages you may receive. Be careful to read the signs not in the way that *you* wish to see them, but in the way that the spirits intend.

Repeat the two previous steps for as many "possible solutions" as you have in mind. When you've divined on each potential outcome, say:

> *Are there additional possibilities in this situation—those I have not previously considered?*

Again, listen to the signs and divine for as long as you need. Eat the apple in front of you and meditate on the messages received. Try blurring your eyes and gazing into the "cross stone" in order to see if any additional messages are waiting to be scryed.

At this point, you should have a more clear direction of the path you should walk. If you didn't get a direct answer of the best possible outcome, take note of the messages you received and continue to practice "informed contemplation" until you make the decision (or realize the decision, I should say).

Thank all entities present for their assistance in your ritual and close the circle as you normally would. For offerings, leave the apples where they are, placing the core of the eaten apple in the center. Without looking back, walk away from the crossroads the same way you came.

Piercing Illusion:
A Clarity Spell to Reveal Truth in a Situation

As mentioned in the previous spell, the Moon is the illuminated eye in the darkness and can be energetically utilized for purposes of clarity and revealing. If you find yourself in a situation that requires a revelation of truth, this spell may be ideal.

This spell is predominantly focused on seeing the intention of others. If there exists the potential that you're being lied to, for example, it's only natural to want to break this illusion and get to the heart of the issue. I've used similar spells to help reveal the actual intentions of others and can attest to its effectiveness! Many factors contribute to a person's desire to glamour and deceive those around them. Just the same, one's own gullibility is likewise problematic. Personally, in my younger days, I used to believe literally everything a person told me. I was malleable, persuadable, and easy to deceive, and a number of people took advantage of me because of it. I naturally expected everyone around me to be as honest as I was! Unfortunately, this caused turmoil and had great "reality check" consequences down the road. Once the lesson was learned, discretion and discernment became my indispensable companions.

This spell can help a person learn truth in the face of possible deception from another person or group of people. Similarly, one can use this spell to reveal truth about an issue that may or may not involve another person. A situation may have occurred that remains unclear. In this case, one must craft the spell while thinking of the event that took place and its possible reasons for occurring. For example, the reason for the death of a loved one (human or animal) may be unknown. With enough effort, this spell can assist in revealing the cause, and should be considered an aid to the active seeking of truth in the situation.

Mystery is part of life, particularly in terms of the larger questions of existence. One shouldn't desire to know everything; some questions are best left unanswered. Before performing this spell, consider the importance of the unclear issue. Is it something that will naturally reveal itself in time, or do you deserve to have the answers revealed to you as quickly as possible? This spell is mostly designed to combat confusion. When performing this spell, a person should be open to multiple possibilities, including those that may have not been previously considered.

Stepping Back & Further Application

If your desire to perform this spell comes from your interactions with another person or people, first consider the deeper issues. For what personal motivations would someone lie to you? Do they feel it's for your greater good, or are they lying for their own gain? If it's for reasons of personal gain, are they trying to get something from you, such as resources, information, or approval? Is it to gain attention or perceived self-importance (a negative aspect of ego)?

Perhaps the answer is easier than you think. Why is the situation unclear, and what options have you not considered? It's essential not to jump to conclusions. Instead, open your mind to all possibilities, both positive and negative. Additionally, keep in mind that few things are black or white, and that there are two (or more) sides to every story.

If this spell is a response to a perpetual situation (such as your regular interaction with a friend, coworker, or family member), keep analyzing the signs. Pay close attention to the other's claims and search for signs of justification. Subtly get inside the other person's head to learn their intentions. Most importantly, know your own intentions.

Supplies

- a few large potatoes
- an athamé or knife
- a purple drawstring sachet bag
- 9 small tiger's eye stones
- a handful of sunflower seeds
- 1 large moonstone
- a brewed cup of black coffee
- any combination of the herbs cedar, eyebright, and marigold (*calendula*)
- a lemon
- a black permanent marker

Notes

- After performing this spell, it's a good idea to carry this bag on you for as long as necessary. The longer its energy is allowed to merge with your own, the more easily this particular spell will work.
- If potatoes are unavailable for some reason, substitute dry beans or something else to represent eyes.

Procedure

Begin by casting a circle, calling the quarters, chanting, or raising energy as you normally would, performing protective exercises, and alter-

ing your consciousness. Clear your mind, bring focus to your breath, and meditate for at least a few minutes. When ready, begin the spell.

With the potatoes situated in front of you, proceed to carve out 9 "eyes." Place these potato eyes in the sachet. To match, add the 9 tiger's eye stones and 9 sunflower seeds (without shells).

Crack 9 additional sunflower seeds and eat them, adding the shells to bag one by one. Toss in the large moonstone and say:

> Lady Luna: eye in the dark,
> I summon your powers of truth.
> Penetrate through illusion, pierce through confusion.
> May I see this situation for what it is.
> So mote it be.

Sip the cup of coffee. Between sips, add pinches of the herbs to the sachet, filling it completely. Right before you're about to take the last sip of coffee, dump it into the bag. Declare the following 9 times, beginning in a whisper and ending in a yell:

> Hail Great Spirit of truth and sight,
> I seek your wisdom on this night.
> My eyes be clear, my intention right,
> may intuition be the guiding light.

Tie the bag and cup it in your hands while thinking about the issue. See if you get any visions or intuitions concerning the situation at hand. Either way, the spell has started to work and answers may reveal themselves to you in many different ways to come.

Picking up the lemon and marker, draw 9 large eyes on its skin. Be sure not to smudge them! When finished, set the lemon on the bag and close the circle as you normally would.

Allow the lemon to sit on top of the bag for at least 24 hours. Afterward, put the lemon in a "seeing" spot of the house (such as on top of the fridge or hanging from the ceiling) and keep the bag close to you for as long as necessary. You might also wish to make some nummy magickal hash browns with the potatoes!

Chapter 3

— · —

MERCURY

— · —

MERCURY

Zodiacal rulership: Gemini, Virgo

Color association: Orange

Sephira: Hod

Number: 8

Day: Wednesday

Archetypes: Magician, Holy Messenger, Scribe, Psychopomp

Themes: Communication, intellect, study, knowledge, travel, perception, logic, dexterity, mystery, technology

Tell It How It Is: Astral Communication

Communication greatly forms our reality and is occurring all the time. From cells in bodies and plants to conversations and reading, from body language to email, from art to music, communication is a constant in reality. This spell is concerned with the communication between yourself and another.

Sometimes it's difficult to communicate in words. Ideas can get bogged down by tangential thoughts. One might have a difficult time forming proper words, or may not want to somehow offend or put off the person they're talking to. According to the results of a variety of 1971 studies by UCLA professor Albert Mehrabian, 55 percent of communication is based on nonverbal cues (body language, facial expression, etc.), 38 percent is based on the tone of voice being used, and only 7 percent of communication consists of the actual words being spoken. Considering this astounding piece of information, it's rational to conclude that *miscommunication* also most easily occurs as a result of nonverbal communication.

When full communication poses difficulty, I always advocate handwriting or emailing letters to communicate thoughts. This allows the writer to clarify, refine, and formulate words and sentence structures that they may find themselves unable to easily formulate in settings of face-to-face communication. In this day and age of representational facial icons :-) and caricatures =^.^=, the tone of one's virtual and typewritten communication can be more easily understood. Written *emphases* help convey tones of messages that could otherwise go undetected or misunderstood. At the same time, written communication is quite limiting and can be easily mistaken without nonverbal cues.

This spell is not only concerned with communication with other people, but can be utilized to hone communication between the practitioner and an external entity, including a deity, a guardian, or someone deceased.

Many present-day Catholics perform the age-old practice of leaving notes to saints on folded pieces of paper. These are left in monument sites like caverns and areas dedicated to particular saints, or at the feet of statues. This practice has been carried over since the time of *defixione tablature* (see page 152) and remains a method of prayer and communication through the planes.

This spell comes into play if other methods of communication seem to have somehow failed or have been incomplete. This working is concerned with subtle communication. The written messages being transmitted here are purely energetic in nature. This method is both a psychological venting for the practitioner and a magickal style of communication to the subconscious mind or energy pattern of another. You may wish to write things that you want to communicate but don't feel comfortable doing ("stop being so bloody irrational!" or "I wish you could see how in love with you I am"), or you may wish to write things that you've attempted to communicate but that have not gotten through for one reason or another.

Stepping Back & Further Application

You are likely to be utilizing this spell in the case that other methods of communication have gone awry. Perhaps you have tried to communicate with certain gods or spirits but are having insecurities and doubts as to the effectiveness of those communications. Perhaps you've been trying to get your message across to a friend or loved one but have been at a loss for words. Maybe you've tried letter-writing but your point still didn't get across as intended.

If you seem to be having communication issues with another *person* in particular, step back and analyze the reasons. Miscommunication occurs between two parties: the deliverer and the receiver. In what ways could you be misreceiving the message? For what reasons could the other person be misperceiving? Keep in mind that both you and the other party are under a similar Universal law: our perceptions are greatly formed by our experience. As an example, my own definition of the word *sister* may be drastically different from your own, and is greatly defined by our individual experiences of the past. Such differing definitions can cause baffling misunderstandings. When communicating, don't be afraid to reword things in other peoples' terms.

If you are wishing to eloquently communicate with a disembodied entity or god (rather than with another person's subconscious), I highly suggest this spell. If one wishes to communicate with the spirit of a departed human, I suggest only performing this spell for personally therapeutic reasons. Souls of the dead may not actually receive the written information, as they best respond to being spoken to directly (much as they would in human form). However, one may wish to subtly communicate unspoken, subconscious messages via this method.

Supplies

- an orange candle
- parchment paper
- a pen, pencil, or quill and ink
- a paper envelope
- an orange pencil, crayon, or marker
- a freshly picked dandelion
- a burning bowl or heat-safe bowl

Notes

- When writing the letter, feel free to use symbols, drawings, or non-word words. This spell is focused on communicating *intention*.

- If a fresh dandelion is absolutely unavailable, substitute a "puffy" dandelion or dried dandelion root.
- If working with a spirit or god, you can anoint the paper with various oils attuned to the spirit's energy after writing the message, or with oils imbued with your intent to help carry the message.

Procedure

Begin by casting a circle, calling the quarters, chanting, or raising energy as you normally would, performing protective exercises, and altering your consciousness. Clear your mind, bring focus to your breath, and meditate for at least a few minutes. When ready, begin the spell.

After lighting the candle, repeat the name of the person or entity you are wishing to receive this "astral letter" to. In a loud voice, say their name 8 times.

Pick up the paper and writing utensil and begin writing your message. Address it as if they will be formally reading it, and take time to formulate your words. Don't be afraid to speak your mind exactly as you see the situation. Use whatever words or terms communicate the messages, and be as deep as you'd like.

When you've finished writing the letter, sign it and read it over. If you've made any mistakes or wish to add or cross out anything, do so now. Once satisfied, fold the letter 3 times, ensuring that the letter will be able to fit in the envelope after being folded. Say:

Folded thrice, folded fast,
through present, future, and past.
Threefold message, break the chains,
Mercury deliver this through the planes.

Open the letter again. You will now notice that the folds have created 8 boxes. Take your orange writing utensil and, in each of these 8 boxes, draw the symbol for the planet Mercury.

After placing the dandelion in the center of the paper, refold the letter (in halves or thirds is fine) and seal it in the envelope. Drip wax from the orange candle on the envelope's back to put a final "seal" on it, and blow it dry.

Next, address the letter to the recipient. Write their name (full name and/or spiritual name) on the front of the envelope and address it any way you'd like.

Finally, light the letter on fire from the flame of the candle. When the flame starts to near your hand, place the letter in the bowl and allow it to finish burning. Keep igniting the paper with the candle, if necessary. While this is happening, repeat the following 8 times:

Delivered to you there, sent off by me here,
[Name], you get this message loud and clear.

When the letter is completely burned, close the circle as you normally would.

Tongue Tying: A Spell to Halt Gossip

Slanderous words can be very hurtful. It can be even more hurtful to discover that people have been saying such things without your knowledge, especially if such talk is a direct betrayal of trust, confidence, or emotional security.

Gossip is part of life. Inevitably, people will discuss others behind their backs. Not everything that is said about another person is gossip, even if it's perceived as such. Part of our culture, particularly in American culture, includes the discussion of those we have come in contact with, take issue with, or otherwise observe. For many people, simply sharing views about another person (whether a friend, coworker, relative, or celebrity figure) can be a platform to observe, compare, and contrast perceptions. Personally, I see no problem with this.

Gossip, on the other hand, can be defined as cruel, critical, two-faced slander. If a person is willing to share deprecating views and insults about another person, yet would *not* say them to the face of the person being discussed, gossip is occurring.

While we need some amount of ego, or "I" identification, to function in this world, a number of psychological factors can lead to the exaltation of the "negative ego." This aspect of ego is both selfish and survivalistic.

One reactive product of fear is the desire to elevate one's own social standing by any means necessary. Unfortunately, one of the easiest ways to do this is to criticize another person or group of people. Such attacks are unwarranted and can injure a person in numerous ways.

Gossip leads to rumors. Rumors lead to even taller tales. This cycle can play out for a long time, and can permanently damage a person's reputation or social standing. What's more, a person's gossip may not only consist of a discussion of their viewpoints, but may actually *originate* from tall tales and lies. What's worse is that some compulsive, pathological liars don't even realize that they're making things up (which is a result of a psychological condition). The social game is indeed complicated, and one must take the most impartial stance possible to correctly analyze a situation of gossip. In all of this, compassion is key.

This spell is focused on bringing malicious and uncalled-for gossip to a stop. There are, of course, many non-magickal methods that can assist in halting such slander, but a spell like this can aid in the process by projecting energy to an intended outcome. As with all projected intentions, the Universe will follow the path of least resistance in order to manifest the energy being sent.

Stepping Back & Further Application

As I mentioned earlier, when gossip is an issue, it's essential for the person being discussed to take an objective stance. From this position, one can most accurately assess the situation. Is there *really* gossip happening here, or has there simply been a miscommunication somewhere along the line? For what reasons would the other person drag your name through the mud, and did they mean to? Is this person only repeating what they heard from someone else? Did you receive wrong information as a result of a "he said/she said" circle? What part did *you* play in all of this?

It's easy to emotionally overreact to gossip. Using a humble, self-analytical approach, try to see if you are truly a victim of gossip or if the other person's intention is genuine. Are the rumors based in fact, simple misunderstanding, or the intention to harm? Is the purpose of the gossip to actually cause you harm or social embarrassment? It may not be.

Though it's easy to react with anger, compassion is one of the best approaches when dealing with a situation of slander and mudslinging. Compassion is also one of the most pure and spiritual approaches a person can take in the face of adversity. If the gossiper wants you to react in anger or cause you upset, wouldn't compassion and even disinterest in the gossip be your best defenses?

Another good step before doing a spell of this sort is to try talking to the person to see things from their perspective. If you are operating under your own misunderstanding when you perform this spell, you may be further damaging the situation, utilizing spellcraft for the sake of revenge. This would not be an intelligent use of magick. If one casts this spell with more force and anger than is necessary, more harm than good could come about in the long run. Cultivate objectivity and understanding before energetically tying someone's tongue.

Supplies

- a yellow candle
- a blue permanent marker
- a long, fresh, unbroken leaf of either mullein or hound's-tongue
- the "essence" of the person or people creating the gossip (see Notes)
- 2 needles or pins
- 64 inches of black thread
- a beryl stone (see Notes)
- any combination of the herbs clove, devil's shoestring, and slippery elm

Notes

- If a fresh, unbroken mullein or hound's-tongue leaf is unavailable, find a different plant and get a long, fresh leaf that looks somewhat like a tongue.
- Beryl stones include the following: emerald, aquamarine, bixbite, heliodor, maxixe (a type of beryl), morganite, goshenite, and golden beryl.

- The "essence" of a person, also called *ousia*, is anything that carries their energy pattern, including DNA (such as hair, fingernail clippings, and excretions), or that has come in contact with the person (this is the Law of Contagion, and can include a person's possession, footprint, handwriting, and so forth). A person's essence can also be tapped into by creating a picture or poppet of the person, or by simply writing their name and focusing on them.

Procedure

Begin by casting a circle, calling the quarters, chanting, or raising energy as you normally would, performing protective exercises, and altering your consciousness. Clear your mind, bring focus to your breath, and meditate for at least a few minutes. When ready, begin the spell.

Light the candle and grab the marker. On the upper side of the leaf, write the name of the person or people who are spreading the gossip. Place the "essence" of the gossiper on top of the leaf. Press these firmly between your palms and declare:

> As this leaf was once of the earth, it is now the gossiping tongue of [Name].

Take the leaf between the thumb and index finger and run it slowly through the flame of the candle. Say:

> Tongue of flame: Spitfire,
> your words of slander come to a halt.
> No more shall you speak such rotten words of me.
> Back-biter, two-facer, shit-talker, trust-breaker, STOP!
> [Name]: DOMEM!
> ABRAKALA!

Immediately roll up the leaf and stick the needles into the roll. The needles should pierce through the leaf in an X formation, securing it tightly.

Take the thread and begin wrapping it around the leaf and pins in a counterclockwise fashion. While you are doing this, wrap the stone and pieces of the herbs along with it, binding their energy to that of the leaf.

Once the thread has run out and the herbs and stones are securely
bound to the piece, drip a good amount of candle wax on the thread and
press it firmly. While the wax is drying, say:

Your words against me are useless.
Your tongue is tied, your gossip bound.
Your slander has no place here.
[Name]: DOMEM!
ABRAKALA!

Close the circle as you normally would, and deposit the spell somewhere that the person will come close to it without actually seeing it
(such as buried near their property or hidden by their desk at work).

Paradigm Shifts:
Safety in Travel

One of Mercury's specialties is travel. As the planet Mercury is the closest to the Sun, its energy is believed to be swift, voyaging, and communicative. One can call forth these agile vibes when constructing a spell
or prayer to aid in travel.

Whether it be via plane, train, or automobile (and sometimes even
foot or bicycle), Mercury can be a guide and protector for travelers. I
draw on Mercury's energy when doing any sort of physical travel and
find the energy to be invaluable. Even during astrological Mercury retrograde cycles, the planet's influence is there to be intelligently utilized.
Of all the planets, Mercury goes retrograde most often because it's the
closest to the Sun, rotating more quickly than the other planets. Retrogrades can make a planet's general energy feel topsy-turvy or backwards
from the Earth perspective and are also said to draw the planet's energy
more deeply inward. People are affected by retrogrades and other planetary shifts at differing degrees of intensity—this is greatly dependent
on the makeup of one's natal chart.

This spell is for creating a Mercury-aligned spellbag. This bag can be
carried during any type of travel and can be reimbued with Mercurial

energies at any time. It would be a good idea to check an ephemeris or zodiacal planner to ensure that the planet Mercury is direct when this spell is either constructed or recharged. Though it's certainly possible to draw on Mercurial energies during a retrograde, it's more advisable to do so when direct.

—— • ——

This sachet spell isn't restricted to physical travel. Physical traveling is only one type of travel! Perhaps you'd like to use the bag when performing astral projection, or to help in your process of learning astral travel. Maybe you'd prefer to keep the bag close when performing trance-channeling sessions, voyaging through entheogenic shamanic work, or achieving ritual Gnosis.

Because sleep and dreaming are a connection between this world, our minds, and other planes of consciousness, you may wish to keep this as a "safety in sleep" charm. There are a multitude of uses for a Mercurial spellbag, and its intended purpose is entirely up to the caster!

Stepping Back & Further Application

This is one of the most general, personally tailored spells in the book. Because you can intend it for any sort of "traveling" purpose, you may want to make a list before performing the spell. Get creative and brainstorm different ways this spellbag can be utilized.

Drawing on the bag's medicine is quite easy: simply keep it next to you. When you feel the need to utilize the bag's medicine, bring it to your face and smell it; this instantly pulls the intended vibrations into your body and energy field. You can also meditate with this bag before trips of any sort, or you can hang it from the rearview window, stash it in a luggage bag, or hang it next to the bed.

Though Mercury can provide protection during both physical and astral travel, still ensure that you take every safety precaution you can when doing traveling of any sort. Put on your seat belt, wear a helmet, don't abuse substances, keep yourself in check during trance states, get enough sleep, and blah, blah, blah. You know the drill.

Supplies

- paintbrush
- dragon's blood ink
- a small sheet of aluminum foil
- a blue or orange permanent marker
- a small orange or blue drawstring bag
- 1 teaspoon of powdered cinnamon
- any combination of the herbs anise, ash leaf, cat's claw bark, comfrey, High John the Conqueror root, Irish moss, kelp, mugwort, oakmoss, olive leaves (or a dried olive), pennyroyal, seaweed, Spanish moss, and wormwood
- 1 stone each of aquamarine (or emerald), moonstone, tiger's eye, and turquoise

Notes

- One simple way to recharge this bag is by meditating with it and envisioning it glowing orange. Hold it to your mouth and intone the word *Mercury* into the bag (as well as any prayers or intentions you wish to enchant it with), or get creative and charge it up via your preferred method.

Procedure

Begin by casting a circle, calling the quarters, chanting, or raising energy as you normally would, performing protective exercises, and altering your consciousness. Clear your mind, bring focus to your breath, and meditate for at least a few minutes. When ready, begin the spell.

Remove your shirt (if you're not already skyclad) and any undergarments. Dip your paintbrush into the ink and draw the symbol for Mercury on your torso. Make the symbol very large, with one nipple at each "horn" of Mercury's upper crescent. Draw the circle from there to a couple inches above your navel, and create the bottom cross so that it intersects at your bellybutton.

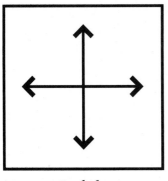

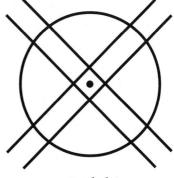

Symbol 5   **Symbol 6**

Lie down and let the ink dry. Next, grab the aluminum foil and draw symbol 5 with marker. On the reverse side, draw symbol 6. Fold the foil three times and place it in the bag.

Add the cinnamon to the bag and declare 8 times:

This charm is of Mercury!

Add the remaining herbs to the bag and state:

Bag of travel, be with me.
Bag of voyage, guide me.
Bag of change, surround me.
Bag of the planes, navigate me.
Bag of Mercury, protect me.
So mote it be!

Add the stones to complete the charm. Tie the bag and lie back down on the floor, placing the sachet in the middle of the symbol on your chest. With your eyes closed, envision the bag surrounded by an orange hue, and see this same energy going into your solar plexus area. Let your energy merge with that of the bag. When you feel a sufficient connection, thank Mercury and close the circle as you normally would.

Mental Clutter, Mental Clarity: A Sachet for Study

We will here draw on another powerful aspect of Mercury, which is study, the intellect, and the mind. Mercury rules Gemini and Virgo, the two most mentally focused, analytical signs of the zodiac.

This spell is designed for people who are undergoing any type of study. For those in school, whether college, high school, or another type of formal educational system, consistently performing magick to bring about mental focus is a good thing to consider. It's easy for the mind to wander or become overwhelmed with an abundance of information. Utilizing magick can help adhere the mind of the practitioner to the studies at hand, encouraging a constant absorption and comprehension of information being presented.

This spellbag can be ideal for a person who is engaging in metaphysical studies. Whether in an occult school, training coven, or other type of structured esoteric program, one can reap particular benefits by creating a charm to aid in the progressive work. Occult information can seem daunting and even incomprehensible if a person is beginning a system of study into new information. Just as the Universe is infinite, the amount of wisdom we can attain is just as limitless. Crafting a bag such as this can help keep the mind focused and inspired, knowing that the endless road of knowledge is being embarked upon.

——— • ———

Discipline is an element of life that is often lacking in the West. Everybody's upbringing and experiences are different, and if you have come to feel that a more disciplined approach to life and study would be beneficial, you may want to craft this bag to keep the inspiration and motivation flowing.

As with all things, there is always a balance. An extreme lack of discipline can create apathy and indifference to progression in life. This can lead to depression and feelings of worthlessness. An overabundance of discipline can lead to rigidity and over-seriousness, and even bitterness and elitism. Everybody responds differently to varying levels of study and devotion, and I believe that pushing the limits of the mind can invoke confidence and accomplishment. Life is change; life is progression. To buckle down and study—both regularly and constantly—is to take the path of personal evolution.

Stepping Back & Further Application

Before performing this spell, be sure that your intention is clear. For what reasons do you feel inclined to craft a spell for study? Are you embarking on a new "odyssey of the mind?" Do you wish to hone abilities you already possess? Are you afraid of failure? It's easy to become discouraged with learning and stop. The demon of looming failure is a powerful one, but one that mustn't be surrendered to. Giving up only breeds more of the same. Courage can be cultivated by disproving your own doubt.

If you approach this spell with fear and anxiety, this energy will naturally absorb into the sachet. Instead, take a breath and realize that you *have* all the ability in the world to learn new information, assimilate it into your consciousness, and progress in life. If you feel you're not absorbing information that's around you, analyze the reasons. Does your mind wander too frequently? Do you *really* want to be learning the information you're being presented, or is it disinteresting? Consider other energetic elements you can add to the bag. If you are in medical school, maybe adding a folded diagram of the human body to the sachet would be beneficial. If you're studying Thelema, maybe ninety-three mustard seeds would be a good addition. As with all spells, craft them to your specific purpose and be creative.

Supplies

- 1 candle each of the colors white, yellow, and orange
- raw benzoin (or storax) incense resin
- a round incense-burning charcoal disk and sand in a dish or censor
- 8 small squares of aluminum foil
- an orange permanent marker
- an orange drawstring sachet bag

- 1 stone each of citrine, turquoise, and moonstone
- 8 black-eyed peas (blackeye beans) or yellow-eyed beans
- any combination of the herbs caraway, cinnamon, clove, dill, eyebright, gingko, jasmine, peppermint, rosemary, sage, spearmint, thistle (milk or blessed), vervain, and white horehound

Notes

- It's a good idea to keep this bag close to you as much as possible. If you take a book bag to school, stick it in there; if you do most of your work at home on the computer, place it nearby.

Procedure

Begin by casting a circle, calling the quarters, chanting, or raising energy as you normally would, performing protective exercises, and altering your consciousness. Clear your mind, bring focus to your breath, and meditate for at least a few minutes. When ready, begin the spell.

Ignite the candles and benzoin incense. Once the incense is billowing, face the east. Raise your arms above you, close your eyes, and bellow:

Spirits of study—hear me now!
Mercury and the Muses!
Those of thought, mind, and intellect!
Spirits of Air and Will,
aid me in my working.
Venerated keepers of the mental plane,
assist in all of my studies hereon forth.

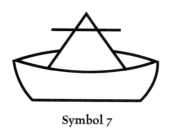

Symbol 7

Grab the aluminum foil and marker. On one side, draw symbol 7. On the other, draw the symbol for Mercury. Fold this three times and place in the bag.

Next, add the stones. While adding the turquoise, say:

Mercury bear witness. Fill this bag, that it may
radiate with knowledge . . .

Add the citrine, saying:

... through all my days ...

Add the moonstone, saying:

... and all my nights.

Slowly add the 8 black-eyed peas one by one. While doing this, think about your studies. Imagine yourself understanding all of the information you're presented, and see yourself succeeding in your chosen area of study.

To top off the bag, add the mixture of herbs. When finished, tie the bag and hold it to the incense smoke. Say 8 times:

Now enchanted, this charm is mine,
I carry wisdom through all time.
From the ears into the mind,
There is no knowledge I cannot find.
So mote it be.

Thank Mercury and any other spirits present, and close the circle as you normally would.

Tapping the Planes: Automatic Writing

Automatic writing is a skill that takes time to develop. It can be described as a process of channeling that consists of the writer receiving messages through themselves and transmitting them on paper.

When automatically writing, the conscious mind of the writer steps to the background. Much like invocation in Pagan traditions, the spirit of that which is communicating is allowed to step forward and dictate messages using another person as a conduit. Instead of speaking, however, all information received is immediately written. Most automatic writers act as "trance channels," though some find success by remaining fully conscious of, and interacting with, their immediate environment (while giving no attention to the hands). Every practitioner has a different method.

Similar to invocation, messages that are received during this process are not filtered through the mind. Instead, they are allowed to flow naturally. When the rational mind filters what the subconscious detects, messages become distorted. Instinctive censorship and rewording can occur as a result of insecurity and uncertainty. Unfortunately, it's easy to mistake *externally received* messages with information of the subconscious. What appears to be a message channeled from an external intelligence can, in fact, be one from the "higher self" or the subconscious—and vice versa!

Some modern surrealist artists practice *surrealist automatism*. This is similar to automatic writing, but the artists generally credit their subconscious or unconscious mind as the producer of such imagery (or music, etc.). *Mediumistic automatism*, on the other hand, is frequently practiced by mediums, and is assumed to be messages from spirits of the deceased.

Practicing automatic writing allows a person to not only tap into their subconscious, but into the other planes. Whether a spirit plane, astral plane, or alternate dimension, information can be transmitted from a variety of "places." However, it's essential that the receiver of the messages does not mistake a simple ghost-communication for musings from Andromeda. Discernment, and even doubt, is key.

——— • ———

When first practicing automatic writing, the final messages can appear to be extremely garbled. It's not unusual for the writer to receive pages upon pages consisting only of random letters, numbers, symbols, and sentence formations. At first, it can be difficult to even decipher the most simple message from all the seemingly abstract nonsense. Even the most gifted automatic writers can struggle with decoding that which is channeled.

Though some people are born with an innate ability to almost effortlessly automatic write (or are born with natural psychic powers, artistic talents, musical abilities, and so on), it is a learned practice for the majority of people. As with all abilities and skills, practice makes perfect.

Stepping Back & Further Application

As mentioned, it can be very difficult to decipher messages received when automatically writing. If you feel that automatic writing is a skill that you are naturally inclined to or wish to develop, keep on practicing. Eventually, messages will come that will be both understandable and significant. Don't rush the process. At the same time, don't feel bad if the messages you *do* decrypt seem to be extremely simple or even silly. Take what you get and keep developing the skill; not every message has to be profound.

Sometimes it's impossible to interpret what's been channeled. Still, many messages can be decrypted by scrutinizing the symbolism of the transmission. The receiver can do this by analyzing what each message could possibly indicate to them personally, or by getting advice from others (especially from the person who the message was meant for, if there is one). One can also research numerology, Qabalistic symbolism, and sacred geometry when faced with symbolism in the form of shapes and numbers. Or you can try an Internet search for strange words or names that stick out.

When decoding the message, beware of anything that seems particularly profound. Maybe you are receiving messages that the Earth is going to explode in a couple of days, or that you're being visited by beings from a distant galaxy. Now, I'm not one to discount the possibility of alien communication through automatism, and I have in fact read a number of "extraterrestrial channeled" books that have highly conscious information throughout. What I mean to emphasize is that one should approach automatic writing with considerable skepticism in order to distinguish likely reality from flights of fancy. One might also want to keep in mind that, much like the Ouija board, should one genuinely channel an external being, that being certainly has the capability of lying!

Supplies

- sandalwood incense sticks
- a white candle
- parchment paper
- a ballpoint pen
- 1 cup of pomegranate juice

Notes

- Pomegranate is a fruit associated with Mercury, and it has numerous mythological associations. Connected with Persephone, daughter of the Greek goddess of fertility, it is said that the god of the Underworld, Hades, tricked her into eating the fruit upon freeing her (following her abduction). This compelled her to enter the terrain of the Underworld for part of the year annually, thus making the story an origin myth for the seasonal cycle.

Procedure

Begin by casting a circle, calling the quarters, chanting, or raising energy as you normally would, performing protective exercises, and altering your consciousness. Clear your mind, bring focus to your breath, and meditate for at least a few minutes. When ready, begin the spell.

Light the incense and candle, and set the paper and pen on a hard surface in front of you.

Cup your hands above the pomegranate juice. Imagine it glowing in a soft white light and recite:

With this juice, I take into myself the ability to journey the planes. Behold! This sacred libation is charged with vibrations beyond my consciousness. As this drink is internalized, I take into myself the ability to expand beyond this waking sphere. Messages now come to me easily and freely. I am open to receive.

Close your eyes and drink the juice. With your eyes still closed, start humming quietly. Find a comfortable, high pitch and continue vibrating this tone for a few minutes. If random thoughts enter your mind, see them disappearing instantly. Keep reentering a space of mental expansion and detachment from ordinary reality. When you feel inclined, put the pen to the paper and stop humming.

Begin writing. Do not become aware of what's being written. You may wish to look around, or you may find the practice easier with your eyes closed. Don't pay attention to your hands; just make sure that the pen is connected to the paper and is still writing. If necessary, put the first piece of paper aside and grab another.

During this process, your hands may be writing letters, numbers, words, symbols, drawings, full sentences, random scribbles—anything. Be open to any and every possibility, and don't limit your thinking to what is "proper." If you find yourself wondering what's being written, distract your thinking by focusing on something else in the room. Over time, you'll discover the method of focus (or lack thereof) and trance that works best for you.

When you feel a sense of completion, set down the pen and close your eyes. Take a number of deep breaths in through your nose and out through your mouth. Lie on the floor, move your body, eat something, or do whatever it takes to ground and center your mind. When finished grounding, close the circle as you normally would, and plan some time in a few days to decode the messages.

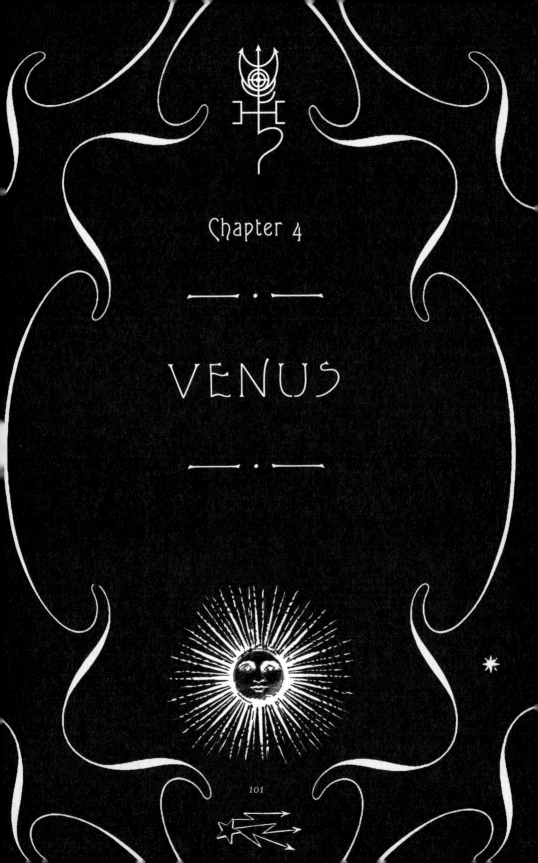

Chapter 4

VENUS

VENUS

Zodiacal rulership: Taurus, Libra
Color association: Green
Sephira: Netzach
Number: 7
Day: Friday
Archetypes: Love Goddess, Fertility Goddess, Sea Goddess, Maiden
Themes: Love, fertility, attraction, relationship, valuables, romance, pleasure, beauty, sensuality, sexuality, affection, friendliness, aesthetics, erotica, luxury

The Twin Flame: Summoning a Lover

Of all the spells that can be performed, love spells are renowned for being the most tricky. All of us want to love and be loved. All of us *deserve* to love and be loved. Of all the emotions in the Universe, love is the most valued, desired, and misunderstood. True love is pure, a spiritual diamond in the rough, and it can be the thing that dictates one's life.

Indeed, there are many aspects and forms of love. We experience different types of the emotion when feeling love for pets versus nature, friends versus relatives, long-term partners versus flings. Love is not limited to one sensation alone; it takes numerous forms and is expressed in a variety of ways. Though the following spell is focused on the romantic variety of love, love in all its many aspects is just as vital for happy and healthy functioning, if not more so.

—— · ——

Playwright Oscar Wilde once wrote that "the mystery of love is greater than the mystery of death." This quote illustrates the divine nature of love as a spiritual connection between souls. It's difficult to understand the feelings that love evokes and, as with all spiritual experiences, love is something that must be experienced to be known.

They say that love is blind. Though it's a most exalted experience, romantic love can injure other aspects of the mind if a person allows it to. Rationality, common sense, and discernment often take a backseat to romantic love. This idealistic approach isn't always best.

To idealize love is to seek it without considering other aspects of the equation. Idealism can be the cause of unhealthy behavior and mental attachment. Because all things are temporary, one mustn't become attached to the sensation of love. Attachment to anything, or to one's perception of it, can lead to injurious decisions and dissatisfaction.

This spell should be performed if you feel that you are truly ready to attract a romantic lover into your life. While a life partner would be ideal, realize that this spell draws the frequency of love and not necessarily an extended duration of it (though it may). People meet and separate for specific spiritual reasons, and everyone has a different set of lessons they're meant to learn in this life.

Stepping Back & Further Application

If you're single and are unhappy with being single (which is an unfortunately common view), consider the reasons. I'm not talking about reasons why "nobody likes you"—such thoughts are based in a "victim mentality" and are highly unrealistic. Instead, analyze the spiritual reasons as to why the Universe would put you in a lonely situation. Perhaps there is an abundance of self-work you need to accomplish now, and doing this spell would only be ignoring its necessity. Consider this, and the benefits of the single life, very wisely and thoroughly. I also recommend looking at the spell *Sacred Body, Sacred Mind: Invoking Self-Love* in this section before performing this working.

Desperation is a palpable, negative vibe to emit when seeking love. If your desire for love finds you desperate and obsessive, examine the reasons behind the feelings and work on those first and foremost.

You get what you give. If you feel hatred toward yourself, how can you expect others to feel the opposite? Loving oneself is important for healthy functioning, and this means loving yourself for who you are.

Keep in mind that for every type of person there is, there are those who are attracted to that type of person on numerous levels. Love is never gone or unattainable. It's never too late to find a partner and enjoy the connection.

Your past experiences of love influence your present perception of it. When performing this working, try your best to put aside perceptions of the past and simply call forth pure love for what it is. Drawing on past experiences can only serve to help them repeat in the future.

In the end, remember to do the follow-up work. Visit places where a potential lover may be, browse profiles online, make an effort to talk to people you find interesting, get involved with local community groups and spiritual centers . . . do the work and have fun doing it!

Supplies

- a burin or another candle-carver
- 2 red taper candles
- lavender essential oil (*not* "fragrant" oil)
- a yellow permanent marker and a black permanent marker
- a large sheet of green paper
- 2 lodestones with lodestone dust (aka magnetic sand or lodestone food)
- 1 rose quartz and 1 bloodstone (or carnelian)
- Mixture 1: an additional, separate herb or herbs (see Notes)
- Mixture 2: any combination of the herbs anise, bloodroot, cardamom, caraway, cherry bark, cinnamon, orris root, rosehips, snakeroot, and vervain as well as a good amount of powdered (confectioner's) sugar
- a red flannel drawstring bag

Notes

- This spell is not focused on casting a love spell on another person in particular. To perform love magick on another without their consent opens a whole new—and very big—can of karmic worms. Manipulating the free will of another is a type of black magick and should be used for defensive workings only, not a love spell. Instead, this spell is designed to summon a lover but no one person in particular.

- For the second herb: If summoning a male specifically, use powdered sugar, calamus (sweet flag), milk thistle, sprouts, and/or lavender. If summoning a female, use powdered sugar, Venus flytrap, red raspberry leaf or fruit, a red flower, and/or rose petals. If gender is unimportant, use an equal combination of lavender and rosehips added to powdered sugar.

Procedure

Begin by casting a circle, calling the quarters, chanting, or raising energy as you normally would, performing protective exercises, and altering your consciousness. Clear your mind, bring focus to your breath, and meditate for at least a few minutes. When ready, begin the spell.

Using the burin, carve symbols 8 and 9 on both candles. Inscribe each symbol 7 times on each taper. Additionally, carve any number of hearts and pentagrams all over both candles. When finished, anoint both candles with the lavender oil, covering them completely. Light the candles.

With the yellow marker, draw symbol 8 on the paper. Hold your hands over the paper and say:

Symbol 8

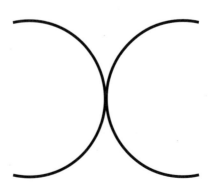

Symbol 9

Star of Venus, stars above,
bring two souls together in love.
In perfect love and perfect trust,
seal this bond between us.

Put both lodestones in the bag. Add the lodestone dust and say:

Magnetic stones and sands of time,
I am [his/hers] and [he/she] is mine.

Drop the other stones in the bag and drizzle a bit of the lavender oil inside. Add Mixture 1 and repeat the following 7 times:

Venus brings you to me.
Bound in the love we both deserve to feel,
this celebration of each other is now made real.
Venus brings me to you.

With the black marker, draw symbol 9 over the top of the other symbol on the paper, in the middle of the sheet. Scatter Mixture 2 all over the paper. Take 7 pinches of this mixture (from the paper) and place it in the bag. Tie the bag and place it in the very center of the sheet.

Picking up one burning candle in each hand, turn them at an angle so their dipping wax meets together on the bag. As the wax drips onto the bag (and paper/herbs), repeat the following chant numerous times until the candles are burned halfway down:

[He/she] is now drawn to me.
By the Star of Venus, so mote it be.

When you set the candles back down, cup your hands over the bag and invoke the feeling of love within you. Smile and feel adored. Imagine yourself gazing into the eyes of another (but not anyone in particular), blissed out with admiration for each other. Feel yourself being safe and secure, happy and fulfilled. Continue to feel this for a few minutes, visualizing the bag glowing in brilliant reds and greens.

When finished, give thanks to Venus and close the circle as you normally would. Allow the candles to burn all the way down and scatter the herbs on the paper to the wind. Hang the bag somewhere outside of your house where it will remain touched by the elements, yet invisible to wandering eyes. After hanging the bag, burn the green paper and declare:

By the Fire of Love—come to me! So it shall be!

Sweeten Up & Chill Out: To Mend Quarrels with Another

Disagreements in life are inevitable. Even the most calm, centered, conciliatory, nonjudgmental person can't avoid the occasional dispute. Though such a person's response to dealing with disagreement might be better tempered, one cannot avoid the occasional tiff.

Arguments, discrepancies, and quarrels result from misunderstandings or differences of opinion. Though everyone has the right to an opinion, it doesn't mean that we're going to agree with them all the time. A quarrel can last as long as either party chooses, or until they simply "agree to disagree."

Disagreements can also have very positive effects. Sometimes it takes intense exchanges to really learn the views of those you associate with. Approaching one's interactions with others should be from a place of balance: not too passive nor too extroverted, not too quick to agree nor too quick to oppose, not too quiet nor too loud, and so on. Balance encourages more balance and inspires others to interact similarly.

When effectively interacting with another person, each party has to make an effort to understand the other person's perspective. Every interaction in life carries the potential to be a learning experience.

——— • ———

Far too often, people approach disputes with a competitive view. In reality, life is not a game of competition; such blatantly animalistic behavior is, I believe, selfish and unevolved. While it's easy to compete in the "who's right, who's wrong" game, much fear and greed can result.

If you find yourself post-argument with a friend, relative, lover, or anyone else, this spell may be an ideal option to encourage an energetic bond of forgiveness and unity.

Peace and understanding are noble goals and should be at the top of everyone's list of priorities (especially world leaders and other people in power). When approaching this spell, be sure not to focus on the disagreement at hand, but the peace you are striving to attain.

This spell greatly assumes that you, the caster, have come to a place of peace and forgiveness, and wish to encourage the other person to do the same.

Stepping Back & Further Application

When analyzing the disagreement, determine whether it was caused from a misunderstanding or a difference of opinion. If caused by a miscommunication of some type, think about ways it can be resolved. Have you tried to clear things up with the person over the phone, in person, or by a letter or email? What, precisely, was misunderstood, and how can you best communicate with them? If the issue is a matter of differing opinion, can you strive to see the other person's viewpoint? Can you communicate your opinions, and the reasons behind them, in different ways than you have? What non-magickal steps can you take toward resolution?

Regardless of who was being irrational and to what degree, coming to a peaceful place on the issue can support you and the other person constructively discussing the point being disagreed upon. However, if both of your views are clarified and there is still disagreement, can you agree to disagree? While it's probably the last possible option, keep in mind that some disagreements are so big and unshakable that parting ways with the person (for a period of time or for good) is the best decision that could be made. As hard as it is, this is sometimes the case with large disputes.

Finally, keep in mind that disputes take time to heal. The more open both parties are to healing, the faster this can occur. Performing this spell can aid in the healing process, and can encourage both you and the other person to calm down, take a step back, and reconsider the value of your connection.

Supplies

- 1 pink candle
- your own hair and fingernail clippings
- a tight-sealing glass jar
- more than enough brewed catnip tea (cooled) to fill the jar
- the "essence" of the other person (see Notes)
- honey
- 1 cup of raw cane sugar
- an ice cube
- a ballpoint pen
- a sheet of parchment paper
- dove's blood ink
- 1 rose quartz stone
- a separate dish of valerian root
- any combination of the herbs broom, cinquefoil, damiana, dandelion, foxglove, High John the Conqueror, mugwort, myrrh, pennyroyal, and rowan (mountain ash)

Notes

- The "essence" of a person, also called *ousia*, is anything that carries their energy pattern, including DNA (such as hair, fingernail clippings, and excretions), or that has come in contact by the person (this is the Law of Contagion, and can include a person's possession, footprint, handwriting, and so forth). A person's essence can also be tapped into by creating a picture or poppet of the person, or by simply writing their name and focusing on them.

Procedure

Begin by casting a circle, calling the quarters, chanting, or raising energy as you normally would, performing protective exercises, and altering your consciousness. Clear your mind, bring focus to your breath, and meditate for at least a few minutes. When ready, begin the spell.

Light the candle and add your hair and fingernail clippings to the empty jar. Add a splash of the catnip tea and say:

I *have entered equanimity.*
I *have entered release.*
I *have entered forgiveness.*
I *have entered peace.*

Add the essence of the other person and say:

I *now encourage you to do the same.*

Add a drizzle of honey and a handful of sugar. Say:

Sweeten up, [Name]*! AREB!*

Add the ice cube. Say:

Chill out, [Name]*! AREB!*

Putting the pen to paper, write your name 7 times and the other person's name 7 times. Fold this repeatedly until it's a little ball and put it in the jar. Add the dove's blood ink, saying:

With the blood of peace, our dispute is no longer.

Add the rose quartz and say:

With the stone of heart, we are connected in compassion.

Add the valerian and say:

With the herb of mending, our dispute is pushed to earth.

Put another dose of the tea into the jar, followed by a handful of the herbal mixture. Finally, add enough tea until the jar is filled to the brim. Cap the jar tightly.

Turn the candle upside-down over the jar, allowing it to drip exactly 49 times onto the jar's lid. Count the number of drips out loud.

When finished, focus on the jar and visualize you and the other person laughing, joking, smiling, and getting along in agreement. Afterward, close the circle as you normally would.

Put the completed spell in a plastic grocery bag and stick it inconspicuously in the back of the freezer, saying:

This cools off our tempers and chills out our stress. AREB! So mote it be!

When resolution is mutually accomplished, thaw the jar, dump all contents into flowing water, and throw the container in the trash.

A Demand for Justice: Winning a Legal Dispute

In the face of the law—whatever kind of law it may be—the truth of the situation is of utmost importance to understand.

In terms of state or federal law, many thousands of people are convicted and punished for victimless crimes each year. America is the top-ranking nation for jail or prison incarceration, even exceeding China in its per capita inmate population. The rate of incarceration in the States is extreme, and the legal system seems anxious to convict. There's a lot of money in it, after all.

This sort of statistic is a prime example of America's generally fear-based, power-hungry approach to life's rules. As a result, people can sue anyone for anything—even the most trivial and commonsense issues—and win. Legal loopholes, fine print, and strict adherence to the written word of the law have greatly replaced the judicial approach of analyzing intention. When caught in a legal situation where intention should be made known, this spell may be of help.

Laws are in place for social reasons. In many other countries, laws exist that do not have the best interest of the people in mind. The judiciary system is a complex beast. If you find yourself in the face of legal adversity, consider all angles of the situation before you decide how best to defend yourself.

———   •   ———

This spell isn't designed only for those facing legal dispute on a state or federal level, and it can be adapted to people facing rule-based conflicts in a workplace, educational institution, and so on. If there is a pending meeting about your behavior, perform this spell beforehand. If someone is constantly tattling to the boss about your actions, or seems to want to get you in trouble, this spell can help bring clarity to the situation.

Venus helps balance situations and lend an energy of social justice. The following spell is to encourage both your intention to be made known and the truth of a situation to come into clarity for all involved.

Stepping Back & Further Application

Though your well-being and reputation are at stake, be sure to take an objective stance to the legal situation. For what reasons did the opposing party get you in trouble? Analyze their intentions as well as your own. Are you demonizing the other party (be it the law, a coworker, boss, or administrator), or are you actively attempting to understand their views of the situation? What was your role in the situation, and are you fully admitting to any of your trespasses or mistakes? Taking responsibility is invaluable and proves that you have self-awareness.

In order for this spell to work, the caster must desire *truth* to come about in the situation. This doesn't mean that the caster should be free of any wrongdoing, but that they should be willing to fully admit to anything wrong on their own side. Additionally, one should be willing to understand how the opposing party came to their conclusion, even if it's something you vehemently disagree with. Be careful not to overdefend yourself or severely criticize the other party. Instead, present your case clearly, with composure, and with the desire for others to understand the truth of the matter.

We all have the right to defend ourselves. Luckily, it's easy to learn from mistakes if one is open to change. Learning these lessons takes humility and a genuine understanding of what went wrong.

Supplies
- a gray candle
- a large gray sheet of paper
- a green pen or marker

- the Justice card from a tarot deck (Rider-Waite, Thoth, Golden Dawn, or one similar is preferable because of astrological and Qabalistic correspondences)
- 1 piece each of amber, bloodstone, and obsidian
- Dr. Buzzard's Court Case powder (see Notes)
- Mixture 1: any combination of the herbs amber resin, aspen bark, cinquefoil, galangal (Low John root), High John the Conqueror root, and lucky hand root
- Mixture 2: any combination of the herbs horehound, rosemary, and sage
- Mixture 3: any combination of the herbs cedar, eyebright, and marigold

Notes

- In the Thoth Tarot, the Justice card is renamed Adjustment.
- The amber stone is actually petrified tree resin/sap.
- Dr. Buzzard's Court Case powder can be obtained from a Hoodoo or magickal supply shop, and has a curious Southern legend behind its usage. For more information on its history (as well as to order it online), you may wish to check out LuckyMojo.com. As an alternative, simply substitute alum powder, which is available in bulk at many herbal and naturopathic shops.

Procedure

Begin by casting a circle, calling the quarters, chanting, or raising energy as you normally would, performing protective exercises, and altering your consciousness. Clear your mind, bring focus to your breath, and meditate for at least a few minutes. When ready, begin the spell.

Light the candle and, on the back side of the paper, draw an enormous eye in green pen or marker. Flip the paper over and write every detail of the case you can think of. Write from an objective standpoint. Note any accusations being made, the time and date of the meeting or trial, and the names of all persons involved to any degree. Take as much time as you need, and read over the list multiple times to ensure that you've covered every detail.

In the center of the paper, place the Justice card with the candle burning on top of it. Place the amber and obsidian at the base of the candle, touching both the card and the paper.

Cup your hands around the candle and state:

Here be the details of this issue.

Sprinkle the Dr. Buzzard's powder all over the paper, card, stone, and candle. Declare:

With Buzzard as my witness and Venus as my judge, this dispute is illuminated in my favor.

Sprinkle Mixture 1 in the same fashion. Say:

Wicked words against me fall only on deaf ears.
The laws are in my favor. Victory and justice are mine!

Sprinkle Mixture 2 in the same way. Say:

With this, I limit outside influence and judgment.
With this, only the knowledge of truth enters.
With this, I invoke common sense into all present in this matter.

Sprinkle Mixture 3 in the same way. Say:

Truth is Law, Law is Truth. Justice from all sides!
May all see clearly the happenings and circumstance.
With utmost precision, only reality can be perceived.
The scales weigh balanced, the scales weigh fair.
In my favor the cogs of justice turn.
As I will, so mote it be!

Allow the ingredients to sit undisturbed until after the legal proceeding is entirely finished.

Thorn in My Side:
Banishing Heartache

The pain of separation is a very difficult thing to deal with. In terms of romantic partnership, separating from someone who was once thought of to be a soul mate or life partner can be emotionally devastating. Though nothing happens without a spiritual reason, the greater picture is difficult to see when parting ways with someone whose connection was originally thought to be a longer-lasting thing.

When separation occurs, idealism falls. Many people build their connections based on an unrealistic sense of who they believe the other person to be. Try as we might, we can never really fully *know* another person, even if we believe that's the case.

The emotions that occur after separation are where this spell comes into play. If, rationally, someone knows that the relationship should not continue, yet feels the desire to keep on trying to make it work, this spell can assist. By no means should one banish another person, and the negative emotions between them, without seriously looking at the situation and determining that relations should cease.

This working can help invoke the energies of acceptance and forgiveness. Even if we feel hurt from the separation, odds are that the other person feels it too. Even in cases where the ex has severely mistreated his or her partner, acceptance and forgiveness still deserve to be felt. These emotions can be exceedingly difficult but are necessary for the sake of moving on and learning the life lessons of the separation.

——— • ———

This spell isn't limited to romantic partnership. This working, or something similar, can also be performed in the case of failed friendship. This spell is not meant to curse or damn the other person, but is designed for the caster's own emotional wellness and acceptance of the situation. More than anything, this spell is intended to help ease the lingering suffering associated with separation.

Breakups of all sorts happen for a million reasons. If both parties have decided, for whatever reason, that the puzzle pieces of "them" and "you" simply don't fit, it should be acknowledged and moved past over time. Holding on to what is not meant to be is unhealthy and can promote obsessive tendencies.

If you are the one who decided to break off the relationship or friendship, take some time to analyze your reasons and decide if you are truly making the wisest decision. If the other person disagrees with the separation, it might be a good idea to try communicating with them even more, ensuring that they reach a place of understanding. If the situation is opposite, try to accept the other person's decision for now, even if you don't understand it. Decide how best to communicate with them in order to come to greater realizations.

Stepping Back & Further Application

Because cases of separation are so individual, personal, and based on a massive amount of relationship factors, it's difficult to comment on such a situation in a general sense. Whatever the details, it's necessary for the person performing this spell to step back from the situation and examine it without emotional attachment.

See what went wrong. Are you jumping to conclusions? Maybe there's more to the situation than is being perceived, and maybe you're not clearly seeing the other person's intentions. If you are a highly sensitive person, be aware that you may be propagating much more drama and heartache than really exists. When heavy emotions come into play, it's easy to become overwhelmed and see things in a skewed light.

Remember that there are two sides to every story. If you feel victimized, realize that such a mentality can lead to bitterness and the holding of grudges. "Victim mentality" is disempowering and is a way to skirt around the real issue. Feeling victimized can cause withdrawal and mistrust, which will naturally inhibit future interactions and activities. It's a *must* to see how you have emotionally responded to the situation and make certain that an increase in negative behavior (including self-deprecating views) doesn't come about as a result. It's also necessary to not cultivate an expectation of these types of breakups. If we expect and anticipate always being screwed over and wounded, that's the exact thing that will result.

If there are legal entanglements to the situation, please make sure that everything is reported and recorded. Additionally, are you relying on friends or other people for emotional support? Sometimes the easiest way to work through something is to discuss it with those you can trust.

Supplies

- a black candle
- a sterile lancet or pricking device to extract blood
- a tight-sealing glass jar
- enough red wine to fill the jar
- a small amount of apple cider vinegar
- 7 red roses
- a boline or serrated-edged knife
- 7 Witches' burrs (see Notes)
- 1 stone each of aventurine, chrysocolla, chrysoprase, garnet, and rose quartz
- any combination of the herbs bleeding heart flower, cinquefoil, feverfew, foxglove, gardenia, lavender, lemon myrtle, rosemary, thistle, and yarrow
- a handful of whole cloves
- coffin nails or rusted nails (see Notes)
- pins, needles, and shattered glass

Notes

- Coffin nails are generally a component of baneful magick and have a rich history in Hoodoo and other magickal systems. However, they (or any nail) can also be imbued with properties of "fixing down" energies or sealing a spell. An iron nail is preferable because of its energetic properties; *real* coffin nails (those formerly used to affix a coffin lid) are a rarity!

- A burr is a seed or fruit that is covered in thorns or sticky spiked hairs. These balls of spikes can be imbued with extreme protection or baneful force. Burrs from any plant can be used, but the more durable varieties seem to carry the most force. (If a burr is particularly sticky, prickly, or painful to the touch, it's said to hold stronger magickal potency.)

Procedure

Begin by casting a circle, calling the quarters, chanting, or raising energy as you normally would, performing protective exercises, and altering your consciousness. Clear your mind, bring focus to your breath, and meditate for at least a few minutes. When ready, begin the spell.

Light the candle and, with the lancet or pricking device, draw a drop of blood from the ring finger of your left hand. Squeeze it into the bottom of the jar.

Next, add a small amount of wine, followed by a splash of apple cider vinegar. Declare:

This represents the spilled and bitter blood of my heart.

Grab the roses and sever their heads. Take the knife or boline and cut off every thorn from the roses, ensuring that each thorn falls into the bottle. Say:

The pain of love broken: banished to this vessel.

Hold the candle upside-down and allow 7 drips of wax to enter the bottle. Set the candle back down and add the 7 Witches' burrs. Next, add the stones as well as the combination of herbs and declare:

My heart has been broken. My heart has been torn. This concoction is the wreckage of my connection with [Name]. I accept this. I move past this. I hereby release these torments of mind and emotion.

Dump the cloves into the jar, followed by the coffin nails, broken glass, pins, needles, and other similar items. State:

I banish and remove this emotional obstacle. No more shall I feel this pain!

Fill the jar the rest of the way up with the wine, cap it tightly, and shake the jar vigorously. While you are shaking, chant the following a number of times:

Mixed up, shaken up, torn up, broken up. I sever this pain from my heart!

Hold the jar to your heart and slowly pull it away, envisioning a green cord between your heart chakra and the bottle. When this is clearly seen, take the boline or knife and sever the energetic cord between yourself and the jar. Push the severed energy into the bottle, and the other half of the energy back into your heart chakra. When this is finished, close the circle as you normally would.

Take the jar to the freezer and set it inside. Say:

With this, I release my attachments. I banish all sadness, anger, jealousy, and self-pity associated with this experience. If love is lost, I allow it. I banish, I let go. I accept.

Slam the freezer door and write down the exact time of day it currently is. Mark your calendar for *precisely* 49 hours from then (which is 2 days and 1 hour) and return to the jar at that time.

When you've returned to the jar, take it from the freezer, look at it briefly, and drop it in the trash can. Seal the spell by saying:

As an icicle falls and shatters, so does the thorn in my heart. Onward I tread, having gained from that experience. Banished. Released. Forgiven. Healed. So mote it be.

Sacred Body, Sacred Mind: Invoking Self-Love

Many practitioners have an extreme amount of power and spiritual awareness, yet lack a key magickal component: love for the self. This element of healthy human functioning is vital for spiritual and magickal folk. If the self is not accepted, a host of issues can surface. Ever mind the age-old saying that the healer must first be healed themselves.

Society encourages shame. This shame, generally, is manipulated to convince people to buy products, pills, and procedures that alter inner reality or outward appearance. Feeling guilty, ugly, ashamed, embarrassed, untalented, or otherwise less than others is a way for marketers to milk us for all the money we're worth. With personal insults coming at us from all angles—often covertly and undetected—it's no wonder America is a nation that despises itself.

From insecurity and the disapproval of self comes the deprecation of others. Simple psychology rules this one: misery loves company. The empathy of feeling another person's suffering is somehow reassuring to the mind—even if it means dragging them to that place to feel it.

If you have determined that a lack of self-love is the cause of some of your issues, you may wish to try the following simple spell, and repeat it as many times as necessary.

—— • ——

The embracing of universal love is a personal and social virtue, and is something that great religions and mystical sects have encouraged throughout time. Feeling love for even the most wicked, maligned, and evil person might seem counterintuitive, but can be the very thing that helps them change their ways. Loving nature, God (however one sees God), animals, humans, and the world and absolutely everything in it is exercising compassion at its finest. It may seem idealistic or unrealistic, but undiluted, overwhelming love can shine through the darkest of experiences, even if it takes serious time and emotional work to reach such a point.

Before one can truly feel universal love, one must love oneself. It's easy to accept everyone but ourself, but it's this lack of self-appreciation that keeps us from feeling universal love to its full extent. Many people agree that you cannot truly love another unless you love yourself.

Stepping Back & Further Application

This spell is only one step in truly cultivating love for oneself. As this is accomplished over time, you must look at the reasons why you might not be feeling self-love. How are you "flawed" in your eyes, and why do you feel that way? Are these your own criticisms, or are they simply extensions of society's judgments? Are you surrounding yourself with people who promote love?

It's necessary to separate from the judgment of others in order to see if your views originate from yourself or from common cultural opinions. Are these conclusions you've come to on your own, or are you only reciting "learned" perceptions? Do you not feel worth and value for yourself only because you believe that others don't feel it? If so, do they unconsciously not value you because you don't value yourself?

What steps can you take in healthfully changing yourself to better fit your ideal self? Do you even *need* to change in the ways you think you do (think that one over well), and will these changes really make you love yourself more—or will you only find other things that are "wrong" with you as a result? Are you seeking approval from others instead of finding it for yourself? If so, do the work to pull back that energy instead of giving it away to the perception of others. Love yourself for who you are now, not for who you think you "should" be. The ideal self can much more easily be stepped into once you first love yourself for who you are, as you are.

Supplies

- any combination of the herbs catnip, flax, ginseng, life everlasting, thyme, rose, rosemary, sunflower, and vervain
- 2 large mixing bowls
- a pot of freshly boiled water
- 1 cup of sea salt
- a couple feet of cheesecloth
- a bathtub or shower

Notes

- The "Blessed be" chant used within is a variation of traditional Wicca's Fivefold Kiss. Please note the [bracketed] words; the first word is what women performing this rite are to say, and the second word is what men are to say. Please note that "formed in perfect beauty" (referring to women's breasts) and "formed in perfect strength" (referring to a man's chest) is not meant to imply that women's breasts aren't strong and a man's chest isn't beautiful. This gender division is found in the traditional Wiccan Fivefold Kiss. You can alter it or stick to the original.

Procedure

No circle needs to be cast for this spell. Instead, raise energy around you in your bathroom. Clear your mind, bring focus to your breath, and meditate for at least a few minutes. When ready, begin the spell.

With the combination of herbs placed in one of the bowls, pour the boiling water on top. In the empty mixing bowl, place the sea salt.

Look into your eyes in the mirror and gaze at yourself—without glancing away—for at least a full minute. Though this may take several attempts, when accomplished, speak very loudly:

I am perfect. I am sacred. I am beautiful. I am love.

Strip naked and dip your right hand in the herbal brew (making sure it's cool enough to touch). Anoint both feet with the water and say:

Blessed be my feet, that have brought me in these ways.

Dip your right hand in the water and anoint both knees. Say:

Blessed be my knees, that shall kneel before the sacred altar.

Dip your right hand in the water and anoint the genital area. Say:

Blessed be my [womb/phallus], without which we would not be.

Dip your right hand in the water and anoint the breasts. Say:

Blessed be my [breasts/chest], formed in perfect [beauty/strength].

Dip your right hand in the water and anoint your mouth. Say:

Blessed be my lips, that shall utter the Sacred Names.

Declare:

Through the shadows I summon perfect beauty.
Through the shadows I summon perfect love.
Through the shadows I summon perfection.
My body is a vessel of perfect beauty.
My body is a vessel of perfect love.
My body is a vessel of perfection.

Look into your eyes in the mirror and say the following very loudly and with much strength:

I *am* love. I *am* beautiful. I *am* sacred. I *am* perfect.

ODIUM

DIUM

IUM

UM

M

MA-MA-MA-MA

A

AM

AMO

AMOR

I *am* perfect. I *am* sacred. I *am* beautiful. I *am* love.

Hold the cheesecloth over the bowl of steeping herbs. Using caution, pour the water from the bowl into the bowl with the salt. Now that you have a bowl of "tea," draw yourself a warm bath. Though not as powerful, you can turn on the shower if you'd rather.

When the bath is created, pour the "tea" into the water before stepping in the tub. If you are running a shower, wait until the brew is cool enough to dump on your head (do this first thing when you enter the shower).

During the process of the bath or shower, repeat the words "I am love" over and over again. Say them fast, slow, in a high pitch, in a low and resounding chant, and so on. Play with the words and say them repeatedly throughout.

After 5 or 10 minutes, step out and approach the fogged mirror (if the mirror is not fogged, fog it by using your hot breath).

In the area of the face, draw a giant heart with the Venus symbol in the middle. Look in your eyes and, once again, say the full "I *am* love" chant (above), ending with a very loud:

So mote it be!

Chapter 5

— · —

EARTH

— · —

EARTH

Zodiacal rulership: None

Color association: Gold, Green-Brown
(or Ochre, Olive, Russet, Black)

Sephira: Malkuth

Number: 10

Day: None

Archetypes: Earth Mother

Themes: Grounding, stability, health, abundance, manifestation, prosperity, life, death, the physical plane

Energetic Entombment: Primordial Physical Healing

Holistic body health is of utmost importance for those seeking balance. From the foundation of the frame (the physical body), other planes of existence can be explored. Being as healthy as possible allows for the mind to bring focus to other aspects of reality beyond the mere physical system. At the same time, many people who legitimately suffer from long-term illnesses and disorders are highly spiritually aware and metaphysically functioning. It boils down to what one does with their predicament, and how one works with the imbalance in their body. Though some imbalances are out of our control (such as genetic factors, lasting physical injuries of the past, and so on), it's up to us to make the most of our situation and ensure the best health possible for ourself.

The following spell is designed for instigating healing of the physical body. Obviously, it should not be used as a substitute for legitimate medical care, but as a complement to other steps you are taking toward greater health.

——— • ———

Fear is a prevalent force, and it's natural to have fear arise when the body is out of alignment. It's easy to overreact and become frightened when the body is not in working order, or is afflicted with a new and uncomfortable sensation. When approaching a situation of physical healing, it's important to take spiritual and physical steps to encourage the healing. Remaining happy and optimistic may be challenging, but these feelings can greatly help in realigning the body. It's also key to remember that the body is designed to rebalance itself when misaligned; our body is designed to continually regenerate to proper functioning. In the case of long-term illness, one can work with their circumstance to come to the healthiest place possible *for oneself,* even if it's medically impossible to do things that others take for granted.

May this spell aid in the process of healing and realignment, whether on a large or small scale, and encourage the body to reach its utmost state of health. Feel free to practice this spell or a variation of it as often as you'd like.

Stepping Back & Further Application

Before performing a spell of this type, make sure you're taking every step you can toward bettering your situation. Are you using herbs, teas, and tinctures? Have you consulted a Western doctor, naturopathic doctor, or other health professionals? Are you receiving massage, acupuncture, chiropractic work, or other alternative healing methods? If not, please do; one's physical health is too significant to avoid proper care.

Consider the life lessons the illness or injury is trying to teach you. Karmically, we encounter various challenges in life as mechanisms for learning deeper truths. Is the Universe trying to force you to pay attention, break certain cycles, or reroute the path you're taking?

Much of the time, ailments of the body are direct reflections of spiritual and emotional imbalances. Because the physical body is the most dense and palpable aspect of our complete self (other bodies include the emotional body, mental body, astral body, etheric body, and so on), illnesses and imbalances can naturally influence other levels and manifest on the physical frame. Consider unhealthy aspects of your thought patterns, including fears, habits, and neuroses, and work on changing them in order to better your physical health. Additionally, try to discover if there are deeper physical causes for the ailments (including diet, physical strain, and substance use), and work on changing them accordingly. Put yourself first.

Supplies

- a brown candle
- a stick of patchouli incense
- 1 cup of steeped chamomile tea
- an array of plant or tree roots, fossil stones, and petrified wood
- 1 stone each of aventurine, bloodstone (or carnelian), hematite, malachite, and selenite
- any combination of the herbs boneset, Low John root, gingko, mandrake, oak (leaf, bark, or acorn), and skullcap
- a muslin bag

Notes

- The "tapping of the cortices" used in this spell is something that originates from the BodyTalk™ system of healing, and is designed to help the whole body "communicate" by tapping on the brain and the heart—the two major engines of the physical frame. For more information, visit www.bodytalksystem.com. (Thank you, Shari, for introducing these cool techniques to our Coven!)
- This spell should be performed at night, outside on the grass if possible.
- For added effect, drape a very long, black veil type of cloth over your body during the ritual.

Procedure

Begin by casting a circle, calling the quarters, chanting, or raising energy as you normally would, performing protective exercises, and altering your consciousness. Clear your mind, bring focus to your breath, and meditate for at least a few minutes. When ready, begin the spell.

Light the candle and incense, placing one on either side of you. Cup your hands over the cup of tea and say:

> Herb of health, water of life,
> enter this body, enter it now!

Place all the stones, fossils, herbs, and such in the muslin bag. Lay on the ground and place the bag on your body, either at the point of the ailment or on your chest. Close your eyes and repeatedly whisper the following chant:

Spirits of fortitude, spirits of healing,
enter this space—enter me now!

When you feel surrounded by these forces, place your hands on the bag and imagine all the energies of the tools being absorbed into your body. Keep this visualization throughout the ritual.

Take deep breaths. With each exhalation, imagine yourself going deeper and deeper into the Earth. See the dark Earth taking the illness from you, absorbing it into itself and replacing the energy with the regenerative health of the soil.

During this process, imagine the various levels of your physical body, including the skeletal system, the muscular system, the nervous system, and the organs throughout. Imagine each of these individually, each receiving and absorbing the healing power of the living Earth.

Spend quite a bit of time on this visualization and emerge from it when you feel the time is right. When you start to come back to your physical body, feel it aligning all the newly received health. To assist in this energetic assimilation, "tap your cortices" by performing the next two steps.

Using the tips of your fingers of your dominant hand, tap the back of your skull repeatedly for about 10 seconds. Afterward, tap your sternum (heart area) repeatedly for about 10 seconds. Take deep breaths while doing this.

Repeat the process by tapping a little ways up on your skull from the place you just tapped, and then tap your sternum again, both for 10 seconds. Continue this process until you reach your brow area, which should take about 5 repetitions. Once finished, tap one side of your head (just above the ears) for 10 seconds, followed by tapping the sternum, and do the same for the other side of the head.

Take a few deep breaths to assimilate the energies, and declare 10 times:

I am formed in perfect health.

Give thanks to the Earth and the spirits of health and healing, and close the circle as you normally would.

Bullshit of the Holy Cow: Purging Impurities & Astral Pollution

The following spell is for leeching toxins from the energetic body, and it will actually aid in leeching impurities from the physical body simultaneously. The odd thing about this spell is that the practitioner is to be covered in cow dung. That's right: cow dung. Though it might be tempting at first to call "bullshit," one must first realize the immense healing properties of the holy cow's excrements.

The average Westerner might be appalled and disgusted by such a thing as utilizing the feces and urine of a bovid (a class that includes the cow, bull, yak, and ox). In truth, using bovine excrements is a regular practice in many parts of the world, most notably India. Hindus worship the cow for a number of reasons, viewing the animal as a most venerated creature whose life-giving powers are virtually endless. Lord Govinda is seen as the one who watches over the cows, and the Vedas cite the cow as the mother of all living beings. In addition to the animal's ability to give milk, assist in farming and travel, and become domesticated, its excrements have long been cited for a nearly endless list of uses.

In Ayurvedic medicine, cow urine is used for a number of ailments and is often viewed as a general "cure all." Being a natural antiseptic, regularly putting the urine on the body as a tonic can clear up skin conditions including acne, psoriasis, and dandruff. The burnt ash of the dung is frequently used for the relief of mouth pain (and is often put in toothpaste), and is smeared upon the body by Indian Siddhus (ascetic holy wanderers) for purposes of divine communion. Internally, cow urine is used—with an astounding rate of documented success—for anything from cancer to impotence. Bottled cow urine can be purchased from a variety of online sources, but fresh is better. Because cow dung is easier to come by, we'll be using it for this spell.

—— · ——

The poop of "organic," grass-fed bovines is ripe with minerals and is, believe it or not, a sterile substance when fresh—after all, it's only digested grass. However—and please note this—most cows in America, for example, are not grass-fed. Instead, they are given a variety of genetically engineered corn, by-product, and chemical feed; their excrements would not be safe to use. For more information on proper poop use, see the Notes section.

The cultural uses of bovine dung are plenty. For starters, the manure is used as fertilizer in many parts of the globe. It also makes a great binding agent for constructing natural houses and huts, and is an insulator and insect repellent for the home. The dried dung is also used to create fires for heat and cooking food. On the skin, organic bovine excrements are used to cleanse and detox, and can be used as a poultice on specific areas of the body.

For our purposes, we will not only be detoxifying the physical body (to some extent, anyway), but will be exorcising built-up astral impurities. Energetically, our auras (and I say this term with as little "New Age" emphasis as possible) collect vibrations around us and can store energies accumulated over time. Many physical body healers emphasize gunk, cracks, or stains on the auric (or etheric/energetic) field, which they see as contributing to physical ailments. If you feel that you could use a serious aura cleansing and are ready to take up the noble challenge of being sacredly shat upon, I highly suggest this ritual.

Stepping Back & Further Application

If you're preparing for this spell, odds are that you have a significant energetic blockage you wish to remove. Feel out your etheric field. Determine where exactly this energy is residual (many carry build-ups of energy around their head and shoulder area, or around the heart, stomach, or hands). For what reasons has this compacting occurred? Perhaps you used to live in a dark, threatening, or energetically dense area that you now wish to "rebirth" from. Maybe you've had negative experiences in the past that still impact your energy and behavior. Or maybe you have a physical ailment and can feel the concordant blockage on your etheric field. Perhaps you have become more negative, pessimistic, bitter, or cold over time and wish to instead become more loving, playful, carefree, and kind again.

Whatever the case, if you're in need of a deep energetic cleanse, this spell can assist. Be sure to follow up on this cleansing outside of ritual to make certain that the energies you're cleansing do indeed continue to wane.

Supplies

- a wand of dried sage
- 1 brown candle and 1 blue candle
- dried or fresh bovine dung
- a large empty mixing bowl
- a large bowl of warm water

Notes

- Because the dung of most bovids is not safe for bodily contact, the practitioner has a couple options. One can track down organic, composted cow manure fertilizer designed for gardening, add water, mush it into a paste, and smear this on the body. If unavailable locally, some online retailers sell this (such as Vermont's www. moodoo.com)—just ensure that it's *organic* and from *grass-fed* bovine. Alternatively, one can find local cow dung and burn it to ash in a fire. By adding a nonchemical burning agent (like grain alcohol), one can ignite the cow pie and transform it to ash. This ash is safe to use on the skin and is not an uncommon practice in many indigenous parts of the world.
- Considering the sacred place that cows hold in Hindu belief, contemplate your own relationship with the cow in our own society. Is it one of compassion or the propagation of injury (such as consuming its meat and milk from factory farms)? Can you easily journey

to a farm or ranch should you wish to observe the cow's gentle, awe-inspiring nature (and even gather some manure)?

Procedure

Begin by casting a circle, calling the quarters, chanting, or raising energy as you normally would, performing protective exercises, and altering your consciousness. Clear your mind, bring focus to your breath, and meditate for at least a few minutes. When ready, begin the spell.

With the sage wand, smudge the area thoroughly after casting the circle. Light the candles and strip naked. If you're using dried dung, use the mixing bowl to blend it with the warm water to form a paste.

Using either the organic cow manure mush or burnt ash, spread it all over your face, neck, chest, arms, legs, back, hair, and everywhere else you can. Give particular attention to areas of the body that are imbalanced, either physically or astrally.

Once covered as much as possible, boldly state:

I *reclaim my untainted self!*
This astral pollution now shall flee!
Cleansed is my body, inside and out!

Meditate on the impurities on both your etheric and physical bodies. See the impurities being channeled into the dung, forced out of your body and adhered to the excrement. Perceive your body getting heavier and heavier—more and more weighed down by the impurities channeled in the dung.

When you feel energetically heavy, declare your intentions. Say out loud the things you are cleansing from yourself. To seal the spell, turn one of the candles upside-down and let a small amount of wax drip on both of your palms and the bottoms of your feet.

Close the circle as you normally would and take a good long shower. Afterward, smudge yourself, dress in fine clothes, anoint yourself with oil, have a drink, or do anything else to center yourself in your newly cleansed body.

Kicking the Habit: Breaking Addictions

According to Buddhist philosophy, sensation (experiencing) can lead to craving (desire), which can lead to clinging (attachment). Being but three spokes on the Wheel of Samsara, these particular points speak a universal truth: addiction and attachment have the potential to occur as a result of simply experiencing something.

Desires for anything in life can be healthy if exercised mindfully; it's only when one becomes dependent on—that is, addicted to—a thing that problems arise. To feel as though we can't function without something (aside from actual necessities like food, water, and shelter) is to enslave oneself to the earthly plane. With these energetic chains on the body, it becomes more and more difficult to reach beyond this world to higher forms of consciousness.

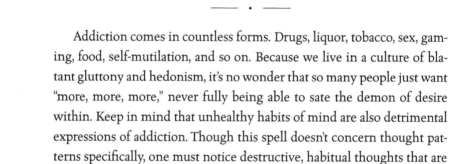

Addiction comes in countless forms. Drugs, liquor, tobacco, sex, gaming, food, self-mutilation, and so on. Because we live in a culture of blatant gluttony and hedonism, it's no wonder that so many people just want "more, more, more," never fully being able to sate the demon of desire within. Keep in mind that unhealthy habits of mind are also detrimental expressions of addiction. Though this spell doesn't concern thought patterns specifically, one must notice destructive, habitual thoughts that are clung to, even unconsciously.

With the realization of addiction, a desire to break the dependency is often simultaneously cultivated. Many people don't know the steps to take in ceasing addictive behavior. There is no one right way to beat addiction; everybody's constitution is different. Various programs offer different numbers and types of steps to recovery, and many are specific to the substance. Every substance we encounter affects us differently, even if the way in which it impacts us is subtle or unnoticed.

For a person kicking a habit, determination is key. Monitor your behavior and see how you react to cravings. Prepare for difficult situations. Discover methods of satisfying those cravings with healthy substitutes (meditation, jogging, painting, yoga, and so on). Find a support unit. Reward yourself for avoiding the substance. Be honest with yourself. With time, effort, and energy in the right direction, an addiction of any magnitude can be broken. May this spell jump-start the process.

Stepping Back & Further Application

Addiction represents the seeking of relief from the mind. Using a substance is an easy way to escape the mind temporarily. Eventually, the addict must either succumb and be destroyed by the addiction, or seek sustainable relief through another method. This requires the dependency on the substance to be released.

For what psychological reasons do you find yourself dependent on one thing or another? Exactly how unhealthy is this addiction—and how unhealthy can it become?

This spell will not instantly break you of any addictive craving. Instead, it can be a step in the process of healing. If your addiction is strong enough, seek out local recovery programs like Narcotics Anonymous, Alcoholics Anonymous, and rehabilitation centers. Seek out a psychiatrist who specializes in the field of addiction. Read all you can on the steps to breaking threatening habits, and follow through with diligence. Find a support group and don't give up on giving it up.

Supplies

- a black candle
- a round incense-burning charcoal disk and sand in a dish or censor
- a loose incense mixture of powdered catnip, dragon's blood resin, and mugwort
- bat's blood ink and a paintbrush
- 2 all-natural, unbleached pieces of paper
- 10 feet of all-natural twine (like jute or hemp)
- a handful of graveyard dirt ("graveyard dust") or its substitution (see Notes)
- something to represent the habit to be broken (see Notes)

- about ½ ounce rue
- a shed snakeskin
- 1 small piece each of amethyst, chrysoprase, and orange calcite
- a piece of jet or charcoal
- any combination of the herbs eucalyptus, frankincense, High John the Conqueror root, ivy, licorice root, and black pepper
- scissors
- honey
- a fresh, organic grapefruit cut in half, plus a spoon to eat it with (adding raw sugar or honey is okay)

Notes

- The substance to be used in the spell can either be the substance itself (like a cigarette with its filter removed, a pill, a splash of alcohol, your own sexual fluids, a video game instruction sheet), or it can be something biodegradable to represent the substance (like a drawing of a video game controller on a piece of paper).
- Because the items will be cast into the water, it's important to use only all-natural, biodegradable items in this spell. You may also use a grapefruit rind in place of the papers and honey.
- Graveyard dirt has long been used in Hoodoo and other magickal practices. For our purposes, it will represent the laying to rest of an old habit. Simply go to a graveyard and scoop up a small amount of dirt (not from someone's grave in this case), ideally from a crossroads area of the cemetery. A common substitute for graveyard dirt is to make a powdered mixture of patchouli, mullein, valerian, and/or sage.

Procedure

Begin by casting a circle, calling the quarters, chanting, or raising energy as you normally would, performing protective exercises, and altering your consciousness. Clear your mind, bring focus to your breath, and meditate for at least a few minutes. When ready, begin the spell.

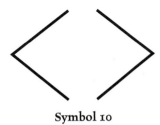

Symbol 10

Arrange the supplies before you. Light the candle and charcoal, putting the incense mixture on the coal. When there is a billowing cloud of smoke, grab the ink and paintbrush and draw a very large symbol 10 on one of the sheets of paper, and a large X on the other. Blow these dry. Flip the papers over and, on one of the sheets, write in large letters EGO IPSE SUM EXPLETUS. On the other sheet, write TO THE DEPTHS I BANISH THIS ADDICTION. Blow the sheets dry and place them with the symbols facing up.

First, cut the twine in half (5 feet). Place one of the ends in the middle of the X paper and put a handful of graveyard dirt on the X, covering the end of the twine simultaneously. Next, place the substance of addiction (or its representation) on the dirt. Immediately thereafter, cover the substance with the rue. Add the snakeskin, followed by the three stones. Next to the stones, place the jet or charcoal. Place more graveyard dirt on top of this, followed by the combination of herbs.

Tightly tie the uncovered end of the twine around your left wrist. Without pulling the twine from under the pile, pull your arm back until the string is straight. Meditate on the nature of your addiction, seeing the cord as a representation of your addiction. The cord is linking you to the components of the spell, and it's your decision to finally sever the ties. When you feel ready, declare 10 times:

> I break this tie. I break this chain.
> No addiction can ever reign.
> My cravings are ceased,
> I banish this beast.

At this point, use the scissors to cut the twine from your wrist. Place it on top of the contents of the paper. Next, take the honey and put it on the uncovered areas of the paper, making sure that you get the honey near the edges. Pick up the other sheet of paper and, with the symbol facing down, press it to the honey. This should seal the pages together, making what appears to be one piece of paper with a bulge in the middle. After the pages are stuck together with the components secured inside, forcefully spit at it and then say:

Leave me now! You are dismissed. You are nothing. You are dead.

Close the circle as you normally would. Eat the grapefruit, feeling its bitter essence chasing all addictive tendencies from your mind and body. Return to the spell the next evening at dusk, having not indulged in your addiction since the night before. Carefully fold the paper and tie it with the remaining 5 feet of twine. Carry this mixture to a bridge with flowing water beneath it and, when no one's looking, throw it off the edge. As you do so, declare the following with utmost confidence:

EGO IPSE SUM EXPLETUS!
You are banished now and forever!
So mote it be!

Leave without looking behind you, and continue to follow up on the spell by taking all possible steps to recovery.

Self-Interment: A Spell for Grounding

A problem that faces many mystically inclined people is that of being ungrounded. In magick, we talk about *grounding* quite frequently. This refers to being centered, anchored in the physical frame, and having one's thoughts and attention brought down to reality. The best time to ground and center is following a ritual in which one's consciousness has been elevated. The traditional Wiccan cakes and ale carry the purpose of grounding one's energy while communing with fellow ritualists.

Some people are inclined to strict rationality and find themselves constantly aware of their surroundings, of conversations being had, and of the sensations of the physical body. This is extreme grounding. On the other hand, some people have tendencies of forgetfulness, a wandering mind, and a "floaty" sense of being. This is an example of ungroundedness. Neither is good or bad; both modes of being serve their purpose.

However, being trapped in either extreme for extended amounts of time can be dangerous and difficult.

One of the reasons I chose to include this spell here is because I suffered from ungroundedness—and all its accompanying difficulties—for many years of my life. Of course, I still carry these qualities to a great extent and feel as though I'm naturally inclined to space-casery. Luckily, I've gotten it under control for the most part and wish to help others in similar predicaments reach the same ends. I've also found methods discussed in the next ritual ("Slowing the Senses: A Walking Meditation") to be of benefit for grounding the mind.

A person must find a balance between being grounded and ungrounded. Ideally, times of meditation, ritual, sleep, relaxation, and artistic expression are the times to unhinge oneself from strictly grounded states of mind (and is indeed one reason people turn to drugs and alcohol to produce this effect). Ideal times to keep grounded and attentive include during one's occupation, during conversations with others, and during academic study.

This is a spell to help one's energy remain grounded. As with all spells, everyday steps must be taken to see its energy through. Paying close attention to your thoughts—your focus from minute to minute—is an extreme benefit in becoming more grounded. With time, you will be able to shift your focus at will. This spell can help jump-start the grounding process and can be used for "emergency grounding" if you must quickly come back down to your body for some reason.

Stepping Back & Further Application

Being energetically ungrounded has benefits and hindrances. In terms of benefits, such a state of being can make a person more aware of the planes of energy and emotion. Being naturally disconnected can give room for highly successful pursuits in meditation and ritual, and can be an amazing asset to artistic work. It can also hone psychic skills and awareness of the spirit plane. On the flip side, this disconnection can make a person unaware of other peoples' intentions, can make serious tasks (like driving a car or working on the job) difficult, and can allow a person to easily forget about important things in life.

If you feel ungrounded most of the time, observe where your mind goes. Are you trapped in memories from the past? Are you thinking about future outcomes? Daydreaming? What is taking you away from the moment of Now? It's important to always observe your mind and be aware of its patterns.

For practical grounding purposes—assuming you feel ungrounded the majority of the time—I recommend frequently eating or nibbling, pausing to take deep belly-breaths, lying on the ground, looking at your feet, putting your bare feet on the grass or dirt, and keeping "grounding" stones near you or in your pockets so that you can handle them frequently. Think of the word *grounding* as you do these things, and center yourself in present-moment awareness.

Supplies

- a prepared wrapping of contained *kalas* (see Notes)
- a large rock
- 2 raw hematite stones
- patchouli essential oil (*not* "fragrant" oil)
- a handful of sea salt

Notes

- The term *kalas* is used by many occultists (and seems to originate with Kenneth Grant) to refer to flows of energy that emanate from various points on the body (and which are also contained in certain bodily fluids). In Sanskrit, *kala* can mean "time," "dark," or "attribute." For our purposes, we'll be trapping kalas by way of various "body bits." Collect each in different tissues or strips of toilet paper: a strand of hair, a fingernail clipping, a drop of blood, a shaving of dead skin (such as from the toe or fingertip), a bit of spit, a dab of earwax, some snot, a bit of urine, some of your sweat, a bit of your fecal matter, and your sexual fluids. If you're female and menstruating, add some of that blood. If you are lactating, add breast milk. The goal is to get as many small body bits contained as possible. With natural twine, tie all these tissues in a large paper towel and

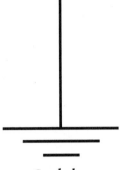

Symbol 11

draw symbol 11 on the bundle with brown or black ink. Now go wash your hands!

- I suggest using all-natural tissues and paper towels in this ritual.

Procedure

Begin by casting a circle, calling the quarters, chanting, or raising energy as you normally would, performing protective exercises, and altering your consciousness. Clear your mind, bring focus to your breath, and meditate for at least a few minutes. When ready, begin the spell.

Hold the bundle of kalas above you in your right hand. Immediately start flailing around the room (or spot in nature), acting as though you cannot stand up straight. In other words, bring your "ungroundedness" to manifest form. Wobble and stumble, trip and stagger, blur your vision, and look all around. While you are doing this, repeat "ungrounded" over and over.

While stumbling around, try to use your left hand to reach the bundle your right hand is grasping. Continually find yourself unable to reach the bundle. Continue to "try" to reach the bundle with much stress and effort. After a few minutes of this behavior, successfully grab the bundle and fall to the floor with both hands grasping the bundle.

Take the large rock and slam it forcefully on top of the bundle. Declare:

I am grounded! I am anchored to land! I am earthbound! Here and Now! So mote it be!

Place the two hematite stones on top of the large stone. Press on this stack with both hands, envisioning brown earthen energy surrounding the whole concoction. When successfully charged, grab the patchouli oil and anoint your wrists, feet, and brow. Follow by anointing the stones and the bundle with the oil.

Close the circle as you normally would. Afterward, walk outside and dig a small hole in the soil. Put in a few pinches of salt, followed by the bundle, followed by the stone, followed by another few pinches of salt. Put a piece of hematite in each of your front pants pockets, and keep these on you for as long as you'd like (I still carry hematite myself). Bury the bundle and stone and clap the Earth 10 times with your right hand. Finish by declaring once again:

> I am grounded! I am anchored to land! I am earthbound! Here and Now! So mote it be!

Slowing the Senses: A Walking Meditation

When a person thinks of meditation, they usually envision someone sitting cross-legged with closed eyes. Indeed this method is widely practiced and should (I believe) be practiced by any spiritual seeker. However, another method of meditation exists that is often more approachable for newbies to the realm of meditation.

Walking meditation is a method of becoming more deeply aware of oneself and the world. In addition to the discussion of walking meditation in the Dharma (the teachings of the Buddha), such a skill is practiced far and wide in numerous areas of the globe. For those who have difficulty practicing sitting meditation, walking meditation is a great introduction to the slowing of one's consciousness and the art of stillness. Some practitioners of sitting meditation always practice walking before a sitting session; others prefer to practice the two independently.

Unlike sitting meditation, the practitioner's eyes remain open while walking. During this process, *contemplation* is the key. One moves very slowly and becomes aware of their body. At the same time, one becomes aware of every aspect of their environment and notices how reality interacts with the senses. This awareness of environment aids a person in practicing meditative techniques of internal awareness and self-observation.

Buddhist schools teach walking meditation as a method of cultivating *mindfulness*. To be mindful is to be conscious and entirely present, keenly aware of oneself and the environment. In a state of mindfulness, a person can witness their thoughts from a third-person or objective perspective, and can come to see any underlying intentions or imbalances beneath those thoughts. When one practices frequent or constant mindful awareness, they then become more able to perceive the intentions and motivations behind other people's actions or words. No spiritualist—and certainly no spiritual teacher—should be without the mindfulness of oneself and one's surroundings. We must constantly strive for awareness in all areas.

You can practice mindfulness when walking, sitting, standing, making conversation, sipping tea, forming plans, working, "partying," making love, and anything else in the world. One of the Buddhist's goals is to cultivate constant mindfulness. This goal is also prevalent in numerous other Eastern and Western spiritual systems, certainly not excluding many schools of magick and esotericism. Awareness is something to work on honing at every moment in life, and this meditation can assist by giving one method of entering a stream of present-moment perception. Such a skill is of immeasurable value to the Witch, magician, or seeker of higher consciousness.

Stepping Back & Further Application

If you have encountered difficulty with sitting meditation, try this procedure. It can seem intimidating to sit in one place for an extended period of time, but walking is an everyday thing. Making one's everyday actions into sacred activities can encourage a person to view all of life itself as a grand ritual or meditation.

The following instructional is just one way to practice walking meditation. Try experimenting with different settings (on a beach, in a forest, downtown in a city, in a club) in order to bring greater awareness to a variety of surroundings. You may wish to first practice this around your home and, over time, advance to different surroundings.

This activity may be difficult and unusual at first, and is something that can be cultivated over time. As with all skills, practice, practice, and then practice some more. The more you do it, the more easily states of expanded awareness can be reached, helping enrich your life, spirituality, and magickal path.

Supplies

- loose, comfortable clothing
- a stick of your favorite all-natural incense

Notes

- Walking meditation should be practiced for intervals of time between 15 minutes and 1 hour, preferably. I recommend performing this at least once a week for an extended period of time, as well as frequently integrating the "meditative awareness" in brief stints throughout daily life, such as while in the shower, driving the car, sitting at the computer, and so on.

Procedure

No circle needs to be cast for this ritual. If you would like to summon your guides and guardians beforehand, feel free to do so.

Begin by getting dressed in your most comfortable clothes (be barefoot if weather permits) and decide where you'd like to perform the walk. Once there, light the stick of incense and begin your trek.

Start walking at normal speed, as if you were simply taking a walk as usual. After a couple minutes, slow your pace and bring focus to your breath. For about 10 counts, count your inhalations. Now do the same and count your exhalations. Eventually move your focus to the environment outside of yourself.

Begin to move even slower. Lighten your steps and slow your pace. Maintain a soft breathing pattern slightly slower than your normal breaths; still, don't give your breathing pattern too much focus; instead, look around you. Use sight to observe the environment. Take note of the sky, the trees, the grass, and anything else. Just observe. Just be.

Now move even slower. Bring focus to your footsteps, noting how slow they are. Notice the feel of the Earth beneath you. Notice the grass, soil, and Earth as it reacts to your step. Observe yourself stepping. As the heel of your foot touches ground, make a mental note: "heel." As your toes touch, make the mental note: "toes." Do the same as you lift your leg ("lifting my leg"), and so on. Move very slowly and take mental notes of your steps. Continue the mental notes of your physical body's actions.

After a while, bring focus back to your breath, making sure that you're breathing slowly. If thoughts of the day (of the past or future) enter your mind, dismiss them silently and bring your focus back to the Now. There is no other place you should be, and there is no hurry.

Let the incense form some smoke in front of you by moving your hand before you very slowly. Smell deeply, letting the smoke drift over you. Keep breathing deeply. Remember to slow your movements. After a few minutes, put the incense in the ground as an offering by slowly bending down (and making the mental note "crouching," "offering," and so on) and sticking it safely in the ground as an offering. Get up slowly and continue your walk.

Bring focus to your 5 primary senses. Spend time on each: sight, touch, smell, taste, and hearing. Individually scan your senses and make a mental note of each. *Hear* all sounds around you: animals, other people, vehicles in the distance, the sound of your breathing and footsteps. *Taste* in your mouth, observing what it tastes like. *Smell* the air around you, experimenting with both shallow and deep nasal inhalations. *Touch* your skin and clothing, as well as any trees, bushes, or anything else you might pass by. *See* the scenery in the far distance, in the sky, from side to side, and on the ground underneath you. Notice details and take mental notes. Observe *very, very slowly*.

Bring focus back to your breath and count 10 inhalations, as well as 10 exhalations. Gradually quicken your pace and take a few minutes to bring yourself out of the meditative trance. Don't shake it off instantly; instead, ease yourself back into a usual frame of mind. Return to the incense to ensure that it burned out carefully, and thank the spirits of nature for allowing you to feel them. You will notice over time that these sensations of awareness will carry over into your everyday life.

Chapter 6

MARS

MARS

Zodiacal rulership: Aries (and Scorpio, classical astrology)
Color association: Red
Sephira: Geburah
Number: 5
Day: Tuesday
Archetypes: Horned God, Warrior God/dess, Protectorate
Themes: Aggression, war, manifestation, inspiration, boundaries, lust, anger, energy, motivation, passion, sexuality, vitality, protection

Blood Magick: Empowering Your Ritual Tools

Blood magick is a subject that even some Witches scowl at. The thought of bleeding oneself for magick seems somehow forebidding and negative. However, I think many of these views are cultural (blood is seen as impure in the West) and may not be entirely realistic.

Though I cover this subject in depth in my first book, *Goth Craft*, I'll review a few points here. Blood is extremely powerful because it's directly attuned to a person. No other substance flows the length of our entire body; its very energetic essence is linked to a person and can serve as a magickal tool like no other. There is immense power in blood and other bodily secretions.

Shamans and indigenous cultures have long made use of blood. To cut oneself, even for reasons of depression (please note that self-mutilation is *not healthy*), is very primal. It's visceral and sensory. Intelligently utilizing one's blood in magick links us to our tribal, primal self, and helps us not fear our body's essence. Dangers associated with drawing blood can be done away with if approached with sterility, caution, and awareness.

Blood is DNA. Our DNA is sacred, connecting us to each other at a base, human level. Many say that memories of human history are stored within the genetic structure, being passed on through generations. Memories of the soul and of past lives can be accessed through blood magick; one can get visions of human history by meditating on the Mysteries of Blood; a person can extract the energy of their genetic lineage at the drop of a hat—er, the prick of a pin. The spiritual use of blood is vast, and is an indispensable tool for any magickal practitioner.

—— • ——

Contagious magick follows the Law of Contagion: that one's essence (be it through blood, hair, fingernails, and so on) is directly linked to the person from which it came. Many spells in this book utilize the Law of Contagion in one form or another. Because of the strict link to the person whose essence is contained, drawing one's own blood for ritual purposes should only be used for *personal* workings. Blood binds whatever it touches to the person who shed it. One of the most appropriate blood magick workings is to enchant one's own magickal tools, which will be explored here.

The planet Mars rules blood and iron, thus the spell's placement here. Mars was originally a god of protection and fertility. He later became chthonic (aligned with death and the Underworld), and was even later aligned as a god of war. Not all his archetypal aspects are aggressive; I believe he would appreciate us doing magick with him that is not strictly related to war. When you experiment with blood magick, ensure safety and act with discretionary intelligence.

Stepping Back & Further Application

When drawing blood, note your intention. If you're cutting yourself frequently due to depression—even if it's masquerading as ritualistic cutting—strive to stop; such behavior is severely unhealthy and counterproductive to healing. I believe that when you cut your skin, the cells respond to your intention. If your intention is ritualistic and self-transformative, the body will aid in the process. Understand your emotional state when approaching any sort of ritual work, blood-involved or not.

Blood magick should not be performed on a constant basis. To do so would lessen its power. Such an act should be reserved for intense personal workings, such as the empowerment of ritual tools. Drawing blood has plenty of risks and dangers, all of which must be considered before performing a ritual with blood.

One needn't shed much blood when performing blood magick. Just enough to be visible is plenty. In this spell, you'll be diluting your blood, which means no more than a few drops is necessary. Personally, I like to regularly dilute a few drops of my blood with dragon's blood ink and paint the edges of my Tarot cards or Book of Shadows with it—something you may wish to incorporate in the following ritual.

As another precaution, don't use an extremely sharp tool to draw your blood—this can be dangerous. I highly recommend sterile lancets that are designed for diabetic testing. Wash your "skin to be pricked" before the ritual. If using a blade or a shard of porcelain or glass, keep bandages nearby. Don't allow the cut or prick to get an infection, and don't cut on a vein or artery. Be smart when drawing blood.

Supplies
- a white candle
- any ritual tools, divinatory tools, or personally protective charms you'd like to enchant or re-empower
- a round incense-burning charcoal disk and sand in a dish or censor
- an incense mixture of dragon's blood resin and caraway seeds
- about 1 cup of lemon juice
- a chalice of purified, spring, or holy water
- a dish of salt or dirt
- a sterile lancet or other pricking device
- tobacco (in the form of either an all-natural cigarette to be smoked or loose tobacco to be burned)
- an herb or herbs to specifically empower tools (optional; see Notes)

Notes
- You can empower any ritual tools with this ritual, from a wand or athamé to a Book of Shadows or a pack of Tarot cards. The only requirement is that the tool(s) be used *by you alone*.
- Suggestions for additional herbs to use when empowering specific tools include the following: use a tea "wash" of mugwort to

charge scrying mirrors and crystal balls, use hemlock juice (deadly poisonous—use gloves and wash the tool after) to empower any blades, or burn cedar to empower wands with its smoke.

Procedure

Begin by casting a circle, calling the quarters, chanting, or raising energy as you normally would, performing protective exercises, and altering your consciousness. Clear your mind, bring focus to your breath, and meditate for at least a few minutes. When ready, begin the spell.

Light the white candle and situate the tools in front of you. Fire up the charcoal and, when embered, place a pinch of the dragon's blood and caraway incense atop. Run every tool through its smoke. As you are doing so, declare the following with each:

I *empower this tool with this creature of air.*

Next, place the lemon juice on each item, rubbing it all over each one. Say with each:

I *empower this tool with this creature of earth.*

Wash the juice off your hands with some of the chalice water. Run each tool through the candle flame and say with each:

I *empower this tool with this creature of water.*

Place salt or dirt on each item, covering each briefly. With each, say:

I *empower this tool with this creature of fire.*

Situate the items in front of you. Blur your eyes and envision the items glowing with pristine white. Take some time to accurately hone this visualization.

Prick your finger with the lancet or other pricking device, drawing a few drops of blood (ideally 5 drops). Let this blood drip directly into the chalice of pure water. When done, stir the blood into the water.

Rub each tool all over with this water. Declare each time:

I *empower this tool with the deepest essence of my being.*

Put a bit of tobacco on the charcoal and run each tool through its smoke. (Or, if smoking an all-natural, chemical-free cigarette, blow a puff of smoke on each item.). Afterward, declare:

Mars! Mars! Mars! Mars! Mars!
Heed my call! These tools are enchanted in the name of swift rebirth and the pulsing magickal Will! Bound to me, these are made sacred in your name!

Charge your tools by any additional method you life (see Notes). Put the items around you and take a few minutes envisioning them glowing red. Declare:

These items are empowered with the glory of the elements, the gods, and myself. Linked to my soul, cleansed and enchanted, these tools are consecrated with the light of the cosmos and are bound to my soul. So mote it be.

Close the circle as you normally would, thanking Mars for his patronage.

Defixiones for Destruction: Cursing a Violator

Now we get to what is probably the most baneful spell in this book. Let me first refer the reader to the "Stepping Back" section following this description—heed well the warnings of cursing. This spell is designed only to harm a person who is legitimately and literally threatening to the practitioner. The caster must take responsibility for their actions and for anything that could result from the working.

This working draws on the ancient practice of utilizing *defixiones*. Defixiones are the most ancient form of written "petition" spells we know of. A *defixio* is an ancient form of spellcraft wherein the caster inscribes various symbols, sigils, divine names, and magickal words (*voces magicæ*) onto (typically) lead tablets. The word *defixio* is Latin for "bound or fixed down." Hundreds of lead defixiones, or "curse tablets" as they are commonly called, have been found buried throughout the Mediterranean area, proving the existence of magickal practice in the ancient world. Most were written in Greek, some in Latin, and date back to between the fifth century BCE to the third century CE. Lead is alchemically associated with the energy of Mars, which carries vibrations of war and vindication. While this may have been an influential factor, lead was actually an inexpensive substance in the ancient Mediterranean world and this is speculated to be the main reason the metal was mainly used in these workings as opposed to other metals. The tablets were folded up and often nailed shut to complete the spell before burying it. Some were also accompanied by clay or metal dollies, some with nails shoved through them, in makeshift lead coffin effigies to amplify the spells. Virtually no ancient defixiones were aimed at actually *killing* the victim; the spells were almost always used to bind or conquer the person for one reason or another, or to attract an unwilling lover to the caster.

New defixiones are turning up regularly at all sorts of Mediterranean sites. Through translation of the tablets, anthropologists have been able to decipher elements of ancient Greco-Roman and Egyptian religions, which were not by any means all love and light.

The tablets have been mostly found in old gravesites (and sometimes in wells). Graveyards were seen as *necropolises*, or "cities of the dead." Practitioners would drop their completed spell tablets into graves through offering pipes. One end of the pipe was above ground while the other funneled to the body underground. Family members and loved ones would leave offerings of food, herbs, alcohol, and precious items to the deceased. Spell casters would drop their defixiones in these pipes in order to contact and employ restless spirits of the dead (called *nekydaimones*) and specific chthonic deities. Leaving defixiones in the graves of those who died suddenly or untimely was preferred simply because of the harsh energy. The spirits of these people actually remained closely connected to the Earth plane and were much easier to control and manipulate to do the biddings of the caster. Black magick indeed!

Stepping Back & Further Application

It can be tempting, especially in youth, to curse other people. Ninety-nine percent of the time, there is *not* a valid reason to curse another person, even in cases of extreme frustration and hardship. If you have a tendency to get worked up or easily upset by occurrences in life, counteract your negativity by cultivating compassion instead. Turn to cursing only as a final outlet.

When you get the urge to curse someone, it's advisable to wait a few days before deciding to actually go through with it. Most of the time, such a thing is unnecessary and only perpetuates a cycle of negativity.

Cursing is absolutely a last-ditch effort, and should be used only under the most dire circumstances—only for self-protection against a person who is threatening your well-being. "Well-being" implies your health and safety—not your ego. Don't curse just to "see if it works," nor because you are simply annoyed by or disagree with someone, or just because they're being a wicked bitch.

If your life is truly in danger from another person (or if this person is brutalizing or is on the edge of seriously harming someone else), *please* follow up legally as well. Talk to people, call the police and protective services, and take all the physical-plane measures you can to stop this activity.

While I can go on and on about the ins and outs of cursing (and have done to some extent in *Shadow Magick Compendium*), I'll stop here and get on with it, hoping that readers will approach a heavy cursing ritual with extreme caution and intelligence—or not at all.

Supplies

- newspaper
- a bowl of water
- about 3 pounds of artist's sculpting clay (ideally air-dry "play clay"—this *must* be all-natural; not Play-Doh™!)
- the "essence" of the other person (see Notes)
- carving instruments to inscribe the clay (a knife, burin, pins, etc.)
- 9 pennies
- a small amount of white wine

Notes

- The "essence" of a person, also called *ousia*, is anything that carries their energy pattern, including DNA (such as hair, fingernail clippings, and excretions), or has come in contact by the person (this is the Law of Contagion, and can include a person's possession, footprint, handwriting, and so forth). A person's essence can also be tapped into by creating a picture or poppet of the person, or by simply writing their name and focusing on them.

- The Greek Gnostic mantra of IAΩ (eye-aye-oh), which is Iota-Alpha-Omega, represents the *Demiurge* (the power of creation) and has numerous correspondences. Its usage here is to petition the power of the Universe.

Procedure

Begin by casting a circle, calling the quarters, chanting, or raising energy as you normally would, performing protective exercises, and altering your consciousness. Clear your mind, bring focus to your breath, and meditate for at least a few minutes. When ready, begin the spell.

Place the newspaper on the floor and the bowl of water next to it. Put the clay on the newspaper and start rolling it around. Smush the clay, knead it, and warm it up with friction. Put some water on your hands to soften it.

Place the "essence" of the person in the clay and knead it around in there. (If you're using a piece of paper or cloth to represent the assailant, you should instead make two tablets and seal the item in between the pieces like a sandwich.) As you are working the clay, envision the person you are working against. See them surrounded by blackness. See their hands and feet tied and bound, unable to cause harm. See them struggling to move but finding themselves unable. Continue to visualize and work the clay for at least a few minutes.

When the clay is malleable, soft, and enchanted, place it on the newspaper and flatten it into a rectangular shape. An ideal size is 10×10 inches.

Use the carving knife to cut off the sides of the clay to form a soft, flat clay tablet. When the tablet is a desirable size, pick up your carving tool. In the middle of the tablet, draw an image of the person you're cursing. When you have gotten it as detailed as possible, write their name across the middle of the image and draw a deep X through both the name and the image.

On the top left corner of the tablet, carve:

PERĪCULUM
PERĪCULU
PERĪCUL
PERĪCU
PERĪC
PERĪ
PER
PE
P

Draw an inverted triangle around the words. On the top right corner of the tablet, carve:

EXITIUM
EXITIU
EXITI
EXIT
EXI
EX
E

Again, draw an inverted triangle around the words. Finally, in the middle of the bottom of the tablet, carve:

TIMEŌ
TIME
TIM
TI
T

Surround this in an inverted triangle. On the right and left bottoms of the tablet, carve IAΩ.

On the remainder of the tablet, carve these symbols five times *each* in random places all over the tablet: an inverted pentagram, a circle with an X through it, a down-pointing arrow, a lightning bolt, and a widdershins spiral. When finished, glare at the piece with a spiteful eye and forcefully say:

PERĪCULUM! EXITIUM! TIMEŌ! [NAME]! ARUR! CURSÈD BE!
Feel the pain of your sting! Drown in the chaos of your torment!
Drink your own poison!
PERĪCULUM! EXITIUM! TIMEŌ! [NAME]! ARUR! CURSÈD BE!
ABRAKALA! ABRAKALA! ABRAKALA! ABRAKALA! ABRAKALA!

Take some deep breaths. Calm and center your energy. When grounded, thank the spirits and close the circle as you normally would, leaving the tablet exposed to the air.

Come back to the tablet precisely 25 hours (1 day and 1 hour) later. The tablet should be considerably dry at this point. Remove it from the newspaper and carefully take it, along with the pennies and wine, to the cemetery.

When you reach the cemetery gates, leave the pennies and wine as an offering. Tell the spirits you are entering for magickal purposes and mean them no harm. Slowly walk to a far area of the graveyard—ideally a crossroads—and stand still. Take deep breaths in, gather your energy, and finally smash the tablet to bits. Stomp on it if necessary. Make sure that pieces fly everywhere and the tablet is destroyed. Seal the spell by saying:

PERĪCULUM! EXITIUM! TIMEŌ! [NAME]! ARUR! CURSÈD BE!
And so it is.

Rusted Protection: Creating a Mars Bottle

Because one of Mars' properties is extreme protection, we'll be taking advantage of this planetary power for this spell.

This bottle is one of the most potent nonherbal protection spells a person can create. Mars is aligned with iron, which is why iron nails are specifically required for the spell. Most nails these days are made of stainless steel, so you may have to do some digging. If nothing else, one giant rusty railroad spike can work for the purpose intended (these are often found at pawn shops, for example). If worse comes to worst, get your iron from a different source—the most important thing is that the item you have is made of iron.

Iron creates rust, which is where this spell comes into play. Rust is both iron and deep red: two things heavily aligned to Mars. Since ancient times, iron and rust have been known to have extreme protective properties.

As an important warning, be careful not to poke yourself with the nails being used, especially if they are rusty. If this happens, go immediately to a hospital to receive a tetanus shot to prevent a potentially deadly infection.

——— · ———

The product of this working—also known as War Water—has long had a reputation of being one of the most powerful and forceful spiritual waters. This water can help project a tremendous punch, be it a curse, energy against a curse, or any pointed, vigorous magickal intention.

This Mars bottle can be kept virtually forever, as it only grows more powerful with time. As the rust keeps on building in the water, the water becomes more potent. Be careful when handling this water: I've discovered that even accidentally spilling a little bit (assuming the bottle is charged with energy) can cause aggressive and Mars-related energies to emerge instantly and unknowingly—and that's just not kosher, man.

In addition to the water being a powerful energetic protecting agent, it can also be used for purposes of projection. If energy is being directed and sent to another source, the water will serve as a unique projective agent. Mars water can also be used for magickal purposes of creation and "impregnation," seeing as Mars is the "penetrator of fate"—just look at Aries' associations with earthen fertility!

Mars Water is also a type of War Water, and it can be used to cause negative chaos of any type. If one wishes to make people quarrel and fight with each other—or with their own minds—this water can be used. However, I advise against doing this unless the need is imperative. One can also sprinkle War Water on an enemy's doorway to get them to flee their property. Because Mars is projective, this energetic boost can be used for either good or ill. The usage of this powerful water is up to the Witch or magician!

Stepping Back & Further Application

I recommend reviewing the properties of the planet Mars (page 148 and Appendix 2) before crafting the bottle. For any purposes associated with Mars, the water can be used. Brainstorm different ways the water can be utilized. Will you keep this bottle on the "fire" quadrant of your main altar? Will you stash it away for emergency magickal use only? Are you planning spells of banishing, protection, or malevolence that the water can amplify? Will you just keep the bottle on hand for possible uses down the road?

Assuming your primary goal is protection, what are you protecting from? Is the protection simply a preventive measure, or is there a greater threat you're specifically guarding against? If the latter, consider whether or not you've taken all the necessary real-world steps to deal with the matter. It's a good idea to protect one's property regularly, and using Mars water is a great thing to incorporate.

Supplies

- a tight-sealing glass jar
- 5 iron nails
- 1 bloodstone (or carnelian)
- enough purified or spring water to fill the jar

Notes

- Again, the nails used in this spell must be made of iron, since it is the eventual rust we're going for.

- After the jar is made, remember to swirl the rust around in the bottle before using it (it's really pretty), and be certain not to cut yourself on the nails or shards of rust.

- As part of an especially potent cursing spell, add to a small pot of boiling water a splash of Mars Water along with a few pinches of Spanish moss, valerian, and sulphur. Let it steep and you have a potent concoction of War Water—use with discretion! Rain water collected during a violent storm adds an extra punch.

- It will take some time for the nails to start rusting; the water cannot be used immediately.

Procedure

Begin by casting a circle, calling the quarters, chanting, or raising energy as you normally would, performing protective exercises, and altering your consciousness. Clear your mind, bring focus to your breath, and meditate for at least a few minutes. When ready, begin the spell.

Call out to the energy of Mars:

O holy Mars in the celestial sphere! He who is five! He who is protection! He who is severity! I call upon you now to aid in this working and lend your sacred quintessence to this rite!

One by one, drop the nails into the empty jar. Say:

By the power of five—the protective pentagram and the vibration of Hod—this iron serves its purpose.

Drop the bloodstone into the jar. Say:

By the power of the blood, and the magick of the living Earth, this jar comes to life.

Fill the jar nearly full of water and declare:

From day to day this power grows in strength. As water and iron create rust, so is this bottle an alchemical charm of the holy and harsh properties of Mars.

Seal the jar tightly shut and shake it around violently. Dance and hop around the space, filling the jar with both physical and energetic energy. While you are flailing about, keep repeating the word *Mars*.

Without breaking it, toss the bottle on the floor so it rolls to a stop. Shout:

The Mars bottle is complete! So mote it be!

Thank Mars appropriately and close the circle as you normally would. The water will increase in strength over time, so check its progress regularly!

Autoerotic Conjuration: Calling a Sex Partner

Sex is a natural human instinct, and is an aspect of being that Paganism celebrates. Sex is a gateway to pleasure, to Gnosis, and it can be used to perpetuate the human species. Unfortunately, due to antiquated ideas greatly associated with Christianity, sex and sexuality have become maligned over time. The debasement of such a sacred and natural thing has resulted in countless sexual imbalances. Sex has become frequently viewed as a "taboo" or forbidden. To view sexuality in a negative light is itself a cause of sexual crimes. It can cause people to indulge in hedonistic spurts, be secretive about their sexuality or sex life, and feel dreadfully ashamed if they have homosexual, bisexual, or fetishistic tendencies. These are just a few examples of the negative effects of sexual repression and demonization. Because they're such intense and psychological subjects, I won't get started discussing the bitter realities of sexual abuse and homophobia. Instead, I urge readers to contemplate the ins and outs of sex and sexuality and how they fit in our present culture—and where such views are headed.

Such considerations are necessary before performing a spell aimed at calling a sex partner. One should know their own motivations for such a working and should think about whether or not such a spell is impulsive or unhealthy. Everyone views sex and sexuality differently, and everyone approaches their own sexuality in different ways.

— · —

One may wish to summon a sex partner to ease loneliness. For some, overindulging in sex is a substitute for feeling love and admiration. Sexual addiction is a common psychological issue (including chronic masturbation), and is severely unhealthy. Please don't perform this spell if you think you may be suffering from a sexual addiction or dependency. Also, if you are looking for a romantic and emotional lover, please skip this spell and reference "The Twin Flame: Summoning a Lover" in the Venus chapter instead. If you are looking for a "bed buddy" or partner to occasionally relieve stress with (that is, with no romantic or emotional feelings attached beyond friendship), this spell might be for you.

Certainly, one should get themselves tested for STDs and ensure that any partner they sleep with has done the same. Sexual liberation is grand and essential in life, but personal sexual *liberalness* is not. One must use discretion and discernment, and *not* have sex with the first person who comes along just because they show interest. Even in the case of flings, both partners' intentions are vitally important. Respect others and respect yourself.

Stepping Back & Further Application

Deeply and honestly analyze your reasons for wanting a sex partner. Why do you want a sex partner and not a romantic partner? What is your sexual history? Do you feel that your personal worth depends on other peoples' attraction to you? Are you in a committed relationship with another person already, and if so, are you wishing to cheat (not recommended!) or are you polyamorous? What are your views on sex? Are you planning on having safe and respectful sex? Do you idealize sex and hold it up on a pedestal, or do you have a realistic view of it? Do you find yourself constantly obsessing or thinking about sex? Are you comfortable with your sexuality? Do you see sex as something naughty, or as something to have fun with?

Are you looking for a magickal and spiritual sex partner? How picky and selective are you with your potential partners? Also, are you seeking out dates with people you meet on adult networking websites?

Sex with another person binds both people's energies together, which is why the motivations of each person, and their general personalities, must match. We are looking for equality, honesty, respect, and respectability here. If you do not respect yourself, or if you are purposefully reliving or repressing sexual abuse or imbalances of the past, please carefully consider whether or not a sex partner would be the most beneficial thing for you now.

Supplies

- 1 red candle
- a round incense-burning charcoal disk and sand in a dish or censor
- about ¼ ounce of the dried herb damiana
- a mixture of lemon juice and orange juice
- a bowl of warm water
- a red permanent marker
- a large sheet of dark green paper
- 1 or more pornographic magazines (see Notes)
- scissors
- honey
- prepared red wine (see Notes) in a chalice or wine glass
- a fresh, chemical-free rose or a banana (see Notes)
- patchouli essential oil (*not* "fragrant" oil)
- 5 cherries
- a combination of black pepper, onion powder, and crushed red pepper
- a small brown paper bag

Notes

- The pornographic magazines can be either softcore or hardcore, gay or straight, vanilla or fetish, as per your preferences.

- If summoning a female, stick your fingers in a fresh red rose while masturbating; if male, grasp a banana. If you're summoning a sex partner of either gender, use both.

- To prepare the red wine, simmer a bottle's worth with a combination of basil, caraway, 5 cardamom pods, 5 clove buds, coriander, damiana, hibiscus, licorice root, saw palmetto, and yarrow. Very slowly warm this mixture on the stove (until it's barely simmering). Strain out herbs and let the wine cool to a drinkable temperature. If you are underage or abstain from alcohol, substitute grape juice for the wine.

- "Willow's Song" comes from the 1975 film *The Wicker Man*, which is, in my opinion, the best Pagan film in the history of cinema! (Don't watch the "remake" version—it's a monumental and degrading waste of time.) The lyrics to the song can be found on the Internet, and the tone, rhythm, and pitch is found in the movie.

Procedure

Begin by casting a circle, calling the quarters, chanting, or raising energy as you normally would, performing protective exercises, and altering your consciousness. Clear your mind, bring focus to your breath, and meditate for at least a few minutes. When ready, begin the spell.

Fire up the candle and charcoal. When ready, place a pinch of damiana on the coal and continue adding pinches to the ember throughout the ritual.

Strip naked and anoint yourself (or rub your body all over) with the lemon/orange juice. Get friction going. Afterward, wash your hands in the bowl of warm water.

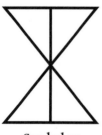

Symbol 12

Facing south, grab the marker and paper. On both sides, draw large images of symbol 12, taking up the full length of the paper.

Take some time browsing through the porn. Allow yourself to become aroused and stimulated. As you reach images that are particularly attractive to you, use scissors to cut out the certain body parts.

Snip out legs, arms, a midsection, a chest or breasts, a penis or vagina, and so on. Try your best to get the images to be matching sizes. When you reach the face, cut out an attractive pair of lips, a nose, different eyes, and a hairstyle.

Now piece together these body parts on the paper to make one amalgamated "person." With the honey, make the back sides of the body parts sticky and adhere them over the symbol in the appropriate places. Continue this with all body parts, forming a very odd-looking solid "person" on the paper. Though each individual part may be attractive, the combination of them looks quite strange. (And it will look quite hermaphroditic if you are summoning a sex partner of no particular gender.)

Once your image is assembled, set aside the magazines. Pick up the image and run it through the smoke. Say:

My desire come to me. My desire cum with me. As I will, so mote it be.

Put the paper down and place the glass of wine atop it. If you have a penis, insert it directly (and *erectly*) into the wine, charging it with sexual energy. If you have a vagina, finger yourself briefly and dip your finger in the wine. Cup your hands around the glass and say:

With this, I take into myself the blood of the gods, bound to my sexual essence. I stimulate my senses, I stimulate my mind. As this enters my body, I am magnetic to the lover I seek. So be it!

Slowly drink the wine as you stimulate your genitals. Softly touch the rose and/or banana (see Notes) between sips of wine. Take time to arouse yourself and feel your body. Intermittently asperge (sprinkle) the image with the wine, using your masturbatory hand. Continue to masturbate slowly, working yourself up. Keep looking at the body parts in the image you've created, allowing it to arouse you more and more. Before you climax, make sure that all the wine has been drunk. If you wish, dump the last splash of wine on your body, rubbing it all around.

When you climax, get the sexual fluids immediately on the image. If you're male, ejaculate directly on the paper. If you're female, smear your sexual fluids from your hands onto the image. (If you are a pre-op transsexual, simply do what feels natural.) Get the image as "wet" from your juices as possible, and wash your hands in the warm water afterward.

Put a drop of the patchouli oil on the image in five places: on the four corners and the center. Anoint yourself with the oil as well, putting one drop on the back of your right hand, left hand, right foot, left foot, and a final drop in the center of your chest.

Put your face close to the paper and sing "Willow's Song" to the enchanted image, slowly and softly. When finished, slowly eat the 5 cherries, depositing the stems on the image. Sprinkle the image with the remaining damiana as well as with the blend of peppers and onion. Say:

> From low and high I summon you!
> From far and wide I summon you!
> From in and out I summon you!
> My desire come to me. My desire cum with me. As I will, so mote it be!

Immediately crumple the paper with the image and ingredients on the inside, making the symbol on the opposite side visible. Toss the spell in the paper bag and put the banana peel (eat the banana) and/or red rose (eat one of the petals) on top of the crumpled spell. Close the circle as you normally would.

Crumple up the brown bag and nonchalantly deposit the bag (which should now look like ordinary garbage) in the trash can inside an adult store, sex shop, or pornographic theatre. Try to find a public receptacle rather than having to ask a store clerk, but do so if one is unavailable.

Fiery Fury:
Releasing Anger

The properties of Mars and the element of fire are aplenty. Some of the most prevalent qualities are war, aggression, and anger. When anger arises in a person, they are overtaken with a rage that has potential to get out of control—much like a fire. Like any strong emotion, anger can be difficult to work with and calm, which is where this spell comes in.

Anger can be considered to be related to Mars. You may then wonder why this spell for *releasing* anger is included here in the Mars chapter. The reason is that we'll be fighting fire with fire. Anger is a piercing, destructive force, and the energy behind extreme banishing is similar. Though it would be a good idea to also incorporate other planetary energies, the essence of Mars can help get the essence of Mars under control! This spell also concludes with a bath or shower. In a sense, the aggressive release (fire) will be cooled off in the end (water). If you're plotting zodiacal alignments, try to incorporate at least a little essence of the element water (Cancer, Scorpio, or Pisces).

Anger requires release; it must be conducted. If bottled away, it only builds: this is exceedingly dangerous both emotionally and psychologically. Many therapies and spiritual paths assert that various steps in awareness can be taken *before* anger builds or gets out of control. While this spell is not focused on these mechanisms, it can provide a small outlet for the fiery fury once it's begun to build. When the escalated rage is conducted, channeled, and gotten under control, it can then encourage a person to change their emotional actions in the future should such a situation arise again.

Releasing anger in a constructive manner is important. If left unchecked, the demon of rage can overtake a person and lead them out of control. Surrendering to one's emotions, including anger, may seem to be empowering in the moment, but this is an illusion. Losing control of one's mindfulness, regardless of the emotion and its intensity, is a serious occurrence. Much like with substance use, a person should remain in control of themselves at all times rather than be swept away by the moment. As this spell provides a method of release, I hope it encourages those with frequent tempers to conduct their emotions before they become too chaotic.

Stepping Back & Further Application

Anger is a secondary emotion that arises from another emotion, usually fear or sadness. The underlying fear or sadness behind anger is the main thing that must be analyzed in order for the anger to eventually lose power, and the reasons for these underlying emotions are different for everyone and every situation. Expressing and working with underlying emotions can keep anger from bubbling to the surface, and can help lessen its frequency by tackling the deeper subjects that require notice.

Anger can easily arise if a person feels they're not being heard. It can perpetuate alongside a notion of proving oneself. Anger is often intricately connected to ego. Various substances can blow anger out of proportion and make communication even more difficult. Blame is a strong component of anger, often accompanying it, and is a method of avoidance. In arguments, try using only "I feel this way because . . ." statements to avoid a vicious and counterproductive blame-game.

Everybody gets furious now and then. However, some of us are more subject to our emotions than others. There is no shame in admitting that you have an anger problem—it's common! If you and those around you believe that the levels of anger you feel are unhealthy, and yet you still can't seem to get a hold on your emotions, I encourage you to consider meditation, therapy, and anger management counseling. Such things can truly be lifesaving and can help a person get to the root of their anger—which is much more empowering than letting the anger run rampant! Know your emotions—know yourself.

Supplies

- 5 organic, cage-free chicken eggs (use only 1 egg if the performance of this spell is frequent, so as to not waste food)
- a red permanent marker and a black permanent marker
- any combination of the herbs dandelion and wormwood
- a few handfuls of sea salt
- 1 can or bottle of beer
- a bathtub or shower

Notes

- If you're underage, substitute apple juice (or hops bath sachet) for the beer. (Beer is known to help dispel negative external influences.)
- There are very few ingredients in this spell for a reason. Like a bonfire, anger can arise suddenly. Thus, gathering tools for a ritual wouldn't necessarily be practical. For those who experience the instantaneous rising of anger, skip to the very last portion of this spell (the bath) immediately when the anger starts to take hold.

Procedure

Don't cast a circle for this spell; doing so in a moment of anger could upset the harmony of the elements/spirits at hand. Instead, immediately grab your egg(s).

With the red marker, draw the symbol for Mars 5 times on each egg. With the black marker, write your feelings. This can be anything from "being ignored" or "disrespected," to "fuck you." Write words that express your feelings and what you feel is wrong in the situation.

Go outside. Briefly hold each egg to your brow and take 5 deep breaths in through the nose and out through the mouth. As you exhale, move the egg to your mouth and imagine fiery red energy being sent into it.

With your right hand, forcefully throw the egg(s) on the ground, smashing with all your might. Kneel on the ground and pound the egg and the ground, pulverizing the shell. Get messy and use lots of force. Purge the anger through the egg. Don't hurt yourself, but do use force.

As you are pounding the egg, see bolts of red lightning exiting your fist, being absorbed by the Earth. While you are smashing, repeat:

> *Fiery fury, anger unjust,*
> *get away from me you must!*
> *Into the Earth this anger is caged,*
> *this egg dies alongside my rage!*

Once thoroughly smashed, put the herbs on the smashed egg. Put a few pinches of salt on the egg to fully ground the energies.

Go inside and wash with soap. If you've been at odds with another person, tell them you need to calm down and will discuss matters later. Grab the beer and salt, and draw a warm bath (or shower). When the bath is ready, dump in beer and salt (or dump them over yourself). Say:

> *Heated water, you shall chill.*
> *Cool my anger: it is my Will!*

While you are bathing, take deep breaths, soaking up the cleansing power of the water infused with fermented hops, yeast, and salt. Allow your anger to be transformed into peace and acceptance. Calm down. Know that you are taking the higher road by not giving in to your anger and are changing your state of mind for the better.

Chapter 7

—ㆍ—

JUPITER

—ㆍ—

JUPITER

Zodiacal rulership: Sagittarius (and Pisces, classical astrology)

Color association: Blue

Sephira: Chesed

Number: 4

Day: Thursday

Archetypes: Teacher, Prophet/ess, Sky King

Themes: Expansion, abundance, philosophy, growth, luck, optimism, prosperity, freedom, opportunity, generosity, justice, higher purpose

Flee, Ennui!:
Breaking Through Stagnation & Sorrow

The term *ennui* is French and refers to a state of disinterest, lethargy, and depression. Periods of frequent crying, feelings of mental and emotional numbness, and an attitude of apathy about life in general can be aspects of ennui. Christian mystic St. John of the Cross coined the term "Dark Night of the Soul" in his sixteenth-century poem of the same name, describing the experience of feeling the "absence of God." In other words, the Dark Night is felt as absolute emptiness, a distrust in reality, and an indifference to anything and everything. The experience is extreme. Pain, despondence, and indolence characterize the constant sensations. Many people would simply call it depression to the extreme. The Dark Night is most certainly a process of initiation ("suffering to learn"), and this spell can utilize such an experience to a person's advantage. It can also help with minor experiences that mirror the Dark Night—shorter periods of ennui are much more common than a severe and lasting sorrow. In fact, combating lesser slumps of ennui can help to prevent the onset of the Dark Night experience.

To experience such slumps from time to time is quite natural to the human experience, and can provide room for inspiration to be reborn from depths of mental isolation. However, the experience can also be held on to—even for an entire lifetime. Unfortunately, many people surrender to the energy of ennui, feeling as if there is nothing else to be had in life.

If a person regularly expends too much energy, slumps of depression and drainage are certain to follow. Not maintaining a balance of energetic exchange can give way to extended depressive slumps. Periods of stagnation can make a person feel worthless, unaccomplished, or guilty for such feelings, simply because the rational mind is telling them to behave oppositely.

Periods of ennui can teach us to reevaluate our lives and prioritize our experiences. If our path has a blockage, we must get to the root of the blockage and remove it accordingly, even if it's difficult, and even if it requires serious life changes. The road must be opened and cleared for success.

—— · ——

Jupiter is attuned to energies of luck, opportunity, and personal growth. Aligning "anti-stagnation" intention to this generous planet's energy is highly beneficial. The theme of this spell is regeneration and new beginnings.

Because Aries is a sign of new beginnings and growth (including flora), one could integrate the energy of Mars with this spell too. However, because of Mars' war qualities—which may be best avoided during a dark time—I feel that Jupiter is more appropriate.

During a depressive tide, all of life can seem hopeless. Paradoxically, during a period of blissful happiness, all of life can seem perfect. Neither view is entirely true; there is always a middle ground. Getting away from the listless energy of ennui requires that one remember life's balance and find reasons to develop the motivation to move forward.

Stepping Back & Further Application

Deconstruct the reasons for this mental and emotional rut. What factors have contributed to your coming to this state of being? Are you making the experience worse by feeling guilt? Are periods of stagnation a common occurrence in your life? How long have these feelings lasted, and are you actually ready to propel yourself out of it now—or are there still lessons waiting to be learned?

This spell can help a person jump out of a stagnant cycle. At the same time, various things in life need to be changed accordingly. This working will help jump-start the energies of motivation, but the practitioner must follow through. Take steps: do things that will get your creative juices flowing. Take a walk, make some plans, immerse yourself in things you enjoy. While you muster back your balanced energy levels, contemplate the things in your life that should be dismissed or released to allow these changes to come to fruition. Honor your period of stagnation as a natural settling of energies, knowing that a sluggish demeanor and bleak outlook are only temporary.

Supplies

- a small potted plant (see Notes)
- 2 small, all-natural pieces of paper
- a ballpoint pen
- a small bowl of warm water
- a small, regular rock
- a timepiece (a timer, clock, cell phone, or watch)
- a blue permanent marker
- a long, transparent glass vial
- any combination of the herbs bayberry, dandelion, dill, eyebright, hemp (or marijuana if it's legal in your area), High John the Conqueror root, jasmine, lavender, lemon balm, lemon verbena, marjoram, mullein, rosemary, St. John's wort, sunflower, thistle (milk or blessed), willow, and yarrow
- 1 piece each of blue agate and orange calcite
- your own hair and fingernail clippings
- a spoonful of honey

Notes

- It would be ideal for the practitioner to buy or transplant a potted plant that is one of the herbs on the list. For example, a person could purchase a potted dill or lemon balm plant, put a garden-growing sunflower or lavender plant into a pot, or find wild mullein or yarrow to transplant.

- Before taking care of a plant, research proper gardening and maintenance techniques. One must make every effort to keep the plant from dying. If the plant does eventually die, discard the biodegradable contents (soil, spell, and all) into a body of flowing water.

Procedure

Begin by casting a circle, calling the quarters, chanting, or raising energy as you normally would, performing protective exercises, and altering your consciousness. Clear your mind, bring focus to your breath, and meditate for at least a few minutes. When ready, begin the spell.

Cup your hands around the potted plant. Declare:

I *charge and enchant this* [name of plant] *with the energy of the cosmos. This represents the conquering of my ennui and the growth from the depths of this rut.*

Press your fingers into the soil. Say:

This soil is my sorrow. This soil is my stagnation. This soil is my slump.

Put your hands gently on the plant, feeling its leaves and vibrant energies. Say:

This [name of plant] *is my strength. This* [name of plant] *is my springboard. This* [name of plant] *is my salvation.*

On one of the pieces of paper, write down everything that characterizes your ennui. Use adjectives, emotions, and fears. Use both sides of the paper, writing words, sentences, symbols, scribbles, and anything else that channels your feelings.

Put this paper in the water. If necessary, weigh it down with the rock. Immediately take note of the time (write it down on your hand). Loudly shout the following into the water at the top of every minute for 16 minutes, beginning at the moment you clock the current time:

Resolve! Transform! Solve et Coagula! Albedo! Albedo! Albedo!

While you are waiting 16 minutes (remember to watch the minutes on the clock and say the preceding line a total of 16 times!), take the other paper and write the positive things you wish to develop in your life. Take note of all your talents, strengths, and abilities, and write goals that you are aiming to manifest over time. Sidestep any feelings of worthlessness in order to bring out your positive qualities. When you feel a sense of completion, use the permanent marker to draw a very large symbol 13 on one side of the "positive" paper and a very large symbol 14 on the other side, covering the words.

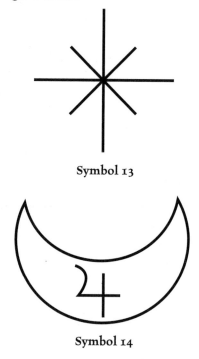

Symbol 13

Symbol 14

With one hand, dig deep into the soil. Take the soaked paper of ennui words and bury it deep in the soil. Put the other, positive piece of paper into the vial, having folded it multiple times. Add your hair and fingernail clippings.

Fill the vial to the brim with the herbal mixture. When finished, stick the uncapped vial into the potted plant with the closed end up (so the herbs at the brim touch the soil). Push this down as far as you'd like, ensuring that it's stable without hurting the plant's root structure. Place the two gemstones in the soil in a similar fashion. (The rock that weighed down the negative piece of paper should be thrown in the trash.) Eat the spoonful of honey, feeling the love and joy of the Universe entering your body and soul.

Close the circle as you normally would and take good care of the plant (water, sunlight, conversation) as you ease your way out of the slump. Remember that death feeds life!

Severing Fears: Cord-Cutting

Fear is a killer. In many ways, our everyday experience is determined by our own internal battle of confidence versus fear. When someone feels able to accomplish something—even the smallest thing—they are likely to follow it through with ease; if someone feels fear toward something, the easiest response is to just give up.

Fear is greatly unconscious and isn't restricted to fears of spiders, heights, and clowns. Fears can be anything from fear of abandonment or fear of relationships to fear of acceptance or fear of a bad public image. For everything that is, there are people who fear it to some extent.

—— · ——

Anxiety and depression go hand in hand, and anxiety is greatly borne of fear itself. These emotions are intricately interrelated, though fear is usually categorized as being more survivalistic and base-emotional, as a response to a threat against one's well-being.

Whatever the wording, fears and anxieties can inhibit our everyday life by making us reluctant to even try. The belief in helplessness and an unavoidable outcome will discourage a person from even attempting to conquer fear. The fear of failure is a heavy weight that can inhibit a person from walking a fulfilling or destined path in life.

Combating fears isn't easy. It takes emotional work—and proof of success—to work with one's trepidations. It's necessary to have both the knowledge of one's own fears *and* the determination to work with them. Without determination and direction, fear can never be fully released.

All things in reality change. That which was painful at one point in time does not have to continue its cycle of inner torment. The body and mind are constantly regenerating, and it's our decision whether or not we hold on to negative belief systems of the past. By getting to the root of fear, the mind can choose to disallow it. For those wishing to sever the restrictive ties of the past and rocket into freedom (with the help of Jupiter!), this spell can be a good starting point in the process.

Stepping Back & Further Application

Fear is not only a painful inner demon, but one of illusion. Fears can bring about ideas of failure, discouragement, and the belief of impossibility. Fear can give rise to irrational and even absurd reactions to things that don't legitimately pose a threat. Additionally, the self-judgment and behaviors of avoidance that accompany fear and anxiety can continue to build on themselves, making a person's reactions to their environment even more divorced from reality. Fear can trigger self-isolation, panic attacks, and suicidal impulses.

Getting to the root of the fear is where the greatest solution to the problem lies. Perhaps a past incident caused a negative imprint of the thing now feared. Maybe you've witnessed someone else fail or somehow sustain injury from a thing or person and have come to fear it yourself by extension.

Testing your fears is important. The fear may actually be gone or changing at this point in time. Taking small steps to combat the challenge can reverse your reluctance in facing the situation, and seeking encouragement from outside sources can provide courage.

Supplies

- a blue candle
- a number of 4-inch-square pieces of paper
- a blue ballpoint pen
- any combination of the herbs basil, nettles, red clover, and St. John's wort
- a burning bowl or dish

- many yards of all-natural string or cord, such as jute, hemp, or even cotton (black if possible)
- approximately 1-inch polished stones; 1 each of amethyst, bloodstone (or carnelian), opal, and quartz

Notes

- When writing your fears, feel welcome to write down things that you feel may or may not qualify. Even if you're uncertain whether or not something classifies as a fear, it's best to focus on its banishment as a safeguard.

Procedure

Begin by casting a circle, calling the quarters, chanting, or raising energy as you normally would, performing protective exercises, and altering your consciousness. Clear your mind, bring focus to your breath, and meditate for at least a few minutes. When ready, begin the spell.

Ignite the candle. On each piece of paper, write one fear. It's likely that you'll be able to think of a few right off the top of your head. After your most prominent fears are written, journey deep into your mind to discover more.

Mentally rewind through the years. Think about instances where fright, anxiety, and uncertainty got the best of you. If you remember any significant, emotionally draining occurrences, take note of the accompanying fear.

Once you have mentally purged all the deep-seated fears you can, set the papers aside and put the herbs in the bowl. Put your fingers in the herbs and mix them around, saying:

Plants of magick, plants of sight,
banish now this anxiety and fright.
My fears can't harm nor cause stagnation,
dissolve my woes with fire of transformation.

On the tops of your hands and feet, draw the symbol of Jupiter. Next, do your best to tie together your hands and feet using the twine. Bind your feet at the ankles and your hands at the wrists. Afterward, wrap

2

your knotted hands and feet together, locking yourself in a wrists-to-ankles position. Fall to the floor. "Struggle" against the cords as if you are attempting to escape the binding. Say:

Fears of restriction, fears of pain,
leave me now as I say his name!

At this point, bellow "Jupiter" very loudly 4 times. Immediately spring out of the binding, ripping apart the twine.

Light each "fear paper," one by one, placing the burning paper atop the herbal blend. When the flame of each paper goes out, say:

In the name of Jupiter, BEGONE!

Once all the papers are burnt, place the stones on top of the ashes and close the circle as you normally would.

Let the spell sit for 4 days (mark the calendar). When you return, pick up the stones and place each at a corner of your bed (under the mattress or under the entire bed). Go outside and throw the entire mixture to the winds of change.

Pieces of Me:
Reclaiming Your Energy

One of the planet Mercury's characteristics is travel—this is also an aspect of Jupiter. Because Jupiter is expansive and progressive, the planet's energy is far-reaching. For this ritual, the practitioner will be journeying back through time and location in order to reclaim energies that were once left behind. This is a significant and potentially deeply healing ritual.

Energy drainage can result from traumatic experience. Shamans tend to believe that trauma can frighten away fractions of a person's soul. Though this spell won't be diving into soul retrieval, it's somewhat similar to the practice of recapitulation. Practiced by Mexican shamans (in the Toltec tradition), psychologists, and a wide variety of spiritualists, a person recapitulates by mentally rewinding their experiences. Many people perform the practice of rewinding and reviewing their day's experience when preparing for sleep. Others rewind longer periods of time in their life at specific intervals. In many ways, this mirrors the long-held notion of a person getting a flashback of their entire life at the moment of death. For this reason, regularly performing recapitulation is said to both lessen the difficulty of the dying process and enrich one's life experience by pulling back threads of energy to the present moment.

——— • ———

When we go through instances of extreme difficulty and stress, psychological imprints can result. These imprints can create fears and neuroses (touched on in the previous spell) that affect us our entire lives. Behaviors associated with traumatic energy trappings will naturally keep surfacing until faced. Avoiding our experiences, no matter how difficult, is avoiding our imperative spiritual life-lessons.

When our spirits are shocked or instantaneously jolted, a part of our energy remains trapped—this ties into the shamanic view of the soul. Through a process of cultivating acceptance and regressing through experience, the psyche can transmute the instances to a higher benefit, integrating and accepting experience into the present moment. Healing difficult experiences can make a person grow in strength and can give them courage to face the future. When a person learns from experience, they can teach others who are in similar circumstances.

This spell is focused on reclaiming your energy from certain places and times. Tapping into the intersection of these two factors is what drives this spell's success. In the spell, you'll be journeying to different places where your energy may be trapped and meditatively time-traveling to the experience to pull your energy back to yourself, even if the location of the experience is different from where you currently live (see Notes).

Stepping Back & Further Application

When thinking about experiences you wish to work on energetically reclaiming and transforming, you're going to want to pick the most significant four. Depending on your experiences, these can be anything from an abusive situation or a physical accident to high school or a bad drug experience.

The traumatic experiences being worked with in this spell do not have to be momentary occurrences. They can be pain felt over periods of time. For example, if you had a bad relationship and think your energy may be trapped on the property you shared with the other person, consider using that location as one of the points. Get creative and think back to determine where the essence of your spirit may be trapped.

Finally, think of ways you can reclaim your energy from these experiences in other ways. Can you talk to certain people involved? Seek therapy? Meditate on where you would be had the experiences not happened? Even the most difficult of experiences do not occur without spiritual reason.

Supplies

- 4 small mirrors (inexpensive and unframed if possible)
- a black permanent marker
- 4 pieces of amethyst
- a small garden shovel
- a bag of wormwood

Notes

- Various suggestions of places to leave mirrors and perform this meditation include the following: your childhood home, a former school (elementary, middle school, high school, college, or other), a former acquaintance's house, a park or playground, or the location of a specific traumatic incident or time in your life.

- If you have since moved to a new location and feel as though the majority of your "stuck" energy may be in a different location or locations from where you currently reside, try finding or creating items that represent these places. For example, say that you've lived in a number of cities over time and feel that you may have unknowingly deposited a significant amount of energy in four particular locations. To draw back these energies, place the mirrors outside of your house facing the directions of these locations. Additionally, place an item *from* or *representing* those locations beneath each mirror. For example, you could use a towel that you bought in Portland for one mirror, a seashell from L.A. for another, a map of London for a third, and a sketch of downtown Cleveland for the fourth. Get creative to tap into the energy pattern of a particular faraway area.

Procedure

Begin by casting a circle, calling the quarters, chanting, or raising energy as you normally would, performing protective exercises, and altering your consciousness. Clear your mind, bring focus to your breath, and meditate for at least a few minutes. When ready, begin the spell.

Assuming you've spend a good amount of time determining exactly which experiences you're going to work with (and have gotten representations of the distant locations if applicable), start by sitting down in front of your altar and placing the mirrors behind you.

Thinking about the first experience, grab a mirror and mark it somehow (using the marker) to represent the location or experience. Meditate on the experience briefly, determining exactly why you wish to reclaim the energy of the experience. Set the mirror aside, face up, placing an amethyst on top of it.

Do this with each mirror. When finished, stack the mirrors on top of each other and hold them in your left hand. Put the stones together and cup them in your right hand. Declare:

> I *now begin this process of transformation!*
> *From near and far, I reclaim and pull back my lost self.*
> *Mirrors of psyche, reflections of the past,*
> *transmute and transform these torments of mind!*
> *Through time and space, through region and place,*
> I *rework my soul to illuminated wholeness.*
> *So shall it be!*

Close the circle as you normally would and go to the location of the traumatic incident the first mirror represents (or use the representation of the location). When there, sit down and look at your reflection in the mirror. Glance up and visually scan the area, and look back down at the mirror. Continue this process and close your eyes whenever you wish.

As you are slowly reflecting, begin to think back about the event or events. Remember the pain, the trauma. If you need to cry, do so and put your tears on the mirror. Reflect on the experience deeply and accurately.

When you are ready, begin moving the mirror in a widdershins motion, facing the area. Feel as though you are transported back in time, reliving the incident. Imagine the energies of the experience funneling into the mirror. See the memories being sucked up through the surface of the mirror. If it helps, assign a certain color to the experience and visualize it whirling into the mirror.

When you feel ready, take the garden shovel and dig a hole about 4 inches deep in the ground. Liberally sprinkle wormwood in this hole. Place the mirror in the hole and cover it with the dirt. Place the amethyst on top of the "grave" as a marker. Look at the stone and say:

> Stone of Jupiter, stone of healing,
> transfer your essence into this mirror.
> Transform this experience to my benefit.
> I am ready to accept, embrace, and integrate my past.
> So mote it be.

Repeat this process in each of the four locations. Be sure to take your time—as long as is necessary for successfully reworking the energy. Once you have conquered all locations, relax and take it easy for the next 4 days. During this time, contemplate the ins and outs of the experiences—and particularly ponder how they could have benefited you in the present day and how you've changed since.

After 4 days have passed, return to each location and unearth each mirror. In its place, leave the amethysts as offerings, buried in the ground. When you've gathered all the mirrors, draw a large X on the face of each, and gaze at your smiling reflection in each mirror before discarding them in the trash, knowing that you've worked to reclaim your vibrations trapped in time.

Push the Limits:
Suffering to Learn

One of traditional Wicca's questions upon initiation is "Art thou willing to suffer to learn?" This speaks a deep truth: oftentimes the most vital life lessons are learned through difficult experiences. It's often within the most trying experiences that the greatest lessons are waiting to be learned.

Many of the spells in this chapter are concerned with working through difficult experiences. Part of Jupiter's energy, which is greatly expressed through Sagittarius, is that of slingshotting through restrictions (similar to Mars, and quite unlike Saturn). Jupiter is a sign of expanded growth and knowledge, on which this particular spell is also focused. Jupiter aids in the development of personal truth. Sometimes it is up to the practitioner themselves to induce personal pain to aid in the development of inner wisdom.

——— · ———

There are many ways to push one's limits to an expanded state of consciousness. For an in-depth description and exploration of these mechanisms, I suggest reading the section on fasting and self-sacrifice in my book *Shadow Magick Compendium*; the information covered there is too much to recite in these pages. Instead, the following ritual will utilize various "smaller" techniques for constructively bringing about stress for the sake of spiritual development.

This spell is not an initiatory experience, nor is it necessarily designed to induce Gnosis. Gnosis—the experience of oneness or unity with God (Spirit)—is accessible in many ways and is indeed something that people of many cultures aside from our own experience regularly. Instead of attempting to push readers to a Gnostic state of consciousness, this working will serve as an introduction to other ways of personally seeking spiritual connection. One must come to know their limits before they can push them.

Mindfully pushing one's limits can be a springboard to expanded consciousness. Western culture is often lazy, apathetic, and filled with excessive desire (for physical "things"). Such a state of being is not conducive to the spiritual experience. Altering one's experience beyond familiar and comfortable boundaries can break down psychological barriers and induce states of consciousness that are divorced, even slightly, from normal operative thought.

Though some of the methods within this spell may seem silly at first, they're in place for good reasons. I can only hope that this serves as a pleasant (well, pleasant-*ish*) introduction to the vast world of self-sacrifice and its benefits.

Stepping Back & Further Application

It can seem daunting or strange to push oneself past places of comfort. It should be understood that countless cultures around the world recognize the spiritual benefits of fasting and restriction. Their main goal is the increase of wisdom and connection to the Divine.

Everyone has something to learn about themselves and about reality—otherwise we wouldn't be here! If you've come to this spell, it's likely that you're feeling a pull to develop your spiritual wisdom. Some of the methods used here can be of benefit in this process, but the real limits to which you allow yourself to be pushed are up to you. It's been said that people who are blind have increased senses of hearing, that people who are deaf have increased senses of sight, and so on. Keeping this in mind, think of physical self-restrictions as techniques for aiding in the development of the nonphysical (spiritual) self.

If this spell resonates well with you, I'd suggest reading the in-depth information on such practices in *Shadow Magick Compendium* and consider performing longer self-sacrifices such as sustained fasting (from food, sight, technology, touch, communication, speech, and so on).

Supplies
- a blindfold
- a drum or drum-like instrument
- a blue candle

Notes

- The ideal amount of time to fast before this ritual is 16 hours. This amount of time can include the hours you slept the night before. However, you may also wish to fast from sleep for a night to aid in consciousness alteration. When fasting from food, permit yourself water or juice.

- If any of the activities herein could potentially be legitimately threatening to your health (such as fasting if diabetic, etc.), speak with your health care professional before attempting. The ritual (and longer, sustained self-sacrifices) are not designed to sabotage a person's health, but to push oneself beyond the ordinary.

- Allow yourself upwards of 2 or 3 hours to engage in the ritual. If you get spontaneous (yet non-risky) ideas for self-sacrifice while in ritual, play with the techniques. If you enter a state of trance and receive visions, allow these to occur.

- Though this spell could be placed in Saturn for its "restrictive" aspects, I've chosen to place it here to utilize the Jupiter energy of expansion and growth, which can be cultivated as a result of ritualizing.

Procedure

Fast all day before this ritual (see Notes). Begin by casting a circle, calling the quarters, chanting, or raising energy as you normally would, performing protective exercises, and altering your consciousness. Clear your mind, bring focus to your breath, and meditate for at least a few minutes. When ready, begin the spell.

Having fasted all day (from food and/or sleep, depending on your choice), your energy should be light and ethereal. Your consciousness should be slightly shifted enough to get the most out of the following activities. To begin, light the candle and declare:

Spirits of vitality and expansion! I am willing to suffer to learn!
Expand my wisdom, allow my knowledge of self to bloom!
My body is temporary and my spirit is eternal!

Immediately blindfold yourself. You will remain blindfolded throughout. Now bring focus to your other senses. Inhale deeply through your nose, smelling the air. Bring focus to your hearing, making even the slightest noises audible. Bring your awareness to the taste inside your mouth. Touch the floor and the altar, feeling every detail. Spend at least a few minutes navigating each sense.

Stand up and lift up one foot. Bend your other knee to maintain balance. (Situate yourself in a corner or by a wall, if necessary, to ensure that you don't lose balance.) Stay in this position for many minutes if possible. When it starts to hurt or feel extremely uncomfortable, bring focus to your breath and allow yourself to keep standing on one leg. Bring focus *away* from the pain and discomfort.

When you finally feel that no more can be taken, collapse to the ground and give yourself a rest. Repeat the process with the other foot.

Next, put yourself in a moderately strenuous yoga position (if you know one). Otherwise, put yourself in "push-up" position (only the hands and balls of the feet touching the ground). Remain in this stance for many minutes, pushing yourself beyond the discomfort. Again, don't give in to the pain: bring focus to your breath.

When no more can be taken, collapse and take a break. Next, grab the drum and maintain a steady beat with 4 counts between each. The rhythm should resonate "(beat)-1-2-3-4 (beat)-1-2-3-4" and so on. Continue doing this for as long as possible, maintaining the precise rhythm and silently counting the beats. I recommend performing this for at least 20 minutes. During this time, you will notice yourself entering a trancelike state. Still maintain the rhythm. Allow yourself to lose track of time and space.

When you lose the plot (so to speak), take a break and soak up the silence. Lay on your back on the floor. Take extremely deep belly-breaths in and out of your mouth. Do this very quickly. While doing this, the increase in oxygen will induce altered consciousness. Do this for only about 20 seconds, to avoid passing out.

Relax in fetal position and return to normal consciousness. When balanced, take off the blindfold, light the candle, and stare at the middle of the burning candle (not at the flame directly). Stare at the candle without glancing away, even slightly. Stare at it and clear your mind. If you look away for even a split second, start over again. Your only movement should be blinking. Don't allow your eyes to blur or shift in any way, maintaining the direct eye contact with the candle.

When you can no longer maintain eye contact, close your eyes and return to usual consciousness. If you have any manifestation spells or prayers to perform, this could be a good time because you are currently energetically "empty" in a sense, and thus more receptive to invocative energies. Consider trying this ritual and discerning variations of it later or on a regular basis. Thank the spirits and close the circle as you normally would. Ground your energy with healthy food and sleep.

O Fortuna!:
Manifesting Prosperity, Wealth & Abundance

Aside from issues of the heart (and genitals), money is probably the most ancient focus of spellcraft. Innumerable things could be said about money and its place in humanity throughout time. Beyond survival necessities, few things are as desired as money and love. It's a shame that humanity has been known for the time-honored practice of hoarding money in elite pockets, thus starving the majority of the population from a comfortable amount of resources. It's even more unfortunate that this practice continues all over the world to this day.

Everyone's desire for money and financial abundance is different. The selfishly brutal demons of greed and fear are to blame for some people's desire to have more, more, and still more cash in their wallets and bank accounts, paying not an ounce of care to those in situations of suffering (er, scratch that, that's just how *business* works, isn't it? Sorry, my bad!). We're taught that the accumulation of "stuff" is true happiness (who cares about the soul?) and that those with more money are of greater social worth. Many of these notions have become second nature, even unconscious, in the group mind.

—— • ——

With all these notions of money as the root of all evil, why have I included a money spell here? Because we all deserve to have it. Though money can propagate wickedness, though it's a fleeting illusion, though it doesn't buy happiness, and though money is a neutral force that can be used for good or ill, it's still nice to have. For now, we are all dependant on the dollar to one extent or another. This doesn't mean we have to become attached to money (which breeds fear and greed), but that we can permit ourselves to feel guiltless for having a full wallet.

We all deserve to have more than enough and to enjoy the pleasures of money without becoming capitalistic slaves. In particular, spiritual people deserve to have money because they are likely to donate, give back, and assist others in need! There is always a balance.

Stepping Back & Further Application

If you frequently find yourself without cash, why is this? Do you feel that this is simply your disposition in life? Your family situation? Do you work yourself to the bone for the buck or do you see it as secondary in importance to the rest of life itself? Do you have ideas against possessing money that may be metaphysically restricting you to its access? Consider your current position and how you can work to change it without burning the candle at both ends.

There are a million ways to manifest money through magick. Obviously, mundane measures must also be taken. I'd recommend taking chances, such as buying a few lottery tickets and intelligently taking up opportunities that present themselves. Again, it's all about balance: don't gamble all your cash away!

Even if you have little money, it's a good thing to give back, even if it's small. Give $20 to someone if you have it and they don't—and don't ask for it back. Give a buck or two to a transient or beggar. Randomly buy someone a sandwich at the shop. Pick up your friend's coffee tab. Donate a few random bucks to an animal shelter or human welfare organization. Budget for donating money frequently and get creative (and have fun) giving it to random causes, people, and projects. Such activities increase positive financial karma, promote generosity, and encourage the Universe to reciprocate. It's fun to share without cause or reason.

Supplies

- a green candle
- a small piece of green calcite (or optical/clear calcite)
- a stick of patchouli incense
- a small loaf of freshly baked organic wheat bread
- green food coloring (organic if possible) and a new paintbrush
- 5 fresh $1 dollar bills (or pound notes, etc.)
- a green permanent marker
- 16 whole bay leaves
- a ballpoint pen
- a small amount of the herb thyme
- about ½ cup of extra virgin olive oil, on a plate
- any combination of the herbs alfalfa, allspice, basil, bergamot, cinnamon, cinquefoil, fenugreek, flax, High John the Conqueror root, jade leaves, moonwort (also called honesty or silver dollar plant), myrrh, nutmeg, patchouli, vervain, and vetivert
- 16 inches of green thread
- a small garden shovel

Notes

- Wear all green clothing or a green robe during this ritual if possible.
- For an added kick of good luck (and a bit of Hoodoo medicine), add a pinch of black cat hair to your altar, wallet, purse, or piggy bank.

Procedure

Begin by casting a circle, calling the quarters, chanting, or raising energy as you normally would, performing protective exercises, and altering your consciousness. Clear your mind, bring focus to your breath, and meditate for at least a few minutes. When ready, begin the spell.

Ignite the candle and place the calcite at its base. Light the incense as well. Hold the loaf of bread high above you, calling out:

Spirits of abundance! Spirits of wealth! Spirits of money! Come now, I summon you!

Using your hands, break the loaf of bread into 4 pieces. Place the candle near the bread. Use the food coloring and brush to draw the following symbols on each piece: the symbol for Jupiter, symbol 15, symbol 16, and a dollar sign.

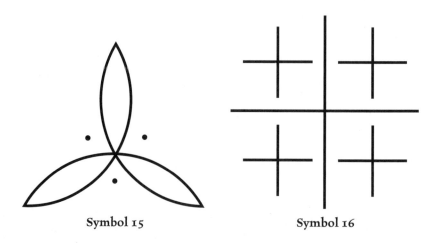

Symbol 15   **Symbol 16**

On *one* of the dollar bills, draw six extra o's after each 1 to create a "million-dollar bill." Make the bill say "One Million Dollars" on it instead of "One Dollar," and so on. Place the bill at the base of the candle.

Take the marker and draw the 4 symbols mentioned above on each bay leaf. Place them at the base of the candle. Cup your hands over the candle, bill, and bread and shout 4 times:

Reverto! Redivivus! Ravah! Increbresco! Cresco! Kavar!

Write the above words on the 4 unmarked dollar bills. Use the ballpoint pen when writing, and write the words around the edges of the bills, so as to not mark them up too much. Set them aside.

Sprinkle some of the thyme on top of the olive oil. Cup your hands over the dish and say the words once again. Take one of the pieces of bread in your hands and say:

My breadbasket is always aplenty. I am abundant and prosperous.

Place the piece in your lap. Pick up another and say:

I *always have more than enough; I shall never hunger, I shall never thirst.*

Place that piece in your lap as well. Grab a third piece and say:

My wealth I share with others, as the gods of wealth provide.

Set that piece on top of the 4 marked-up dollar bills. Grab the last piece and say:

With gratitude do I accept the money I manifest. So shall it be!

Wave that piece through the incense smoke, burn it briefly with the candle flame, and dip it in the olive oil (with thyme). Finally, sprinkle some of the herbal blend on the bread and place it on your altar, leaving it there for a month or more as an offering.

Take one of the pieces of bread on your lap and slowly eat it, dipping it in the olive oil. While you eat, visualize yourself being happy having more than enough money. See yourself buying luxurious items, having absolute financial security, and helping other people with the cash. Once finished, drink a sip of the olive oil, offer some to others, and anoint your forehead with a dab.

Thank the spirits of abundance and close the circle as you normally would. Roll up the "million-dollar bill" and tie it with the thread. Stick this inside the other piece of bread that was on your lap. Also smash the calcite into the bread. Using the garden shovel, dig a hole on your property (in front of the front door if possible). Sprinkle the rest of the herbal mix on top of the bread and bury it all. This will secure the spell's magick in your home.

Take the bread that you put on the bills and put it outside for the animals to find and devour. This will recycle the spell's energy in nature.

Finally, take the 4 marked-up dollar bills to a grocery store. Place each bill in random locations in the store (behind a bottle of soy milk, between two boxes of cereal and so on) so that others will eventually find them. This will amplify the spell's energy in society. Be sure you buy something at the store so your covert magickal operation of generosity and abundance doesn't get exposed!

Chapter 8

— ⋅ —

SATURN

— ⋅ —

SATURN
Zodiacal rulership: Capricorn (and Aquarius, classical astrology)
Color association: Black
Sephira: Binah
Number: 3
Day: Saturday
Archetypes: Dark Mother, Father Time, Death God/dess, Underworld God/dess, Destroyer, Crone
Themes: Karma, restriction, discipline, life cycle, death, initiation, responsibility, perseverance, limitation, sacrifice, fear, binding, harshness, destruction, aging

Don't Fear the Reaper:
Severing That Which No Longer Serves

Though all of the spells in this book are aligned to the given planet's energy—and integrate specific alignments attuned to each planet—this one pays utmost attention to its planet. In this spell, the practitioner taps into the essence of Saturn through various archetypes of the planet. For this reason, a variety of deific names are used rather than one alone.

Life is a process of change, which is one message that Saturn clearly delivers. For the most part, change is feared in our society. It's easy to form an idea about something, someone, or oneself and cling to that notion continually. The Greek philosophical saying *Panta rhei; ouden menei* (everything flows; nothing is stagnant) can be seen as Saturnian wisdom.

This spell is designed to help sever and destroy those energies that no longer serve you. Drawing on the concept of Life as Change, this working is designed to connect you to the energy and necessity of sacred death. Because this rite is directly concerned with the potentially overwhelming energy of Saturn, allow me to first give some history.

—— • ——

Before the discovery of the outermost planets, Saturn was viewed in classical antiquity as the farthest planet from the Sun, earning it metaphysical associations with death and the cycle of life itself. Naturally, mythological deities representing death and the overarching life cycle were ascribed and aligned to its properties. Pluto, in modern astrology, now additionally carries many of these associations.

As deities of life, light, and fertility exist, they must too have their equal-opposite counterparts. Without death there would be no life, and this often maligned force of nature demands equal observation. All pantheistic structures include one or more representatives of the vibration or occurrence of death, be it the death of the land or the death of humans and animals. To be sure, Saturn had no option but manifest as an enigma, for death itself is a grand mystery.

The ancient Greeks recognized the deity Kronos as the first-born Titan. His name is also spelled "Cronus" or "Kronus," and should not be confused with the deity Chronos, who is Father Time. The Titans were the mythological offspring of the primordial deities Gaea and Uranus. Because of his divine associations—which are comparative to that of Horus, the son of Isis and Osiris in Egyptian mythology—Kronos was especially honored during antiquity's Golden Age, and he continued to be celebrated in Greco-Roman harvest festivals.

The Roman agricultural deity Saturn (or Saturnus) was aligned with Kronos as the Greek and Roman cultures merged. Saturn was the father of Ceres, Veritas, and Jupiter. In the mythology, Saturn overthrew and castrated his father Uranus. Later, because of a prediction that one of Saturn's sons would in turn overthrow him as universal sovereign, Saturn devoured his children as a preventive measure (much as the Egyptian sky goddess Nuit "devours" her children, the Sun and the stars, each night). However, Saturn's mother Ops hid her sixth child, Jupiter, on the Mediterranean island of Crete. Later, Jupiter overthrew Saturn and the other Titans. (Note that in Greek mythology, Jupiter is equivalent to Zeus and Ops to Rhea.)

Saturnalia was the Roman festival associated with Saturn, and it took place around the time of the Winter Solstice (the zodiacal transition into Capricorn, which Neopagans call Yule) as a festival of the harvest. Saturnalia was a celebration of Earth's bounty, as well as a time to feast. Fascinatingly, common culture went topsy-turvy during the holiday, as the slaves and lower caste individuals were allowed to "turn the tables on their masters" and be free to do as they pleased.

———— • ————

Later in history, as the experience of death was anthropomorphized into a deific form, associations were drawn between the folkloric Grim Reaper and Kronos/Saturn. Azræl, the archangel of death in Islamic belief, has also been associated with these deities, though he seems to have a livelier and less corpselike depiction.

Saturn is known as Sani (or Shani) in Hinduism, one of the nine planets called Navagrahas. The deity that rules Sani is the karmic judge.

Some modern Wiccan traditions draw associations between the Saturnian archetype and the Holly King who rules the dying year. The common Wiccan imagery of the Oak King and Holly King is derived from *The White Goddess*, by Robert Graves, which is itself a poetic account of ancient histories interwoven with modern myth. Indeed, the archetype of death is a universal phenomenon because death itself is life's doppelganger.

Stepping Back & Further Application

For starters, are you ready to release the things you feel no longer serve you? Are you clinging to past ideas? Do you have perceptions of self that are unrealistic? It may be a good idea to reflect for a certain period of time before performing this working. Think about what kinds of things no longer serve your path—and this can be *anything*. What restricts your happiness and the pursuit of your goals? Are you willing to begin the process of allowing these things to slip away, and thus be replaced with different energies, ideas, and so on?

Keep in mind that Saturn also works subconsciously. If there are things in your life you don't realize are inhibiting, this spell will still set the ball rolling on severing these things from you. Don't resist the change, but be aware of how the ritual's effects carry onward.

Supplies
- a black towel and a black blanket

- black body paint, greasepaint, a body marker, or bat's blood ink with a brush
- a black candle with the symbol of Saturn inscribed on it
- any combination of the herbs agrimony, alder, asafoetida, basil, bay laurel, belladonna, bistort, black pepper, boneset, cedar, comfrey, cypress, datura, elecampane, elm, eucalyptus, galbanum, hemlock, hemp, henbane, ivy, kava-kava, mandrake, mullein, nightshade, patchouli, poplar, skullcap, slippery elm, and valerian
- a fresh rose
- a boline, athamé, or sharp blade
- 1 whole beet (not pickled!)

Notes

- Substitute mandrake (either *Mandragora* or American mandrake) for any of the toxic herbs on this list, if you'd rather. If you do in fact use the deadly herbs (belladonna, nightshade, hemlock, and henbane), use extreme caution, ensuring that you don't ingest, inhale, or touch them with bare skin.
- If you can't settle on a timed alignment for this spell, you may choose to perform it on a Satur(n)day at either 11 pm or 3 am (ideally with the Sun or Moon in Capricorn or Aquarius). If performing at 3 am, do so on a Friday night so that the ritual will technically take place on Saturday.
- To represent Saturn, wear all black for this ritual or simply go skyclad.

Procedure

Instead of casting a circle, hop in the bath (or shower if a bathtub is unavailable) with the black body paint, marker, or bat's blood ink set aside. Spend some time meditating on Saturn. Reflect on what Saturn represents as a planet, and on the variety of mythologies aligned to the celestial body.

After bathing or showering, dry yourself with the black towel and remain naked. Look at yourself in the mirror, connect your eyes with their reflection, and take 3 deep breaths to center your energy. These breaths should be taken in through your nose and out through your mouth, and should be very long and deep.

The symbol of Saturn represents the deity's sickle. With the body paint or marker, draw a large symbol of Saturn on your chest. Take some time to perfect this design. Make it thick and visible, painted with the "cross up" and "tail down." If you are a more seasoned occultist, draw the Seal of Saturn on the back of each hand.

To continue attuning to Saturnian vibration, draw the Saturn-aligned numbers 3, 6, 9, 11, 15, 30, 45, and 52. Put these on various places on your body, such as the arms, legs, and belly. Whether or not you understand the numerological correspondences of these numbers is unimportant (though doing serious studies into the associations could be of benefit).

Grab your black towel or blanket. Wrap it around yourself, concealing your nudity. You can choose to stay nude for the ritual, or you can put on black clothing or robes. With your tools in hand, journey outside to an area where you can be undisturbed in nature, even if you have to journey to get there.

Once in a good spot, unwrap the blanket or towel, standing nude (unless you've chosen to wear black clothing instead) and your body covered in symbols. Looking up at the night sky, take 3 more long, slow, deep breaths, filling your body with the energy all around you.

At this point, light the black candle and set it in a secure spot. Lie with your back flat on the ground, your flesh touching the ground. Cover yourself with the blanket from the neck down, and sprinkle the herbal mixture atop the blanket. Finally, lay the rose across your chest to, in a sense, symbolize death. Once again, take 3 deep breaths to center your energy and feel yourself in this symbolic ritual setting.

Once you feel appropriately grounded, either whisper or roar (depending on how you feel inspired or how vocally conducive the setting is) 3 times:

*Saturnus . . . Saturnus . . . Saturnus! Great Reaper and Lord of Karma,
he who oversees time, and the death of all things great and small. Great
Saturnus, great Kronos, great angel Azræl, I connect with you now on this
most Saturnian night. I invite you to surround me, to deliver messages I
must hear, and heed my prayers. Come now, take from me that which no
longer serves my path. Saturnus . . . Saturnus . . . Saturnus!*

Close your eyes and envision a grim reaper in a long black hooded
cloak. Sickle in hand, his influence is that of reaping the harvest, declaring reign on the fruitful land by taking its life to the Underworld. He is
Saturn, Kronos, Father Time, Azræl, the Grim Reaper. He is the archetype of the dying year. He is Death.

Face this deity straight-on, making out his features and telling him
your wishes of severance. Psychically tell him your reasons for wishing
to contact him, making clear the things you wish to sever from your life.
Open your psychic and perceptive channels to see if you receive any
messages from Saturn. You may receive messages having to do with any
qualities or properties that Saturn represents.

When you feel this meditation has continued for as long as is beneficial to you, speak aloud any personal prayers you have to Saturnus, Kronos, Azræl, and the Reaper. When finished, keep your eyes closed and
pluck the rose from atop your body. Hold it high above you and say:

*Great Saturnus! With the severing of life in this rose, I too ask you to sever
and break issues in my life that no longer serve me. Great Lord of Karma,
and Bestower of Divine Justice, I ask you to assist me in harvesting that
which restricts my development, that it may fall before me to analyze,
understand, and banish. Saturnus, with your mighty sickle, I ask you now
to oversee this severance of my dead past.*

Using the boline or blade, cut the rose in two, whether it be in the
middle or at the top of the stem. With a piece in either hand, let your
arms fall, hitting the ground with force. Close your eyes and slip into
meditation. Again, allow any visions to fill you, and simply be in the
presence of the energy at hand.

When you are finished, reenter your normal waking state of consciousness, get up, shake the herbs off the blanket, and throw the pieces of the flower in opposing directions. Snuff the candle in the dirt, declaring "So mote it be." End by thanking the deities, bowing to each direction, and leaving the beet as an offering.

Downward Spiral: To Cause Failure & Misery

Here we come to another cursing spell. I must reiterate that spells for crossing another person should only be done in the most dire of circumstances, and after all other efforts to resolve the situation have been exhausted. Destructive magick toward others should not be used for revenge, but for self-protection and defense. Please approach such workings with intelligence and solid ethics. To magickally harm another without damn good reason is to lay a curse upon oneself. The practitioner must take full responsibility for their actions in the spell and for anything that could potentially result from performing it.

One of Saturn's archetypes is the Lord of Karma. It would be entirely egotistical to think that other peoples' karmic lessons are up to us to determine, but sometimes a push in the right direction is what's needed when our well-being or that of others is legitimately threatened. Stopping a perpetrator in their tracks can in fact be the best way a person learns the lessons they're actively avoiding.

——— · ———

Magick focused on love, sex, money, and cursing are some of the most prevalent types of ancient spells. There's nothing wrong with these things in and of themselves, but an attachment to these forces can lead to unethical decisions and an unhealthy attachment to the physical plane and its components. I advise practitioners to perform all magick, benign or severe, with a foundation of morality and conscious thought.

If you would like to learn more about cursing in a Neopagan context, I suggest Dorothy Morrison's acclaimed *Utterly Wicked: Curses, Hexes & Other Unsavory Notions*. This book contains numerous ideas and methods of cursing and is one that I feel should be read by morally inclined Craft practitioners, even if there is never a need to utilize the workings.

Stepping Back & Further Application

Cursing magick is serious. Aside from the obvious reason that it can cause damage to a person, the subject is serious because the motivation of the practitioner is highly significant. Yes, some people who are "into" magick will throw curses and hexes out like nobody's business. This can be a psychological assertion of power, an ego-based domination tactic, or a whole slew of other inner issues on the caster's part. If you're considering a curse, approach the situation from the most objective stance possible, clearly defining where you stand in the mix. More often than not, genuine compassion and the desire to heal are the energies that can truly mend a difficult situation. Get inside the person's head and see if a curse really is the most ideal solution.

Think about other ways you can follow up on the situation that you may not have tried before. Use your real-world magick to influence change before turning exclusively to esoterica. Remove yourself, your subjectivity, and your bitter emotions from the situation and analyze it from that vantage point. If you've honestly tried other methods of influencing change and feel that wishing deep ill upon a person *is* the best option *for them*, give yourself time to reflect on the working and modify the magick to fit the situation. Finally, wait at least a few days to perform a curse after you get the initial idea to do so; sometimes you'll realize that a curse may actually be counterproductive.

Supplies
- 3 black candles
- the "essence" of the other person (see Notes)
- a black poppet that has one side open (or an old black sock or fabric that has been made into a doll)
- 1 or more *Solanaceæ* herbs (see Notes)
- a coffin nail (see Notes)
- a small stone of opal and/or obsidian

- a small, empty cardboard box
- a black permanent marker
- graveyard dirt (see Notes)
- a small amount of powdered sage

Notes

- The "essence" of a person, also called *ousia*, is anything that carries their energy pattern, including DNA (such as hair, fingernail clippings, and excretions), or has come in contact with the person (this is the Law of Contagion, and can include a person's possession, footprint, handwriting, and so forth). A person's essence can also be tapped into by creating a picture of the person, or by simply writing their name and focusing on them.

- Coffin nails are generally a component of baneful magick and have a rich history in Hoodoo and other magickal systems. However, they (or any nail) can also be imbued with properties of "fixing down" energies or sealing a spell.

- Graveyard dirt has long been used in Hoodoo and other magickal practices. For our purposes, it will represent the laying to rest of an old habit. Simply go to a graveyard and scoop up a small amount of dirt (not from someone's grave in this case), ideally from a crossroads area of the cemetery. A common substitute for graveyard dirt is to make a powdered mixture of patchouli, mullein, valerian, and sage.

- A *Solanaceæ* herb is any herb belonging to the plant family of that name. This includes the nightshades, encompassing belladonna, henbane, datura, mandrake, and tobacco. If none of these are available to you, substitute (or add) tomato, potato, eggplant, or petunia, which are mostly nontoxic members of the *Solanaceæ* family.

Procedure

Begin by casting a circle, calling the quarters, chanting, or raising energy as you normally would, performing protective exercises, and alter-

ing your consciousness. Clear your mind, bring focus to your breath, and meditate for at least a few minutes. When ready, begin the spell.

Light the black candles and situate them in a triangle in front of you; the uppermost candle should be farthest from you, with the other two closer to you, and about a foot apart from each other. Grab the "essence" of the person. Close your eyes and bring to mind all the negative things that make it clear this person should be cursed. Feel the upset rise inside you. Become angry and sad. Have confidence in your curse. When ready, open your eyes and put the contents in the poppet (or makeshift poppet). Glare at it and say:

[Name]: *this is you.*
[Name]: *this is you.*
[Name]: *this is you.*

Add the *Solanaceæ* herb(s) and the stone(s) to the poppet and seal it up as needed (by sewing it, dripping candle wax on it, or tying it shut). Place it in the center of the candles. Envision a black line connecting the candle flames into a perfect triangle, energetically trapping the poppet inside. Stare at the poppet and envision the person as being helpless to your magick. Say:

If you continue on this path, you'll fall farther down the black hole.
If you continue on this path, the Earth shall swallow you whole.
If you continue on this path, you'll reach the deadliest end.
If you continue on this path, you'll find only suffering again and again.

Grab the coffin nail and briefly dip it in the hot wax of each candle. Hold the nail in your right fist with the spike pointing downwards. Stare at the poppet and shout the following,

Dēstrŭctus! Dēstrŭctus! Dēstrŭctus!
Detritus! Detritus! Detritus!
Dēstrŭctus! Dēstrŭctus! Dēstrŭctus!

Immediately slam the nail into the heart of the poppet, seeing all the dense and destructive energies plummeting into the victim. Shout:

♄

Grow or Go! Grow or Go! Grow or Go!
[Name]: ARUR! [Name]: ARUR! [Name]: ARUR!

On the inside- and outside-bottoms of the box, draw symbol 17. On 3 other sides (such as on the lid—it's your choice) write AŌROS. On all other sides of the box, draw a large X. Sprinkle the graveyard dirt into the bottom of the box. Place the poppet inside the box and say:

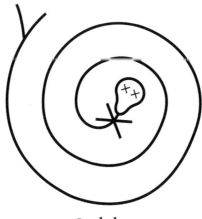

Symbol 17

This is your coffin if you don't change your ways.
This begins for you a downward spiral of self-destruction.
But: should you make an effort to grow and to love, you will be blessed …

Sprinkle some of the powdered sage over the poppet. Say:

However: if you stay as you are, you are cursed, hexed, bound, and dead.

Forcefully spit at the poppet and declare:

See the light! Be the light! Or perish if no effort is made! So mote it be!

Put the lid on the box and seal it with black wax. Drip some of the wax on the top of the box to form a cross shape. Close the circle as you normally would, allowing the candles to burn fully down with the "coffin" in the middle. (But keep an eye on the flames, of course.) Once the candles are extinguished, leave the box in a dark, hidden corner of your house so that you can release and "unbind" the spell if necessary.

Second Saturn Return:
A Dedication as a Crone or Sage

A Saturn return is the time in a person's life when Saturn's original placement in one's natal chart returns to its original position. Saturn takes approximately 29.5 years to make a complete cycle around the sun. Depending on its position when a person is born, the time of its precise return can vary. In more simple terms, every time we have a birthday it marks a solar return: the Sun coming back to the same position it was in when you were born. A Saturn return is our Saturnian birthday. This ceremony celebrates a person's second Saturn return.

Most people experience two or three Saturn returns; the first one at somewhere between the ages of 27 and 30, the second between 58 and 60, and the third between 86 and 88. When these returns occur, the influences of Saturn, including Karma, destiny, purpose, and direction, become illuminated in a person's life. The initial Saturn cycle (from birth until the age 27–30) can be seen as the Maiden or Son cycle, the second (beginning at 27–30) as the Mother or Father cycle, the third (beginning at 58–60) as the Crone or Sage cycle—which this ceremony is focused on celebrating—and the fourth (beginning at 86–88) as the Transcendent, Transitioning, or Spiritual Merging cycle. The exact time of the return can be calculated by a reliable astrological source.

If you are searching for a natal chart (birthchart) astrological casting, I personally recommend the and fun and extremely accurate *MoonCat! Astrology*, whose contact information is located at www.catoverthemoon .com. MoonCat is a globetrotting astrologer extraordinaire whose cosmic insights are like none other. I also heartily recommend Calantirniel, whose professional chart castings have keenly assisted those in need (myself included) more times than I can count! She can be found via www.thehiddenrealm.org or www.myspace.com/aartiana.

— · —

One thing to keep in mind is this: *chronological age* and *spiritual age* are not always synonymous. For many, the two go hand-in-hand (and that is what this particular rite of passage is focused on) because life experience can, and should, encourage the deepening of knowledge, which is wisdom. Still, some people are well aged and have little wisdom; others are little aged and have much wisdom. This ritual honors the convergence of these two forces: the physiological/biological and the spiritual/experiential. Also, the entrance into becoming a Crone or Sage is *not* synonymous with becoming a Priest, Priestess, or Craft Elder—such titles are separate and generally depend on a person's tradition and Craft training.

Some women begin to observe the "Entrance of the Crone" just after the final period of menopause, and perform a Croning ritual to mark the achievement. Men's biological times are not as clearly marked, so many perform a "Saging" at the time their intuition (and community) deems it appropriate. Most importantly—and even more important than precise age or Saturnian time—a person should have a deep sense of knowingness regarding their dedication into the next step of life's mysteries.

As mentioned in the Introduction, all ceremonies in here are designed for solitary practitioners but can be modified for group work. Because the Eldering position of Crone or Sage has implications of wisdom, ability, and experience, many "new Elders" are involved with a working group or will solitarily utilize their skills to help others in need. To conclude a Croning or Saging ritual, the newly dedicated Crone or Sage can present themselves to their community by going to a metaphysical shop and other magickal circles and mentioning their willingness to assist community members in need.

Stepping Back & Further Application

One does not have to perform this spell precisely at the moment of their second Saturn return, though it would be ideal. People transition into the Crone or Sage aspect of their lives as the Fates guide it to occur. This cosmically occurs upon the second Saturn return, but if one performs this rite give or take a number of years, its effects are still significant. That is, if the Universe aligns your elevation into this most venerated level, you will clearly perceive the transition regardless of Saturnian position. Just the same, marking one's physical age in this rite is almost as important as marking the wisdom earned.

Are you being objective in your desire to dedicate yourself at this time? Is this the most ideal time to leave behind aspects of your past and enter what's next? Have you accepted your experiences of the past and are you willing to embrace the unseen future? If now is the time, plan your solitary rite of passage accordingly. Put a lot of thought into the preparation and modify the ritual to fit you. Decide if you wish to practice fasting during the experience, if you wish to perform it skyclad, if you wish to paint your body, or even if you wish to do a vow of silence during the twenty-four-hour period (in which case you should "mentally speak" the ritual words). Make this "rebirthday" highly significant and reflective.

Supplies

- a small tent or supplies to construct one
- camping tools, sleeping supplies, and fire-kindling tools
- a pen and sketchbook
- supplies for building a campfire
- any combination of the herbs eyebright, High John the Conqueror root, ivy, lotus, mistletoe, mullein, Solomon's seal root, thyme, and woodruff
- drums, rattles, shakers, and other trance-inducing instruments
- jugs of fresh water (to drink and to extinguish the fire)
- a bottle of cooled gingko tea (see Notes)

Notes

- You will be spending a period of 24 hours alone in the wilderness for this ritual. Plan this carefully, plotting a campsite area where you won't be disrupted (if possible). Bring all the food, water, and sleeping supplies you need. If you choose to fully fast for the 24-hour period, permit yourself water, tea, and/or juice. At the very least, you should not eat any meat or dairy during the experience, to keep your energies merged with the Earth rather than with other animals' energies. Also, camp in a safe area.

- Please note the [bracketed] words in the spell and use the appropriate words depending on your gender. In instances of "[God/dess]," men can pray to the God alone and women to the Goddess alone *or* both men and women alike can certainly say "God and Goddess" if they'd like. As with all rituals, it should be personalized depending on one's own spirituality and deific alignments.

- Gingko is one of the most ancient trees in the world. For this reason, it's said to hold the memories of the world. Ingesting the tea slowly throughout the duration of the experience represents imbuing oneself with the wisdom of the ages.

- It's best to have scoped out a campsite well before the ritual. I recommend setting up your tent in the early afternoon and remaining there throughout the ceremony until that same hour the following day. Also, be sure that you're in an area with a fire pit and that there are no fire restrictions in effect at the moment.

Procedure

After setting up the tent, cast a circle around it, call the quarters, chant, or raise energy as you normally would, perform protective exercises, and alter your consciousness. Clear your mind, bring focus to your breath, and meditate for at least a few minutes. When ready, begin the spell.

Facing the Sun, raise your arms fully and declare:

> As the Sun swings from day to night and back to day again, so does the pendulum of my life and censor of my soul swing to rebirth. I currently stand in the liminal—the place in between this and that.

For the next hour or so, perform a walking meditation (see page 142 for an example of this). Fully observe and absorb your environment and slow your senses so you enter a sacred and reflective state of mind. In your own way, communicate with the spirits of the area and leave them offerings as you see fit. Merge with the land.

During the course of the next few hours (assumably leading to dusk), spend a lot of time with your sketchbook. Sketch a number of pictures that represent various points in your life. For example, you may wish to sketch a picture of you as a baby, in grade school, in high school, working at various jobs, raising children or getting married, practicing rituals, and so on and so forth. I recommend sketching at least 13 pictures. (Don't worry; no one but you and the spirits will see your doodles!) These sketches should all represent significant phases in your life's experience leading up to the present. Try to encompass as many experiences as you can.

When the Sun begins its descent, kindle the fire. Use the sketches you've drawn by placing them under the kindling sticks and logs, igniting them to start the fire. Try to gather some fallen branches from the immediate area (if that is allowed in your camping area—be sure to check first!) to add to the fire pit. When the fire gets going, say:

> *Entering this terrain, I hold the Sacred Flame! These experiences of my past are transformed by this fire at the down-going of the sun. I offer my past to the mightiest of spirits, petitioning the [Lord/Lady] of Karma to usher me into the next phase of life. Great [Father/Mother] of Time and Transition, I am being transported to your terrain. I welcome your comforting embrace. As the Moon wanes to sliver in due course and the sun wanes to winter as it does, so too do I enter the perceptive and peaceful world of the Aged, Golden, and Wise. Take me in! Let me know and live the Wisdom of the Ages!*

As the fire roars, intermittedly throw the herbal blend to the flame. Use your drum, rattle, shaker, or other instruments to help summon the change. Channel the energy into the fire of transformation, simultaneously heightening your consciousness. Take time to commune with the Aged God and Goddess, as well as those spirits and ancestors that you've come to know as guides in your life. Perform work on your energy body. Meditate deeply. Astral project. Divine. Do all sorts of spiritual work, and allow yourself to become spontaneously inspired. After these and any other activities you wish to perform, properly extinguish the fire and go to sleep for the night. As you drift into sleep, repeat "Sage" or "Crone" over and over again until you are asleep. As you get closer to sleeping, simply repeat the term in your head rather than speaking it aloud.

The moment you wake up the next day, emerge from the tent with a feeling of renewal. Go straight to the Sun, raise your arms, and declare:

♄

*From this day on, I am aligned to my utmost divine nature. This Rite of
Passage marks me as a guide; a holder of experience; a Seer. Behold my
ascent! Behold my descent! To the timeless [God/dess] of Wisdom I forever
dedicate my soul. I hereby enter the world beyond words and invoke the
Wisdom of the Ages. Experience has left its mark on this body. These
marks, these wrinkles, these thin and gray hairs, are all sacred marks of my
Wisdom: a mark of my Beauty and Strength!*
I am [God/dess]. I am [God/dess]. I am [God/dess].
I am golden. I am purified. I am [Sage/Crone]. Blessed be!

Piercing the Veil:
Summoning the Ancestors

All magick finds its roots in shamanic and indigenous spirituality from
one part of the globe or another. A common thread of virtually all indigenous religious practice is the honoring of ancestors. Those who have
crossed the veil before us hold a special place in society. No longer with
us on the operative plane, their spiritual existence can be interpreted in
many ways.

Neopaganism honors the ancestors most prominently around Halloween. Still, they can be contacted and connected to at any time. Views
of the afterlife vary from culture to culture and person to person. In reality, no one on Earth can possibly know what happens to individual
consciousness once life ceases. We have to rely on our own conclusions
and experiences to determine our beliefs in the beyond.

Ancestors should always be called forth with a purpose. In the case
of this working, the purpose is up to the practitioner. Many people feel
that deceased relatives and beloved friends (or animals) become spirit
guides for them once they've left the physical plane. If this is your case,
you may wish to call upon those guides in order to receive messages and
advice. For those who have recently lost someone, it can be beneficial
to call upon their spirits to make peace, leave offerings, say your final
words, update them on your goings-on, and so forth.

Keep in mind that, though every culture has a different view, it's
likely that earthbound spirits of the deceased retain "ego/self-identity"

qualities that were present in their human form. In other words, death does not necessarily imply increased knowledge or spiritual insight. It's also good to keep in mind that long-dead ancestors may appear differently than the recently dead. If you follow a belief in reincarnation (or a similar theory), the souls of the long-dead are most likely reincarnated. If they appear to you clearly, is this an act of magickally reaching through time? Or is it a mental projection? Are they "ghosts" (earthbound disincarnates)? It's good to think through some of death's most curious questions when considering an ancestral summoning.

Stepping Back & Further Application

Okay, I admit it: many years ago when I had a television, the show *Charmed* was a guilty pleasure of mine—particularly the first season. In one of the episodes, the family performed a "Wiccaning." During this, the ancestral line of familial Witches was summoned to observe the child-blessing. Though the show is far-fetched and silly, some of the information and spells in the program are based on true magick. If you wish to summon your own line of ancestors for a particularly significant purpose, go for it. At the same time, such a thing would take proper planning: look at a family tree, gather information for those ancestral spirits you wish to call (some of the spirits may *not* be okay with your doing so), and look at old family photo albums.

For this working, you may wish to only summon one or two ancestors, or you may summon individuals whom you feel are now spiritual guardians of yours. Do as you will, but be mindful of the spirits you're working with. Plan your intention carefully, and remember to treat them as you knew them (if you knew them) rather than as gods. Don't supplicate yourself before them, don't command them to do your bidding . . . just exercise respect and humility.

Supplies

- 1 black candle and 1 white candle
- an image or representation of the being(s) being summoned

- Mixture 1: a combination of the herbs henbane, periwinkle, poppy, rowan (mountain ash), thyme, tobacco, wormwood, and yew
- a round incense-burning charcoal disk and sand in a dish or censor
- Mixture 2: a combination of the (dried) herbs basil, myrrh, sandalwood, and willow
- a piece of paper with symbol 18 drawn on it
- a loud bell or chime
- offerings for the summoned (see Notes)
- pen and paper (and spirit-recording devices if ghost-hunting is one of your specialties)

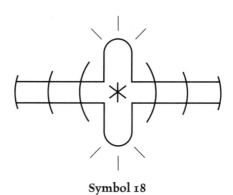

Symbol 18

Notes

- The herbs henbane and yew are optional in this working because of their toxic qualities. As always, don't ingest, inhale, or touch with bare hands.
- Think about the most ideal offerings you can leave for the spirit(s) being summoned. Is there a favorite food they preferred when incarnated? Can you bake some bread or prepare something special? If nothing else, apples are a traditional offering to the dead.
- It's best to begin this ritual either at the moment of sunset, at midnight, at 3 am, or at a nighttime hour of Saturn (see page 16).

Procedure

Begin by casting a circle, calling the quarters, chanting, or raising energy as you normally would, performing protective exercises, and altering your consciousness. Clear your mind, bring focus to your breath, and meditate for at least a few minutes. When ready, begin the spell.

Light both candles and place them on the altar. Between them, situate the images or representations of the being(s) being summoned. Sprinkle Mixture 1 around the candles and around the images of the dead. Ignite the incense charcoal and, when glowing, place Mixture 2 on top. Remember to add more incense to the charcoal throughout the ritual. If you have any spirit-recording devices, turn them on now.

Stand facing the west. Place the paper with the symbol either on the floor in the west or on the western quadrant of your altar. Raise your arms and say:

> Hail Guardians of the watchtowers of the west. Holy Zepherus, Western Wind, rush upon this space. Mighty setting sun—he who guides lost souls—lend your power to this rite. Spirits of water, spirits of change, spirits of the dead, hear my calls! I seek to commune with those who have gone before me. As I, too, will eventually take the hand of death, I seek to converse with inhabitants of the world beyond while I am still in the flesh. Almighty Bringer of Death, I ask that you grant me permission to consult [one/two/some] of those you've already ushered forth. Hail! Hail! Hail!

Ring the bell 9 times. Sit on the floor, close your eyes, and bow to the west. Absorb the energies around you and sense yourself in your body, your physical frame. Sense the western spirits and the soft, peaceful energy of death. Expand your senses, slow your breathing, and become entirely present in the moment.

When ready, sit before your altar and look at the images or representations of those being called. At this point, say whatever you'd like to communicate with the deceased. Spend a good amount of time stating your intention, speaking directly to the dead, just as you would as if they were still incarnate. Say anything you'd like to get off your chest. Tell them anything you think they'd like to know. Ask for their blessings. Tell them they're loved.

When you've said your piece, begin communicating open-ended questions to them. Tell them that you may have difficulty understanding them, but that you are patient and will try to understand. Record any sensed responses on the paper if you wish. Don't allow your rational mind to justify the experience: take what you get and trust your first impulse. Trust the energies you feel, and have a conversation based on what you *believe* is occurring. The results may be crystal clear or utterly incomprehensible. Whatever the results, you *are* making contact and can perform this ritual again in the future. Open yourself as much as possible, entirely immersing yourself in whatever you can perceive in the communication.

When you've finished your conversation and have recorded what you'd like, thank the spirit(s), leave them the offerings you've prepared, and send them on their way. When ready, face the west again. Say:

> *Guardians of the Gates of Death. Holy and venerated spirits of the west.*
> *Thank you for allowing this most sacred communication between my*
> *world and yours. Please aid me in my life's quest for Truth. Know that I*
> *approach you not with fear, but with love. Thank you for your patronage*
> *this evening. Be blessed in all you do. Spirits of death, spirits of the west,*
> *Guardians of the Gates, hail and farewell.*

Leave any additional offerings at the west and close the circle as you normally would.

Passing Away & Crossing Over: Guiding the Dead & Dying

Losing those we love can be an incredibly difficult experience and can stay with us for the rest of our lives. The term *psychopomp* refers to a deity or spirit who guides the souls of the dead. This archetype appears in virtually all mythological systems and is seen as one of the characteristics of Saturn. Though psychopomp deities work between the planes and are seen as existing beyond the physical, we can draw upon this archetype and use it from our earthly vantage point. This is a ritual of Crossing Over, helping a dying (or recently deceased) person to the next phase of their experience.

So what happens to the soul when it leaves the body? For Christian societies, the soul is seen as either having gone to Heaven or Hell. Older cultures didn't usually make such strict divisions of the afterlife (and indeed the Christian version of the afterlife is a variation of more ancient views). Many of the world's oldest religions see the soul as traveling through a series of liminal realms of existence following death (Tibetan Vajrayana Buddhism calls these *bardos*). Many have very rigid superstitions regarding proper burial, spiritual conversation, and strict ritual observances following death. These views tend to accompany the perception of ghosts, attributing a very influential sense of power to the souls of the deceased. Some cultures visually mark their mourning for many years (by wearing certain clothes, cutting the hair, and so on). Some erect permanent altars and representations of the deceased. Some practice ritual observances to keep the souls of the dead from possessing those in mourning. The observations and ritual practices surrounding death and dying are vast, varied, and endlessly fascinating.

Whatever your own procedures for honoring the dead, and regardless of your perception of the afterlife, this particular working is focused on those who are *in the process* of dying (and can be modified for those who have *recently* passed on—as in the last week or two). No matter what happens after the moment of death, this working is centered on the transition between physical existence and the next stage. The working is appropriate for friends or family members who are passing due to old age or illness, or for pets who are trying to leave their bodies or are approaching euthanasia to end suffering.

For those who wish to further research death and dying in a Neopagan context, I recommend *The Pagan Book of Living & Dying* written by Starhawk, M. Macha Nightmare, and the Reclaiming Collective. Additionally, for those who particularly resonate with magickally working with death energy, I recommend Michelle Belanger's *Walking the Twilight Path* and Leilah Wendell's *The Necromantic Ritual Book*, among others.

Stepping Back & Further Application

A ritual for guiding the dying is a serious and heavy topic. A rite like this should *only* be performed if the person is medically confirmed to be in the process of dying. It can also be modified to use soon after the actual occurrence of death.

When guiding the dying, it's absolutely essential to have your emotions in check. Are you and those around you emotionally okay with the person dying—is it accepted by those around them, at least for the most part? Would the dying person be alright with you helping them leave their body? If your intentions are not aligned to that of the ritual, you shouldn't perform it. If you know that you must perform the rite, do personal ritual work beforehand to both ground and center your energy and to release emotional ties that may restrict the person from leaving their physical frame. The focus of guiding the dying should be entirely on the dying themselves. Unless you were hired by someone to perform the spiritual work—which Witches, Priests, Priestesses, and Pagan clergy/ministry sometimes are—it's likely that you have emotional ties to the person. These ties shouldn't be neglected, because they are part of the dying person's experience. However, your own insecurities and emotional attachments that are *not* directly connected to the dying person's perceptions should be expelled prior to helping them leave their body.

Supplies

- a fresh pomegranate (or pomegranate juice)
- a small, vibrant potted plant
- a cup of steeped thyme and mugwort tea
- any combination of the herbs benzoin, rose petals, sandalwood, vervain, and wormwood, all placed in a small black drawstring bag on a necklace cord
- a raven or crow feather

Notes

- This working should never be used unless it's absolutely certain that the person is in the process of dying. If you're working with the spirit of a recently deceased individual, simply modify the ritual to fit your purposes (such as using a picture or representation of the person, and so on).

- Be certain to communicate to the beloved dying in a manner they understand and appreciate. For example, if you are helping a dying person die who follows a Christian belief system, you wouldn't want to talk about the Great Goddess as they die—it would simply be inappropriate and disrespectful. Alter your words and modify the actions to that which is appeasing and comforting to the dying individual. This, as it is written, is a Neopagan ritual and can be personally modified to fit the individual situation. The psyche of the dying person is of utmost importance.

Procedure

Begin by performing protective exercises and altering your consciousness. Clear your mind, bring focus to your breath, and meditate for at least a few minutes. When ready, approach the dying person to begin the working.

This ritual should be performed slowly. As a person enters the Otherworld, their body processes slow and eventually cease. Be in a peaceful and comforting state of mind. Put on some music that's pleasing to the dying. Ensure that their beloved friends and family members are present (if they wish). Make them comfortable. Calmly ensure that all the proper people and institutions are notified of the occurrence. Double-check that everything is in place to peacefully aid in the process.

Place the pomegranate and the plant near the dying. Take sips of the tea. When ready, put the sachet necklace around your neck and begin speaking slowly to the dying. Notice their experience. Ask if they are comfortable. Quiet any distractions in the environment. See if they are perceiving anyone who has died before them (the known departed are often noticed by the dying). Don't discount their perceptions of the Afterworld as the two planes begin to merge for them; the distinction between worlds blurs as they proceed to the next plane. Encourage them to discuss visions. Pay close attention to the person's eye movements and words if they are able to use them. Surround them with comfort.

In a way that's most comforting to them, inform the person that they are in the process of dying. Tell them that they're loved and supported in the process. Encourage them to relax. Tell them that they're safe. Tell them to breathe. If the person struggles with any of your statements, take some time to ease their mind. If they're visibly struggling to stay in their body, keep encouraging relaxation and change the subject to something more mental (to draw their focus away from the physical), such as recounting experiences of the past. Talk in a comforting, soft, and slow manner. If the person is uncomfortable at any point, pause and see to their comfort. Remember that everybody dies at their own pace.

When you feel the person is ready to receive the blessing, tell them that you're going to help bless their soul as they pass on. Pick up the feather and lightly wave it above them, all around the body. Say:

> I call upon the ancestors. I call upon the gods, goddesses, and watchful
> spirits that protect and guide souls on their journeys through the planes.
> Come now, descend upon this space so that [Name] can peacefully ascend
> and join your beautiful and peaceful world.

Put the feather down and softly touch the dying with your right hand. Place your left hand on the soil of the potted plant. Say:

> As the sun rises in the eastern sky, so too must it go down in the west.
> As all life springs into existence, so too must it return to the Source.
> As the most immaculate flower blooms, so too must it wither into soil.

Turn your voice directly to the dying. Slowly say:

> Beloved [Name], you are preparing to enter the Hall of the Ancestors. Now
> is the time to allow yourself to slip into the Dreaming in Perfect Love and
> Perfect Trust. Your body has served you well. Your life has been a sacred and
> perfect experience. Those who have gone before you stand in waiting, gently
> summoning your spirit to the Great Mystery beyond this world. You are
> purified and prepared. You love and are beloved. Peace and joy surround
> you. The Afterworld, the Otherworld, the Summerland, and the Heavenly

Realms are inviting you … take your time … relax and be at peace. Your
friends and family love and support you, and are all at peace with your
passage, we are all okay. It's time for you to take a step beyond this world.
Go at your own pace. Go in comfort, love, and peace.

At this point, close your eyes and slip into meditation. Disengage
from the dying person and focus your attention on the energies of the
room. Sense the air above the dying person: this is where the dying often
perceive the heavens opening. Turn your focus to the spiritual energies
of the dying and vibrations around them. Visualize their etheric body lifting up from their person, merging with the astral planes. Visualize their
body glowing in a dim, pale blue light, softly losing hue. Work the energies as you see fit. Don't overextend yourself if you feel any resistance.

After pausing for awhile, reengage with the dying. Say to them:

Your transition into the infinite world beyond this one shall be free of pain.
Allow yourself the confidence to join the ranks of the ancestors. Slip into the
Dreaming. Take the next step on the journey, for this is the Great Initiation
and you are blessed. Now … rest … enjoy this transition into the Great
Beyond. A whole Otherworld awaits, and we here on earth celebrate your
ascension. Go, good soul: enter the Sacred Beyond with love in your heart,
and you will be carried forth on the softest wings. Thou Art [God/dess].
Blessed be, and congratulations.

Slowly lean your face down to the face of the dying. Kiss (or air kiss)
each cheek and give a heartfelt smile. Back away and perform any remaining energy work you wish. Spend a good amount of time with the
family and make sure both the living and the dying are dealing with the
process. Support friends and family after the beloved has left his or her
body. Know that you are blessed for the good work you've just done.

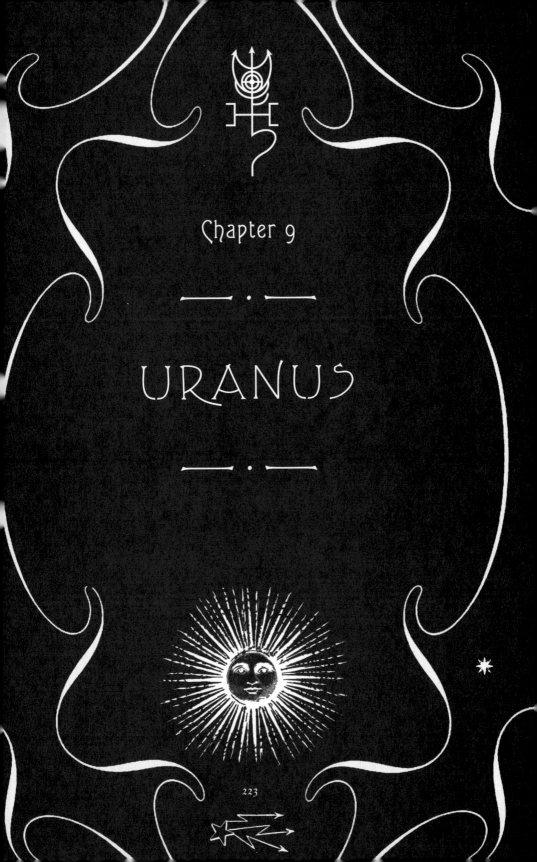

Chapter 9

— · —

URANUS

— · —

URANUS

Zodiacal rulership: Aquarius

Color association: None (ineffable)

Sephira: Da'ath

Number: 11

Day: None

Archetypes: Trickster, Sky God

Themes: Creation, newness, freedom, nontraditionalism, intuition, trickery, invention, revolution, science, change, excess, individuality, discovery, deviation, eccentricity

The Evil Eye: Warding Against the Covetous Gaze

When you think of medieval accusations of Witchcraft, things come to mind such as ill health, barren animals or people, and misfortunes of all types. Much of the time, these people were said to be cursed by the dreaded "evil eye." This foreboding term became aligned with (negatively viewed) Witchcraft in many parts of Europe, and the superstitious or fearful would seek any measure through folk magick or physical action to counteract the curse. It is also called "the art of fascination," "overlooking," and "seduction" (bewitchment). The influence of Uranus is appropriate for escaping a curse and crafting wards against it.

There is no one method of creating or deflecting the so-called evil eye. According to many, the evil eye is simply a name for that metaphorical (or actual) death-gaze that is born of one person's highly focused negative emotions toward another. When this scorn impacts another person, an unintentional (or intentional) bitter astral link is formed. One can quite easily drain another person's subtle life force in this manner. Indeed, many celebrities' energies are erratic, escapist, and imbalanced simply because of the number of people sending them silent astral "messages" on a daily basis.

The evil eye is recognized in areas of the world including South Asia, the Middle East, and the Mediterranean area of Europe, and is said to be put on a person in the form of a covetous gaze. In other words, staring at a person while feeling envy, spite, jealousy, and a desire for what they have (in addition to the desire for them *not* to have it) constitutes the evil eye. It doesn't necessarily have to be delivered through eye contact (it's energetic), and is not always a conscious act of black magick. There is much superstition around the belief in the evil eye and an equal amount of paranoia in terms of how to reflect it, deflect it, and dissolve it. While modern Witches aren't so obsessed with these antiquated and superstitious views, there is certainly still some validity to the belief: all energy is transferred through thought, emotion, and action, whether destructive, constructive, or indifferent. This spell is a charm to reflect such heavy influence and guard against any future fascination.

Stepping Back & Further Application

So, do you think the evil eye has been put on you? If so, *why*? Investigate all possibilities in the situation. It's best to practice active skepticism: in all likelihood, you're free and clear of fascination. At the same time, the evil eye can be put on someone unintentionally via a heavy direction of covetous energy. If this is occurring, do you feel its influence is significant enough to warrant a charm against it? Do you feel the curse in your astral body? Are you just being paranoid?

Examine the subject from all angles. Unless you have solid evidence of the evil eye occurring, don't assume the negative energy you feel is coming from any one particular person; if envious vibes aren't *actually* coming from a single individual, focusing your charm against one particular individual would be restricting. Instead, use this charm to boost your preexisting walls of protection and allow it to halt any evils directed at you from any direction. Regardless of whether or not you are truly bewitched, this charm can ward against its future influence and can be a fun and important project for Witches, covens, and magickal families.

Supplies

- a circular piece of cardboard (such as those from frozen pizzas)
- a black sketch pencil
- a small amount of flour mixed with water (see Notes)

- a circular piece of blue construction paper, exactly the same size as the circular piece of cardboard
- a number of chicken leg bones or oak twigs (see Notes)
- a spool of red thread
- a squeezable container of honey
- a blue stone, such as lapis lazuli or sodalite
- a bit of black cat hair
- medicine or a representation of either the fox (foxglove, fox hair, etc.), the bat (batwing petals, holly leaves, bat's blood ink, etc.), or the cat (cat whiskers, more cat hair, cat's claw bark, catnip, etc.)
- some small cowrie shells, blue beads, porcupine quills, amethyst, or tiger's eye stones
- a number of full (unbroken) star anise pods
- a separate bowl of lavender buds
- a very fine powdered combination of any of the herbs acacia, hyssop, marigold (*calendula*), rue, vervain, and white horehound
- a small amount each of black pepper (ground or whole), garlic powder, powdered sage, white sea salt, and black sand or black salt ("Witch's salt")

Notes

- The chicken bones and porcupine quills suggested in this spell can be purchased at various online retailers, including the Bone Room (www.boneroom.com). The number of chicken leg bones or oak twigs to be used in this spell should be double the number of places you wish to protect in this spell, as these will be tied in a cross. For example, say you wish to hang a cross of bones or twigs in front of every window and door in the house, as well as one dangling from your car's rearview mirror. In this case, if you have 7 windows in the house, 9 doors, and 1 vehicle, you would need 34 bones or twigs in total. However, you may only wish to protect 2 doors in the house (the doors that open to the outside world, for example), in which case you would only need 4 bones or twigs for the spell. Decide for yourself what requires the most protection in your general area.

- The mixture of flour and water should be the consistency of a gummy mush. This is a good binding agent for items used in the spell that honey won't hold (like the shells and stones).

- The symbol used herein is a variation of a traditional Pennsylvania Dutch hex sign that has the purpose of deflecting the evil eye from one's property. Various other symbols can also be used, and I encourage practitioners to add their own protective symbols to the charm.

- The purpose of having a variety of separate herbal powders, salts, spices, and the like, is not only for their magickal properties, but for practical use: each powder is a different color or consistency and will aid in the formation of this artistic charm.

Procedure

Begin by casting a circle, calling the quarters, chanting, or raising energy as you normally would, performing protective exercises, and altering your consciousness. Clear your mind, bring focus to your breath, and meditate for at least a few minutes. When ready, begin the spell.

Sit in a meditative position, close your eyes, and bring focus to your energy body. Observe if you feel any inconsistencies in your Ki (or Qi: energy flow) that may be influenced by someone else. When you sense this, hold the cardboard to that area of your body and shout:

Evil from the outside: HERE!

Keep directing bad external juju into the cardboard. Do this also on your third eye. When finished, write, in very large letters, the words LO THA-CHEMOD on both sides of the cardboard. Next, grab the flour-water mixture and smear it all over one side of the cardboard. Affix the blue paper atop the cardboard and flour adhesive, rubbing it down with your hands to smooth any lumps. While this dries, get your other ingredients in order.

Get the bones or twigs and begin to lay them into X formations. Bind them together with red thread at the intersecting point. Make as many of these X charms as is appropriate for your home (see Notes). Once constructed, place these all around your ritual space to absorb energy. Raise your hands and shout:

Gaze of covet! Gaze of ill!
Eye of envy! Eye of evil!
Deflected, Reflected, Rejected!

Grab the pencil and draw symbol 19 on the entire piece of blue paper. If your intuition tells you to make modifications to this symbol, go for it. You may wish to add dots, additional lines, and other protective symbols. The most important part of the piece is the giant Middle Eastern double-eye in the middle.

Begin making the ward. Use the honey to squeeze sticky lines on top of the pre-drawn image. Carefully re-create the image in honey. If you wish to work portions at a time (begin with the innermost eye section first), it may help avoid the honey drying too quickly. Also use the sticky flour-water mixture on any portions of the charm that require heavier

Symbol 19

objects on it (like shells or stones) that honey may not securely hold. At the very center dot of the charm, place the blue stone, affixed with the paste. On the 12 outer dots, affix the cat hair as well as the fox and/or bat and/or cat medicine. On the outermost diamond, affix the stones, shells, quills, anise pods, and other items. On all other portions of the image, use your intuition to decide where all the powders should be placed.

When you've fully constructed your artistic ward against the evil eye, sit down and balance the charm on your head. Once carefully balanced, put your hands in the "prayer" mudra position and repeat:

> *Gaze of covet! Gaze of ill!*
> *Eye of envy! Eye of evil!*
> *Deflected, Reflected, Rejected!*

In your mind's eye, see the symbol absorbing any negative vibes being sent from outside sources. See it capturing and deflecting any ill influence. Once completed, set the charm on your altar to dry and close the circle as you normally would. The next day, hang the charm on the wall in an area of the house that sees much human traffic, or hang it up outside your front door. Hang the cross charms in the appropriate areas and perform any additional protective magick you deem fit.

That Old Black Magick: An Uncrossing Spell

Uranus is a sign of freedom and revolution, and it oversees the breaking of bonds. For this reason, a few anti-evil spells are included here.

Saying a person is "crossed" is the same as saying a person has been "cursed." If you feel this has happened to you or someone you know, this spell may be of benefit. Drawing mostly on Hoodoo practices, a working such as this can help clear one's energy regardless of curse. In all likelihood, no curse has been placed. Just the same, if you feel it has been, this type of working can ensure a rampart of protection, just in case.

In most instances, the "curse" a person senses on themselves is actually an accumulation of internal energy that hasn't been dealt with. Unless the signs make it extremely apparent that bad magick has been worked from an outside source, consider the probability that internal emotional and energetic work should be done before confusing it with external juju.

The power of thought is amazing. Magick is sent through the mental plane constantly and even a buildup of particular thoughts projected in one direction is a magickal working in and of itself. Manifestation occurs unconsciously, and formal magickal arts are methods of consciously honing that creative power. If you believe yourself to be crossed, consider that the person may be sending bitter, harmful energies to you without realizing that they're actually causing harm. Nonetheless, the energy can still become manifest, "actual" curse of not. Uncrossing spells help remove these energies and are good to practice frequently if you interact with a number of people on a regular basis or are somewhat well-known. If the energetic body is receiving adverse vibrations and is not cleansed regularly, the energies are at risk of building to a damaging degree.

Stepping Back & Further Application

Don't get too paranoid that a spell has been put on you. In most cases, the two parties (your and the assumed caster) are actually both performing energetic protection against each other! Most magicians aren't unwise enough to throw out curses like candy (though there certainly are a handful who enjoy this sort of feeble power-play).

Just as with unsolicited psychic vampyrism, harming another person magickally is usually nothing more than a pathetic attempt to assert power. Cursing has its time and place, but it's very rarely warranted. If you believe someone in particular has put the bad stuff on you, consider not a counterattack but additional protection and reflection magick instead. An uncrossing spell can go a long way in lifting negativity thrown at you, but your protective shields must be reinforced on a regular basis to guard against any future attacks, conscious or otherwise.

Supplies
- a large black candle
- a separate bowl of the herb rue

- a large muslin drawstring bag (or another bag suitable for bathtub use)
- a small black fabric drawstring bag
- a small amount of black sand or black salt ("Witch's salt")
- any combination of the herbs angelica, chamomile, cinquefoil, dragon's blood, galangal (Low John root), hyssop, juniper, marshmallow root, nettles, poke root, snakeroot, thistle (milk or blessed), and vetiver
- black hen feathers (see Notes)
- a small sheet of waxed paper
- a bathtub or shower
- a bowl of sea salt
- a bit of Four Thieves Vinegar (see Notes)
- any number of freshly cut citrus fruits (halved)

Notes

- Four Thieves Vinegar, a component of many Hoodoo workings, is said to have gotten its name from the time of the European plague (approximately CE 1334–1350). Many people at the time would rob bodies of their jewelry and other valuables, and legend says that a band of four thieves were able to ward off the plague by rubbing their bodies with a vinegary concoction before robbing the corpses. Four Thieves Vinegar is now used as a strong protection and banishing formula and is available through many occult supply shops. Substitute apple cider vinegar if unavailable.

- Black hen feathers have a long history in Hoodoo. Historically, if a person were to "lay a trick" (such as a line of magickal powder) in front of another person's door, that person could get a black hen to scratch and claw away the powder that was laid for them, thus rendering the original caster's spell broken. Black hen feathers in spells have similar effects. These can be purchased at various online retailers, including Lucky Mojo (www.luckymojo.com), who sells very traditional, handmade magickal items of Hoodoo, Santería,

Vodoun, and other African diaspora systems. If black hen feathers are unavailable, substitute with a black-dyed chicken feather, available at all kinds of craft stores . . . *and* Craft stores!

Procedure

Begin by casting a circle, calling the quarters, chanting, or raising energy as you normally would, performing protective exercises, and altering your consciousness. Clear your mind, bring focus to your breath, and meditate for at least a few minutes. When ready, begin the spell.

Ignite the black candle and sprinkle a handful of rue all around you. Next, place a good amount of rue and black salt in the muslin bag and the black bag. Add the herbal mixture and fill both to the brim. Tie the bags shut and state:

> Herbs of uncrossing, herbs of hex-breaking,
> be all around me and lift this black magick.

Set the bags aside—the muslin bag will be used in the bath and the black bag should be hung above the most-entered doorway of the house.

Place the black hen feathers and a pinch of the remaining herbs (including rue) on the waxed paper in front of you. Take the black candle and drip almost all of its wax onto them. As you're doing this, use your other hand to form the wax, feathers, and herbs into a big round ball. (Don't let the wax dry without your sculpting it!) The wax ball should contain the herbs and feathers all throughout it. When the candle has almost burned down completely, set it aside.

Get naked (if practical) and rub the ball of wax all over your body. Envision any and all negativity sent from others absorbing into the wax, freeing you of the burden. See your aura shining brightly after the wax touches certain areas. Focus hard while you do this. If the case is extreme and deep-seated, ask another practitioner to help you draw the energies into the ball.

After you spend some time doing this, close the circle as you normally would and go draw yourself a bath. Place the wax ball on the side of the tub. Throw in the sea salt and add some of the Four Thieves Vinegar. Place the citrus fruit halves in the tub and remember to squeeze them on your body throughout the bath. Finally, put the muslin bag in the bathwater and submerge yourself. Work the bag with your hands and squeeze water from it all over your body. (If you don't have a tub, simply dump the vinegar and salt on yourself and squeeze the saturated bag all over you in the shower.) Keep repeating:

> *Broken jinx!*
> *Uncrossed cross!*
> *Severed bind!*
> *Lifted curse!*

When finished, drain the bathwater and allow yourself to air dry rather than towel dry. This ensures that the spell's energy is fully adhered to one's person and isn't absorbed into the towel. When fully dried, get dressed and go downtown to the most prominent intersection of roads (one that sees the most traffic, both human and vehicular). When no one is looking, sneakily throw the ball into the middle of the crossroads. Walk away without looking back.

Free Your Mind: Undoing Social Conditioning

Social norms are a tricky one. The term *social mores* (pronounced MORE-ays) refers to commonly accepted social customs in a group of individuals. The West has all sorts of mores, influenced from a number of sources over time. Every culture and society has their own set of mores, most of which aren't even recognized as being exclusive to the society in which it occurs. Cultural taboos and deviations from socially acceptable behavior are viewed as antisocial and often cost a person respect from others. At the same time, various subcultures exist within greater societies all across the world, making particular group behaviors more acceptable within each individual unit.

Everyone is socially conditioned. No one is entirely free from social conditioning. Most conditioning is unconscious. Behaviors and viewpoints deemed "acceptable" and "normal" are constantly reinforced. If someone gets out of line, society tries to put them back in the box. I once heard a quote (I don't know the source) that said "the sheep don't even need a shepherd; they herd themselves!" At times this is extremely beneficial (as in the case of violent crime and such), and other times it's exceedingly harmful to individuality. Being "different" in the world requires a certain amount of sacrifice and usually comes with questioning and even cruelty from those who have been conditioned a certain way. People keep themselves in various closets for fear of being socially ridiculed or humiliated. This working is designed for those who feel restricted and trapped by social labels, social demands, and social inequality. It can help instill confidence in uniqueness.

This is a very strange magickal working and can be creatively modified in an endless number of ways. Because of its eccentricity—which is in place for a very good reason—I suggest that this working be performed alone and that there's no risk of you being seen or heard.

One of the most interesting aspects of this working is the inclusion of *glossolalia*. Glossolalia is also called "talking in tongues," and is the act of entering an ecstatic trancelike state and speaking in incomprehensible "languages." Yes, it's gibberish: a piecing together of various familiar sounds and syllables. Some musicians use glossolalia as a vocal instrument (bands like Dead Can Dance, Sigur Rós, and Cocteau Twins do this frequently), but "tongue-talking" is most commonly known for occurring within sects of Evangelical Christians—most of whom don't realize that glossolalia isn't exclusive to their ecstatic religious acts. Engaging in an odd practice like glossolalia can help combat commonly enforced modes of behavior.

Stepping Back & Further Application

This spell alone is *not* enough to completely undo a lifetime of social conditioning! Such a thing is basically impossible, and coming close to an entire "undoing" takes a heavy amount of work, self-awareness, and even extended counseling and therapy. Shame, deep depression, regret, and all sorts of other emotional negatives are results of heavy social conditioning and greatly affect those who are inherently "different."

Everyone is uniquely individual. Yet, no one is individual—we are all the same. This paradox may seem contradictory at first; however, esoteric truth quite often lies between seemingly opposing ends of the spectrum. Keeping perspective can help a person remain balanced.

If you'd like to further study ways of undoing social conditioning, I suggest *Undoing Yourself with Energized Meditation and Other Devices* by Christopher Hyatt, as well as *Astonish Yourself: 101 Experiments in the Philosophy of Everyday Life* by Roger-Pol Droit. Please note that Hyatt's book is heavily occult-based, and Droit's is centered on fun and lighthearted experimental psychology.

Supplies

- a white or beeswax candle
- dragon's blood ink and a paintbrush
- an empty cardboard box large enough for you to fit in
- a blindfold
- a full jar of honey
- a discarded beehive or wasp's nest (see Notes)
- any combination of the herbs eyebright, High John the Conqueror, lotus, mistletoe, mullein, Solomon's Seal root, and thyme

Notes

- Be sure that you don't let other people see or hear you performing this spell. Also, it's best to begin this spell about 20 minutes before sunrise.
- If you don't currently have a discarded beehive or wasp's nest, don't go searching; it can be very dangerous (and disruptive) if there are any creatures still living inside them. Instead, substitute some hive-shaped beeswax or a beeswax candle.

Procedure

Begin by casting a circle, calling the quarters, chanting, or raising energy as you normally would, performing protective exercises, and altering your consciousness. Clear your mind, bring focus to your breath, and meditate for at least a few minutes. When ready, begin the spell.

Strip naked and light the candle. With the ink, write only on the inside bottom of the box:

TOKH

HTOK

KHTO

OKHT

On every other side of the box, both inside and out, draw a large symbol of Uranus. When the ink has dried, tie the blindfold tightly over your eyes. Pick up the honey and beehive, one in each hand, and step inside the box. Leave the candle *far away* from the box and put the bowl or bag of herbs next to the box (within arm's reach).

Still standing, put yourself in a trance state, using your familiar method or methods. Additionally, jump up and down and visualize yourself standing on top of the world. As you jump, see your head driving high into space and your feet landing on the top of the Earth. Stop jumping and start humming. Start your hum in a very low, resonant pitch and eventually work the pitch up higher and higher. Do this repeatedly.

When you're somewhat tranced out, take the honey (eyes still closed) and dump it all over your body. Do not focus on trivial things like making a mess. Instead, simply *feel* its sticky consistency covering you high and low. Smear it all over your body using the contents of the entire jar. Say:

> This honey is society's demands and expectations sticking to me!

Let a feeling of discomfort rush over you. Invoke disgust and paranoia at the thought of society's norms, expectations, and demands being placed all over you. As this sensation arises, break apart the beehive and stick it in random locations on your skin.

Grab the herbs and pour them all over you as well (the excess should fall into the box). Now that the herbs and hive are stuck to you, say:

> These herbs invoke freedom! Dissolve this mess! I am not like the rest!

Rub the herbs all over you, mixing with the honey. Feel their harshness against your skin, but absorb their energies of freedom and transcendence into yourself. Next, crouch down into the box and close the lid. If this is not possible, overturn the box so you're under it completely and covered in darkness.

Feel a sense of sadness rush over you. Think about various instances in which people have tried to make you fit in or have ridiculed you for being unique. Remember those feelings. Recall instances of your attempting to fit into various molds but failing because they didn't suit you. Think about the box that others try to put you in.

At this point, start saying random things. Say partial words. Say things that don't make sense. Say random syllables. Whisper and scream. Clap and pound. Chant and act crazy. Don't even *think* about what you're saying or how loud you're saying it. Don't say anything that "makes sense." Just *speak*! Let your emotions conduct your voice. Feel and experience. Enter an ecstatic state of trance and keep yourself in it by acting "insane" and erratic. Go all out. Be crazy.

Once you've reached a peak of extreme disconnection from reality and your vocal cords are tired, hit your chest and continually shout:

I am me! I am free! I am that which I am!

Aggressively break yourself out of the box. Tear it apart at the seams. Throw pieces of the box around the room. Rip off the blindfold. Free yourself. Keep repeating the above words. When you've ripped apart the box and have stood up, take deep breaths to calm down. Once grounded back into the moment, smile to yourself and feel a renewed sense of self. Before closing the circle and taking a shower, pick up the mess, ending with a powerful:

So mote it be!

To Be or Not To Be?: Removing Restrictive Labels

Society works in labels. Young, old, boy, girl, right, wrong, sane, crazy, true, false, black, white, straight, gay, good, evil, and everything else under the Sun. Though these are examples of polar opposites, even the array of "gray area" in between each is subject to definition and categorization. Everywhere we turn there are descriptive—and limiting—definitions for everything. Usually if a group of people agree on one definition as "correct," others are influenced to believe the same (this is the group mind).

So, how are you labeled? How do you label yourself? How do other people label you? This can include "obvious" physical descriptions like *girl, short, muscular;* active terms like *athletic, talented, indecisive;* and *adjectives* like *optimistic, naïve, delusional,* and so on. Some labels are positive and complimentary, while others are cruel and patronizing. This spell will focus on both.

——— • ———

Labels provide easy reference and categorization. Descriptive terms are constantly used in spoken and written words, and have been since the beginning of time. Labels are important. At the same time, they can be extremely limiting. As I've discussed, words hold an immense amount of power. They convey symbolism and communicate mental ideas based on a person's understanding of the terms. Different terms mean different things for different people. The most important aspect of this particular spell is what certain terms mean *to you.*

Because labels are easy points of reference, they will never be done away with socially. They are unavoidable. For this reason, they should be worked with rather than entirely escaped. The intention with which labels are used is the most important factor. This spell requires the participant to think about both self-imposed labels and labels from outside sources.

Stepping Back & Further Application

If there are only a few labels you specifically wish to banish, modify the spell by writing them repeatedly on numerous strips of tape. Otherwise, spend a good amount of time thinking about different labels that you've given yourself or that have been put on you—these should be both complimentary and insulting.

For example, I have no problem with terms like *male*, Priest, Witch, Goth, *queer*, *tall*, *artist*, and other things being used in reference to my character (either by myself or others), so I wouldn't want to banish them if I was performing this spell. Because they carry positive meanings for me—even if they have negative connotations to other people—these are terms I have no issue with keeping affixed to my character. Still, I mustn't allow myself to become attached to these labels—they're only descriptive in terms of reference and don't encompass the entirety of my being. Indeed, the soul is transcendent!

Use the above example to mentally sort your own labels and descriptions. Decide which labels are inhibiting and release them accordingly. Pay particular attention to this question: what inhibiting labels do you give yourself, and how might they be restricting your personal development?

Supplies

- 2 paper plates
- a black permanent marker
- a roll of heavy transparent packing tape
- scissors
- a large bowl of the herb mullein
- a small piece of yellow calcite (or optical/clear calcite)

Notes

- When tearing the tape from your body, you will be ripping off some body hair and dead skin, and so will experience a small amount of pain. These factors are important because the hair and skin will link you to the labels and the small amount of pain will help project energy.

Procedure

Begin by casting a circle, calling the quarters, chanting, or raising energy as you normally would, performing protective exercises, and altering your consciousness. Clear your mind, bring focus to your breath, and meditate for at least a few minutes. When ready, begin the spell.

On one of the paper plates, draw a large circle that covers the whole area of the plate. On the other plate, write the following in large characters (on both sides of the plate):

ανωνυμία

ανωνυμι

ανωνυμ

ανωνυ

ανων

ανω

αν

α

Strip naked. Now is the time to express your labels. Think about labels that have been put on you over time, either by yourself or others, and divide them into the categories (labels!) of *beneficial* and *harmful*. When you think of labels that are complimentary, positive, and beneficial to you, write them inside the circle on the first plate. Cram as many in there as come to mind, even if you have to overlap words.

When you think of labels that are critical, negative, and belittling to you, write them individually on pieces of tape using the black marker. The pieces should be at least a few inches long. Write only one label on each piece of tape. As you write them, stick them on your body. Put them on your arms, legs, neck, back, tummy, and upper body (but not on your hair, armpits, or genitals, of course).

After you feel as though you've gotten out as many possible labels as you can, move on to the next step. Begin chanting:

These are not me! These must flee! As I will, so mote it be!

Rip off one label. Feel the sting. Read it and immediately dip the sticky side into the bowl of mullein. Now that pieces of the herb are stuck to the label (along with some of your body hair and dead skin), put it on the second paper plate (the one with the Greek on it). Assert:

[Label], *you are not me. You must flee. As I will, so mote it be!*

Continue doing this with all of the other labels. Stack them in a sandwich formation on the "banishing" plate, making sure that you stick each label in the mullein, stack it on top of the previous label, and say the words of power.

Once you've done this with all negative labels, put a handful of mullein on the uppermost label and declare:

These are not me! These must flee! As I will, so mote it be!

Crumple the plate around the labels and mullein, and throw it in the trash after ritual. Fold up the "positive" plate with the piece of calcite in the middle, and store it somewhere in your bedroom, to keep that energy present in your sphere. Close the circle as you normally would.

Sky Sorcery: Practical Weather Magick

A fun and simple form of magick on the physical plane is working with the weather. New Witches often have fun with this because it can quickly provide results and can help connect the practitioner to the larger natural world.

Cloudbusting is a fun form of magick practiced by young Witchlings and metaphysically inspired children (and those of us who are forever young at heart). With this, a person finds a tiny cloud in the sky and imbues it with an intention they wish to banish. After projecting that negative energy into the cloud, the practitioner sits or lays on the grass and stares at the cloud, intending it to break apart and disappear. The practitioner can blow wind toward the cloud and use their fingers to wave it away. Soon the cloud disappears along with the intention it was imbued with.

—— · ——

Weather influences mood much more easily than we usually notice (I'd suggest trying to observe weather's effects on your psyche from day to day). Weather is also the single most binding force between people; all individuals can relate to and discuss the phenomenon of weather as a consistent point of reference. Great friendships and relationships have begun with a simple comment on the weather, which is certainly an affirmation of its profound effect. When all other conversations fail or an ice-breaker is needed to end an uncomfortable silence, people talk about weather! There's a reason for this: weather affects all of us. It's Mother Nature at her finest. Pagans honor the tides of nature. Many cultures, as well as everyone's ancestors, live(d) in direct conjunction with the cycles of nature and their area's ever-changing weather pattern, entirely dependant on weather for survival.

Although fun, it's good to approach weather magick with a distinct purpose. Don't do it just to see "if it works." Instead, consider it a type of magick that can help the Earth. Numerous native cultures practice rain dances and other types of weatherworking to influence the growth of crops, avoid drought, and achieve other survivalistic aims. These ceremonies are usually performed by ritual specialists and are of utmost importance to a culture's sustenance.

If weather conditions in your area are severe, consider working with the weather to help better the environment. If you're in an area that gets extreme wildfires, consider summoning the rain and calming the winds. If you're in an area where rain is causing damage, consider working with the forces send the rain away to an area that needs it.

The weather won't instantly change when weather magick is performed. Such things are better reserved for Hollywood portrayals. Instead, weather magick is best worked continually over time. Weather isn't "controlled" or "commanded"—it's worked with. Weather is a force much more powerful than our little human bodies, and its spirits deserve our respect.

Stepping Back & Further Application

Effectively altering weather patterns takes steps. Most weatherworkings need to be performed daily over a period of time. Additionally, consider the possibilities for the weather to shift: is there rain geographically close to you that you wish to bring to your area? Are there heavy winds nearby that you can try to summon to your area? Do weather conditions ensure that the outcome you're looking for is a possibility? What are the odds of the weather helping you?

Keep in mind that all intention—all magick—works through the path of least resistance. After researching current weather statistics in and around your area, consider "weather" or not (ha!) the outcome you're hoping for is attainable and in your favor. Ask yourself if it's truly in the best interest for the environment or if it's an unnecessary expenditure of energy. The actual *need* to perform weather magick is infrequent unless your life is directly tied to the harvest of the land or weather conditions have become threatening. Contemplate just how your desired change in weather will affect others in the vicinity (even hundreds of miles away), water supplies, animals, and crops.

Supplies

- a shaker or rattle
- the appropriate tool, candle, herb, and/or stone (see Procedure)
- a large blue sheet of paper
- a black permanent marker
- a lighter

Notes

- Depending on the weather you're calling, you may be using beryl. Beryl stones include the following: emerald, aquamarine, bixbite, heliodor, maxixe (a type of beryl), morganite, goshenite, and golden beryl.
- This working should, of course, be performed outdoors.

Procedure

Begin by casting a circle, calling the quarters, chanting, or raising energy as you normally would, performing protective exercises, and altering your consciousness. Clear your mind, bring focus to your breath, and meditate for at least a few minutes. When ready, begin the spell.

Think about the weather pattern you are trying to cause. Now, bring to mind the opposite condition of that weather pattern, its antithesis.

For example, if you are working to bring rain, the opposite of rain is dryness. In this case, dryness will be called the antithesis.

Now that you know what you're working with, link your mind to the spirit of the antithesis weather pattern (that is, the one you're experiencing an abundance of and are trying to banish). Connect to the antithesis by physically mimicking the force. For example, lightly flail your body around to mimic air and dryness, cover your head to mimic rain, and so on. Begin mentally communicating with the force, explaining to it why you wish for it to go away. Don't be aggressive, but do be assertive. Communicate respect and appreciation, but tell it why you'd like for it to be on its way and return at another time. Conclude:

Hail and farewell.

Do the same with the force you are summoning. Mimic it, link your mind to it, and persuade it to come. Speak to the spiritual forces that govern the force and convince them to come to the area. Explain why it's significant and exactly why you'd like to experience the force. Shake the rattle and construct a chant. Dance around and communicate with the desired force. Visualize it coming, negating its antithesis. Additionally, use the following brief guide for suggestions:

Symbol 20

Bringing rain: Burn cotton and send prayers in the smoke. Throw rice in the air while focusing on rain. Use a sword to summon and direct the clouds. Draw symbol 20 on the blue paper and burn it. (Don't worry; birds won't explode if they eat uncooked rice—it's an urban legend. They actually quite enjoy it!)

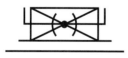

Symbol 21

Stopping rain: Focus energy in a beryl stone and leave it outdoors (see Notes). Use a sword to summon and direct the clouds. Draw symbol 21 on the blue paper and burn it.

Symbol 22

Bringing snow: Throw crushed ice cubes in the air while focusing on snow. Burn a white candle outside and focus your intention in the flame. Use a sword to summon and direct the clouds. Draw symbol 22 on the blue paper and burn it.

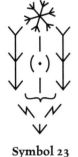

Symbol 23

Melting snow/ice: Burn a yellow candle outside and focus your intention in the flame. Use a sword to summon and direct the clouds. Draw symbol 23 on the blue paper and burn it.

Bringing wind: Burn the herb called broom. Throw kelp and other seaweeds in the air. Use a besom to summon in the wind. Draw symbol 24 on the blue paper and burn it.

Symbol 24

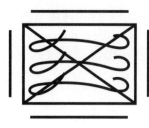

Symbol 25

Stopping wind: Focus energy in a beryl stone and leave it outdoors (see Notes). Bury the herbs broom, kelp, and other sea-weeds. For extreme purposes, bury an entire wooden besom in the ground. Draw symbol 25 on the blue paper and burn it.

Symbol 26

Bringing storms: Sprinkle the herb lobelia on the ground. Use a sword to summon and direct the clouds. Draw symbol 26 on the blue paper and burn it.

Symbol 27

Stopping storms: Focus energy in a beryl stone and leave it outdoors (see Notes). Use a sword to dismiss and direct the clouds. Draw symbol 27 on the blue paper and burn it.

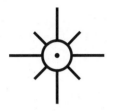

Symbol 28

Bringing sunshine: Burn a yellow candle outside and focus your intention in the flame. Draw symbol 28 on the blue paper and burn it.

Symbol 29

Bringing clouds: Burn cotton and send prayers in the smoke. Burn a white candle outside and focus your intention in the flame. Draw symbol 29 on the blue paper and burn it.

There are many types of weather patterns; should your intention not be listed above, use the list to generate ideas for summoning the weather you're wishing for. Repeat the working frequently and cultivate a sense of knowingness that the weather pattern is on its way. Frequently communicate with the force you're summoning throughout the day, encouraging and casting for its appearance. When it does arrive, leave an offering to the spirits.

Chapter 10

— · —

NEPTUNE

— · —

NEPTUNE

Zodiacal rulership: Pisces

Color association: Gray

Sephira: Chokmah

Number: 2

Day: None

Archetypes: Sacrificial God, Sea King

Themes: Love, intuition, psychic ability, healing, creativity, illusion, empathy, imagination, sensitivity, transcendence, compassion, dreaming, vision

A Ritual Bloodbath: Releasing Suicidal Desires

If you are experiencing absolute hopelessness, a loss of faith in everything (including yourself), a feeling of numbness and disconnection, and are toying with thoughts of ending your life, you are most likely experiencing a "Dark Night of the Soul." (This term was coined in the sixteenth century by the mystic St. John of the Cross. See page 172 for more information.) Allow this. Allow yourself to question anything and everything in your reality. What you are experiencing is very much a natural part of the mystic's journey and is something that all aware and conscious souls have experienced, and still experience from time to time in varying degrees. All sensitive, mystical, psychic, empathic, and healing souls experience the deepest, darkest levels of inner pain at one point or another. We experience misery to learn from it, not to be devoured by its chaotic allure or comforting torment. You are sacred. You have a purpose. There are solutions to every issue; it's just a matter of getting back on track toward those resolutions. *Panta rhei; ouden menei* (everything flows; nothing is stagnant): life is a process of change.

If I can offer any consolation to those readers who may truly be contemplating suicide as a solution, allow me to admit that I've entertained this thought at various times throughout my life. Even for those who are steadfastly devoted to spiritual seeking, the expansion of consciousness, and the path out of suffering, the temptation to leave this world altogether can still rear its ugly head. We are all subject to such emotional patterns. Experiencing thoughts of suicide should not be seen as spiritual failure; instead, we must allow it to confirm the fact that we're sensitive and deeply feeling individuals. By the same token, we have the responsibility to not give in to these feelings, as tempting as they may be. Our spirits—our higher selves—are connected to our mind and our emotions, yes, but these things don't constitute the fullness of our beings. Observing our minds and emotions objectively allows us to step back from thinking that we *are* our thoughts and emotions. Actively navigating and working with even our most painful experiences enriches us. There is only change, and even the heaviest weights are usually not as burdensome as they may appear. We must work ourselves out of emotional attachment. Every trial in life is an initiation.

When experiencing the depths of misery, perspective is of the utmost importance. When cultivating perspective, I sometimes think about the Buddhist Monks of Tibet, for example, who have been brutally tortured, whose families have been slaughtered, who have been forced out of their country, and on and on, and yet they have come to terms with their pain enough to smile and still altruistically help others in their lives. I use this example in particular because Buddhists do not hold a "faith" view of God, the Universe, or reality itself. Instead, the Buddhist view is an "experiential" view—one that is intricately connected with the psyche. It's not that "faith" kept and continues to keep these people going through the most indescribably horrific hardship, but that their experience has shown them that suffering can be ended through diligence and trust. Experience has disproved hopelessness and cultivated inner strength.

This is only one example. Indescribable evils exist all around the world—but so do indescribably beautiful acts of good. A person *must* keep perspective if suicidal thoughts are present. Change is the only constant in life, and those in desperate situations must trust in and activate inevitable personal changes for the better. This spell is simply one way to do that.

——— • ———

This spell calls for the use of a representation of blood. This is not your own blood, not someone else's, and not an animal's. (Though Pagan animal sacrifice—where the body is respectfully killed and eaten, and the spirit of the being is offered to gods or spirits—is noble, there runs too great a risk of salmonella or pathogenic infection if real blood is used in the spell.) The representation for blood I suggest is Clamato™ juice—a combination of tomato juice, clam broth, and spices. Yes, I'm aware that the "Vampyre clique" in *South Park* drank Clamato™ juice instead of human blood, but that's beside the point! I suggest Clamato™, or a similar store-brand blend, because of its contents. The tomato juice carries the energetic properties of tomato, a fruit that's in the *Solanaceae* (night shade) family, which is the best type to use for death-related magick. Clamato™ also contains clam broth, which is water that was once sealed inside a clam. When shucked, this water is collected. This water carries some amount of death energy as a natural result. Additionally, the sodium content in Clamato™ is considerable, adding an energetic cleansing element to the bath. Finally, the potent spices in the drink help "chase out" blockages.

Some practitioners substitute actual blood in a spell by using a small amount of bat's blood ink, dove's blood ink, dragon's blood ink, or a bottle of any red wine. As an aside, I may as well share my thoughts on *actual* animal sacrifice, as some spells (none in this book, however) do make use of real animal blood. Though the majority of practitioners won't be using animal blood for any spell, whether it calls for it or not, allow me to expound. Animal sacrifice has been practiced in native, indigenous, and Pagan societies since the beginning of time, and is a highly respectable and sacred ritual procedure whose purpose is to petition a deity for a particular outcome (avoiding illness, ensuring crop growth, and so on). When sacrificed, the animals are eaten and their spirits are offered to gods, spirits, ancestors, or sacred items. Modern Western culture is quite the opposite: animals are most frequently raised under torturous, inhumane conditions, brutally slaughtered, and widely distributed to feed the public.

If you are using animal blood for any type of working, the blood should be fresh and must be from an animal used for food. (It should also be handled with rubber gloves, to avoid skin contact and its potential risks.) Those who live on a farm, for example, could directly send the soul of the animal to the gods. Personally, I've gone to a local free-range cow slaughterhouse and asked for fresh blood from the slit throat of the "daily cow." It was for use in an ancient spell, but I told them it was for a recipe of traditional English blood sausage (also called black pudding or *Blutwurst*). However, this may not be a very feasible option for those living in larger cities. For practical and sanitary purposes, it's generally best to use a substitute in place of real blood.

Stepping Back & Further Application

Keep in mind that suicidal thoughts are an indication that a *part* of the self has to die—not the *whole* self. What aspects of self can be put to rest in a spell such as this? Do some serious thinking about your situation and its intricacies. Suicide is a *permanent* response to *temporary* problems. Suicidal impulses are just that: impulsive. Even if we hurt on the deepest levels, we are here on Earth for a good reason and have a lot of positive work to do—and that work begins with ourselves. Even those in the most tragic dispositions can discover healing. If there's a will, there's a way. Also, keep in mind that the vast—and I mean *vast*—majority of suicide attempts are not successful. Instead, the person is either left alive and intact with none of their issues solved, or is physically damaged for life (such as brain injury). There's a reason for this "failure" rate: the body wants to be alive.

Above all, I recommend speaking to a therapist or professional counselor if you're truly experiencing suicidal thoughts. It's hard to see the forest for the trees, and sometimes it takes the aid of another person to help us find the way. Do some research online, get recommendations from people, and find a therapist that suits you. Even if you live in an area of the world that doesn't have a readily available health care plan, do your best to save up for at least one or two sessions with a compassionate counselor. If you don't have much spare cash or your insurance doesn't cover therapy, research low-income or free therapists in your area. Yes, they exist, they are trained, and they can help. You can also talk to loving peers or spiritual clergy. The world would be a much better place if we all had a compassionate soul to talk to. Activate the healing you deserve.

Supplies

- 2 large muslin bags (or others suitable for bathtub use)
- Mixture 1: any combination of the herbs dandelion, dill, eyebright, gingko, High John the Conqueror root, lavender, lemon balm, lemon verbena, mullein, nettles, rosemary, sunflower, vervain, wormwood, and yarrow
- 1 piece each of blue agate and bloodstone (or carnelian)
- Mixture 2: a combination of marjoram, St. John's wort, thyme, thistle (milk or blessed), and willow
- a bathtub or shower
- Clamato™ juice (see above)
- an empty bottle or jar with a tight-fitting lid

Notes

- This is a simple spell to aid in the process of healing. Suicidal impulses are severe, serious things and are best tackled through professional therapy. Performing a spell like this can only help get the ball rolling in the right direction—the rest is up to you.

Procedure

No circle needs to be cast for this spell. Instead, raise energy around you in the bathroom. Clear your mind, bring focus to your breath, and meditate for at least a few minutes. When ready, begin the working.

Fill the muslin bags with the individual mixtures. Inside the Mixture 1 bag, add the bloodstone. Inside the Mixture 2 bag, add the blue agate. Set the bags and the empty jar aside.

Start drawing a bath. (If you don't have a bathtub, modify the working by dumping the ingredients on yourself while standing—or even sitting—in the shower.) Get the water as hot as you can stand it, but not hot enough to scald you. When the tub is full, add the "blood" (Clamato™) to the water. Enter the bath and get comfortable. Gazing into the water, say:

> In this vessel, in this womb, my blood is spilled. On all sides of me, my sadness. Oh Spirit, how I wish to leave this plane … to end this life … to cease to be. Deeply I have been thinking of leaving this body … cutting ties to this world … moving to the next experience … This blood surrounding me is the blood of my sorrow. This is the blood of my agony and pain.

Take a few deep breaths and grab the Mixture 1 muslin bag. Soak it in the water and squeeze the drippings all over yourself. Spend quite a few minutes doing this. Throughout, contemplate your reasons for wanting to die. It's best if you cry and *seriously release*. If no one's in earshot, wail, moan, and scream. Mourn your life. Think about the weight of your deepest life issues. Feel the pain of existence. Push the energy of this torment into the water around you—don't let it dissipate; conduct it. Let the squeezed contents of the bag pull the sadness from your pores. Release.

After you've spent quite a few minutes releasing your sorrow into the water, declare:

> I find myself on this Earth, in this body, in this place. With reluctance, I know I must be here. I must learn the lessons of Earth. Make me pure, release this agony. Show me the way from this darkest place. Revive my will to live. Illuminate my path. I deserve happiness, I deserve direction, I deserve balance. Get me out of these depths.

Fill the empty jar with the bathwater and squeeze water from the bag into it. Seal the jar and start to drain the bathwater. While it's draining, repeat:

RASHITH!

Afterward, stand up and start the shower. As the water rushes over you, see it cleansing and purifying your pain. Grab the bag that holds Mixture 2 and squeeze its essence all over you. See it purifying and uplifting your spirit. Spend as much time doing this as you'd like. When you emerge from the shower, allow yourself to air dry. Step outside and soak up the energy of the Sun or Moon. Finally, make a list of what you can do to actively and accurately work with your sorrow and regain a footing. The next day, take a trip to a cemetery and dump the bottled bathwater on the ground (but not on someone's grave), ideally at a crossroads location. Toss out the contents and turn around without looking back.

Sharpening Intuition: Crafting a Psychic Oil

One of Neptune's associations is psychic power. Everyone in the world is capable of using psychic power, it's just a matter of honing it. There are numerous guidebooks and teachers available that can help a seeker fine-tune their psychic power. The recognition of psychic power and its validity dates back to the earliest of times and can be seen in every culture imaginable. Divination, astrology, mediumship, augury, and other psychic work has been performed since the dawn of time.

There is so much superstition and skepticism surrounding the word *psychic* that the term's real meaning has been distorted. A common mistake when approaching psychic work is assuming that it's a separate force from one's everyday state of mind. Simple things like noticing synchronicity, having intuitions or hunches, or getting a "feel" for something or someone *is* psychic in and of itself. There are varying degrees of psychic prowess, and different people are born with different psychic aspects and abilities. Still, no level of psychism is unattainable for those who put their mind and heart into the skill.

Physical reality is only one aspect or level of reality. Having a sensitivity to the other, more subtle parallel planes is not supernatural or paranormal. Everything in reality is interconnected. The view of everything and everyone being separate is true in a sense—for example, I know that I am separate from this bookshelf and am a different person than my buddy—but as with all things, there is a paradoxical dichotomy. We share a group mind. Everything shares a similar physical constitution. There is Oneness, even if appearance and function tell us otherwise. As a result, tapping into the "unknown" is really tapping into that which is already known on other levels. If I see something that reminds me of an old friend on Tuesday, and she ends up sending an unexpected email on Wednesday, I'm not surprised: that's just how it works. The Universe is an immaculate cosmic dance, and it's only natural to tap into the interconnected energies that bind everything. The degree to which this connection is realized is, however, personal.

——— • ———

Psychic powers are intricately connected with our physical senses: seeing, feeling, hearing, smelling, and tasting. As such, psychic powers and ESP (extrasensory perception) can manifest through these: *clairvoyance* is the ability to psychically "see," *clairsentience* is the ability to "feel" surrounding energies or gain psychic knowledge through touching something, *clairaudience* is psychic power made manifest through hearing, *clairalience* is the acquisition of psychic knowledge through smelling or via "phantom smells," *clairgustance* is the ability to perceive psychically through "phantom tastes," and *claircognisance* is the ability to simply know or have inherent psychic intuition (and is related to clairsentience).

For more information on developing and understanding psychic powers in an occult (read: non-New-Age-fluffy) sense, I highly recommend Michelle Belanger's *The Psychic Energy Codex*.

Stepping Back & Further Application

Remember that we are all psychic. Crafting an oil such as this can indeed help awaken powers, but these powers are within our own minds and perceptions. If you feel as though you have no psychic ability, consider that you've simply not realized precisely how to ignite the skills inherent in all of us. Monitor how your mind operates in everyday reality: is it self-focused? Focused predominantly on physical reality? On the ego? If so, play with shifting your focus regularly—become a "watcher" more often rather than a "player." Study psychism and follow up on the methods that personally get you results.

How and when will you use this oil? Unless you are on a regime of deeply studying and developing psychic power, I don't recommend wearing it daily. Instead, you may wish to reserve the oil for sessions of divination, channeling, before sleep, as a ritual anointing oil, or while counseling others. The choice is yours! Monitor how the oil alters your consciousness and how you can utilize that energetic shift.

Finally, remember that you should *not* use "fragrant" oil. A good percentage of the ingredients that constitute the word "fragrance" are literally biohazardous waste that have been blended with other ingredients. True essential oil is what we're going for, not unnatural poison!

Supplies

- a couple small labels or pieces of tape
- a blue permanent marker
- an amber-colored oil vial
- a combination of the following essential oils (*not* "fragrant" oils): 1 part lemon, 2 parts rosemary, 2 parts ylang-ylang, 2 parts lemongrass, 2 parts bay laurel, and 3 parts base oil (see Notes)
- a small tiger's eye stone (small enough to fit in the vial)
- a small combination of the herbs cedar, eyebright, frankincense, mugwort, peppermint, and yarrow

Notes

- You will need to dilute your finished oil with at least 30 percent base oil to avoid burning the skin. For this mixture, the 3 parts base oil will exceed 30 percent of the mix (the essentials total 9 parts). Base oil can include grape seed, jojoba, or mineral oil. If none of these are available, you can use olive oil (though it doesn't keep nearly as long as the others).
- At least 24 hours before using the oil, do a "test dab" on your arm or somewhere. This is to see whether or not you have adverse or allergic reactions to any of the ingredients. Safety first!

Procedure

Begin by casting a circle, calling the quarters, chanting, or raising energy as you normally would, performing protective exercises, and alter-

Symbol 30

ing your consciousness. Clear your mind, bring focus to your breath, and meditate for at least a few minutes. When ready, begin the spell.

On a piece of tape or a label, draw symbol 30. On another, draw the symbol of Neptune. Adhere these to the vial. If you have an extra piece of transparent tape, it would be a good idea to put it overtop the symbols so they don't get smudged if oil spills down the side.

Facing the west, mix the oils together. While you are mixing, chant repeatedly:

Neptune, Pisces, day, and night,
I summon forth my second sight.

When the blend is complete, pour it into the vial carefully. Sit in a crosslegged position, close your eyes, and sniff the blend. While smelling, envision its subtle indigo energy traveling upward. See it entering your nostrils and filling your brain with its power. See it radiating out of your brow and up your head. When you've reached a semi-trancelike state, bring the oil away from your nose and envision the energies bursting out like an explosion. See the indigo energy radiating from your head and shining out into every nook and cranny of the world.

Come back to center. Add the tiger's eye stone, cap the oil and, still facing the west, blur your vision and declare:

This oil ignites my psychic flame,
and can be used again and again.
Neptune, Pisces, powers of the west,
I develop my powers to their mighty best.
There is nothing I cannot know,
there is no skill I cannot grow.
I am psychic; my third eye Sees,
as I will, so mote it be.

Finally, close your eyes again and see the indigo energy that surrounds your face and head. See it returning to the bottle. (Don't try to redirect the energy you sent outward, only pull the energy around your head into the bottle.) When finished, dab a bit of the oil in the west (on your altar or on the wall) and store the bottle in a dark spot, resting atop the herbal blend. Close the circle as you normally would. Only use this oil when you wish for your psychic powers to come out!

Sleeping with the Gods: A Prophetic Dreamtime Elixir

When we sleep, our bodies and minds—and thus our spirits—are rejuvenated. As the arms of sleep allow our minds to drift within themselves, our energy rebuilds and is revitalized. It's said that sleep is the brother of death—this is likely a reference to the god Hypnos (sleep) being the twin of Thanatos (death) in Greek mythology. We do brush up against the energy of death after every dreamtime, yet we reenter our body, the shell that allows us to function and interact on the manifest plane.

Though many would say that sleep is the "interlude" between moments of waking life, I (with my beloved Pisces Moon!) would like to think that *wakefulness* is the interlude between moments of rest. The realm of sleep is a magickal place, unbound by the trappings of waking reality.

If you have made the psychic oil from the previous spell, you may wish to anoint your third eye with the blend before bedtime. Incorporating an elixir like this can also be of benefit if you're trying to gain prophecy and psychic insight from dreams.

——— • ———

I admit that I'm not the best interpreter of dreams. Some people are highly skilled at dream interpretation, however, and I like to get their opinions on the matter if a dream stands out as significant. You may wish to interpret on your own or find someone who's successful at dream interpretation. There are also numerous books on dream interpretation.

Dreams are made up of many things. Experiences of the day (most of which are subconscious or momentary thoughts) rewind and purge themselves. Hidden thoughts make themselves apparent through symbolism. Interesting scenarios come to life—and even the most unusual dreams are felt and believed as if they're actually experienced. Indeed, perception (and the mind's reactions) while dreaming and perception in waking life are *not* very different. In that sense, dreaming is real.

Rarely do psychic messages in dreams work in a direct, straightforward manner. Because dreams so frequently manifest through symbolism, it's essential to research those symbols when interpreting dreams that may have psychic significance. Keep in mind that your own symbolic associations are the most pertinent—because you're the one having the dream! At the same time, it's a good idea to research universal symbolism. This is simply an aspect of magickal awareness. Because all minds are connected, meanings of symbols (including colors, words, gods, and such) are stored in an unseen superconscious. All "things" have *egregores*: unseen collective thoughtforms. Different cultures interpret different symbols in different ways. Dreams can be interpreted through personal symbolism, Jungian psychology, crosscultural religious views, and other shared perceptions.

Stepping Back & Further Application

Do you have prophetic dreams? Everyone has experienced this at some point. As with any inherent psychic power, it's just a matter of honing the skill and becoming more disciplined in bringing it out.

Remember that not every dream that you remember is significant; many are just the results of mental purging. However, there is in infinite amount unseen energy in our unconscious mind, and sleeping is an ideal platform for those messages to become manifest consciously.

Most of us have significant dreams but, upon waking, instantly jump into "this" world and forget about the experiences we just had. Brutal alarm clocks, a rush to get in the shower and wake up, and other time constraints on this plane keep us unfocused on the unconscious and its manifestations. Examine your relationship to dreaming: are your dreams trying to tell you more than you're actually hearing? Are you prepared to spend a little time each day immediately recording your dreams (even if they make no sense at the time)? Stay disciplined to bring out your psychic dream skills; it will aid in your development as well as the development of those who come to you for dream advice and interpretation.

Supplies

- 4 unbroken bay leaves
- a blue permanent marker
- about 1 gallon of spring water
- any combination of the herbs bay, dandelion, mugwort, peppermint, poppy seed, rosemary, and rose (flowers or rosehips)
- a stovetop cauldron, dutch oven, or boiling pot
- a large glass jar
- a small amount of brandy
- 1 stone each of amethyst, opal, and tiger's eye
- a large sticky label
- a bedside dream journal and pen (or recording device)

Notes

- Instead of keeping a dream journal, you may wish to keep a recording device by your bedside. I personally prefer this method, because I can press the "record" button and ramble uncensored about the dreams.
- You may also wish to create an affirmation to say before falling asleep every night. A simple example is "Tonight, I will remember and record all of my significant and prophetic dreams." Every night, repeat this out loud and then in your mind while you drift off into sleep.

Procedure

Begin by casting a circle, calling the quarters, chanting, or raising energy as you normally would, performing protective exercises, and altering your consciousness. Clear your mind, bring focus to your breath, and meditate for at least a few minutes. When ready, begin the spell.

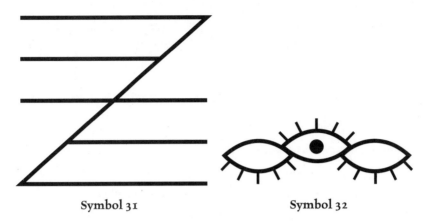

Symbol 31   **Symbol 32**

On 2 of the whole bay leaves, write the words THARA THARŌ on both sides. On the others, draw symbol 31 on one side and symbol 32 on the other. Set these aside. Put all other herbs in the cauldron.

Pour about ½ gallon spring water in the cauldron and make your way to the stove (or fire). Boil the mixture until only a small amount of water remains in the bottom. While the brew is bubbling, chant intermittently:

> *Boil, bubble, transformation,*
> *in dream give me vision and confirmation.*
> *This potion opens the gates of mind,*
> *stretching through space, piercing through time.*
> THARA THARŌ!

Allow the brew to boil until there's about 1 cup of water remaining. Extract this by straining the herbs. (You can utilize these "used" herbs by either placing them outside, in a stream of water, or dry them and put them in a sachet by your bed.)

Next, fill the jar 30 percent full of brandy. Add the cup of herbal potion followed by the stones. Fill the remaining space with fresh water and cap the jar tightly. Shake it vigorously while once again saying the above chant (replacing "potion" with "elixir") 4 times in a very loud voice. Be sure to direct your voice at the bottle.

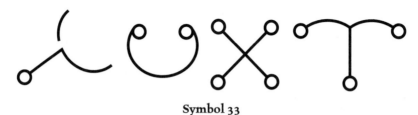

Symbol 33

Write symbol 33 on the sticky label and affix it tightly to the jar. This will aid in causing prophetic dreams and a restful sleep.

Close the circle as you normally would. Keep the bottle by your bedside and take a single sip of the elixir before falling asleep each night, for as long as you desire (however, discontinue use if you notice any adverse reactions). Keep the enchanted bay leaves by your beside (you can hang them up or keep them underneath the elixir jar itself). After a few weeks, begin to smell the jar before you go to sleep—if it smells sour or tainted at all, don't drink the mixture (however, the brandy should preserve it). Finally, remember to write your dreams down in the journal (or record them on a recording device) immediately upon waking. It doesn't matter if the dream ramblings make sense when you're recording them—they can be analyzed later in the day.

Behind Mine Eyes: Scrying in Shadow

Scrying is a type of divination that makes use of a luminescent surface. Scryers gaze at a surface, usually in darkness or near-darkness, to gain vision, prophecy, and insight. Much of this insight appears in the form of symbols, shapes, designs, and patterns, though some psychics and experienced scryers see full scenes play out before their eyes (all three of 'em).

Scrying links one's unconscious mind to the surface scryed upon. In a sense, it's subtle projection: the deeper mind projects itself on the surface and the conscious mind interprets. The surface being scryed, then, serves as a bridge between the unconscious and the perceived. Unlike tarot cards, runes, and other divinatory tools, the surface gazed upon is unchanging: it doesn't reveal meanings by way of direct symbolism or conscious categorization.

One of the forms of scrying within this ritual is a direct scrying in one's physical shadow. In *The Book of Mephisto*, Left Hand Path occultist Asenath Mason suggests completely darkening a room and, by the light of a single candle, performing divination in the body's reflected shadow. This, along with other scrying methods, can be extremely beneficial in reaching into the unconscious mind to retrieve messages. For more information on activating internal shadow work, please refer to the first chapter of *Shadow Magick Compendium*.

——— • ———

Also called a black mirror or *speculum*, a scrying mirror is a darkened piece of glass, mirror, or other reflective surface. The practitioner gazes into the mirror and blurs their vision in order to receive messages. Divination by gazing into a magick mirror is called *catoptromancy*. Many Witches prefer this method over the traditional crystal ball.

Crystal ball gazing is called *crystallomancy* and is one of the most well-known forms of divination. The crystal ball seems to have been made famous by John Dee and Edward Kelly, the founders of the Enochian/Angelic system of magick. Kelly preferred a large crystal ball as his divinatory instrument.

Many Witches use "crystal" balls made of either glass or another stone like calcite, selenite (celenite), or any kind of quartz. Some prefer opaque balls, while others like clear. This is entirely a personal preference based on what works best for you. Not to mention, actual crystal balls are quite pricey. If you do decide to save up for a crystal ball, ensure that the crystal (or other mineral) is naturally mined. I tend to believe that stones cultivated with Earth-damaging chemical processes actually put negative and damaging vibes into the stone and thus the user, which has potential to taint any reading.

Stepping Back & Further Application

For the uninitiated (and by this I mean "unfamiliar"), scrying—and indeed any form of divination—can be somewhat frightening and even risky. Accusations of divinatory tools being "doorways of the Devil" aside, the risk is more or less one of insight-gaining. Because divination works so much on the subconscious and unconscious planes, unsettling or suppressed information and insights can come to the surface in the process. In a working such as this, which incorporates a direct scrying on actual shadow, those risks are particularly high. Honestly, I'm not too worried about any readers of this book trying shadow-scrying and don't believe there's too much risk involved. (If a person has chosen to be on a magickal-spiritual path, it's likely that they're willing to face their inner shadow should it wish to be faced.) However, it's not a party trick and should be approached with seriousness. Unlike scrying and divining for other people, divination by way of one's shadow is strictly personal.

Supplies

- a purple candle
- a round incense-burning charcoal disk and sand in a dish or censor
- a large surface (see Notes)
- a small amount of mugwort
- a mug of steeped mugwort tea
- a notepad and pen or recording device (optional)
- a black scrying mirror or *speculum* (Latin for "mirror"), crystal ball, or other scrying tool

Notes

- For the "surface," I refer to something huge and monochrome. The best surface is a blank wall, but a big piece of cardboard or something similar can be used.

Procedure

Begin by casting a circle, calling the quarters, chanting, or raising energy as you normally would, performing protective exercises, and altering your consciousness. Clear your mind, bring focus to your breath, and meditate for at least a few minutes. When ready, begin the spell.

Light the candle and incense coal and turn off all the lights in the room. Facing the surface or wall, situate the tools next to you. After the coal turns to a glowing ember, add the mugwort. Throughout the ritual, add pinches of mugwort to the coal and take sips of the mugwort tea.

Sit down and place the burning candle a couple feet behind you until the shadow of your body appears on the surface in front of you. Gaze into the area of the shadow where your eyes would be and say:

> *Shadow self, make yourself known to mine eyes.*
> *[He/She] who is the culmination of that which I repress, suppress, oppress.*
> *[He/She] who is my unconscious, my subconscious, my superconscious.*
> *[He/She] who is the assemblage of my unseen, my hidden, my forbidden.*
> *Shadow self, make yourself known to mine eyes.*

Blur your vision and look at various aspects of the shadow before you. Take some time letting your rational mind slip to the background, bringing your subtle senses to the surface. See if you get visions visually (such as symbols or words), in your mind's eye, or any other way. Clear your mind and don't rush the process.

After a few minutes, jot down notes about what you received. Turn to your other scrying device(s) and, after a few minutes of gazing, see if they reveal other messages and whether those messages are clearer or more convoluted than those from the previous method. Experiment with different scrying methods to discover what works best for you.

Do the same with the mug of tea: gaze into its surface, blur your vision, and see if it reveals anything to your conscious mind (*hydromancy*). Do the same with the smoke of the incense (*libanomancy*). Repeat this process for as long as you'd like, and be certain not to rush yourself.

Conclude by turning your gaze back to the shadow on the surface. Once again, slip into a trancelike state and record any messages you may receive. Now is not the time to interpret the messages, but to record them for future analysis. If you're relatively successful in your scryings, ask your shadow to show you different aspects. You can say "show me the shadow of my past," "show me the shadow of my relationship," "show me the shadow of my spiritual progress," or anything else. Some diviners get more specific answers by asking more specific questions. Because this ritual is largely one of experimentation, remember which method works best for you and return to it at another time. For now, thank the spirits of the unseen and close the circle as you normally would.

Cauldron of Creation: Art of the Subconscious

For æons, numerous artists and creators have said that their work is divinely inspired. Most of these "channelings" aren't directly related to religion, but are often aligned to emotion. Being a supremely spiritual force, the emotional body is connected to the soul and its progression. Emotions are tied into thoughts, behaviors, and personal expressions such as art.

Whether the medium is music, film, painting, drawing, writing, or photography, where there's creativity, there's emotion. Where there's emotion, there's spirit. This working is focused on tapping into the subconscious mind and becoming a creative conduit of unseen energies.

——— • ———

This spell makes use of a cauldron. One of the most renowned Witches' tools, the magickal cauldron is a holy vessel of creation. Even Shakespeare's *Macbeth* features three Witches making a "hell broth" over a cauldron while petitioning the aid of Hekate.

In Wicca and other Neopagan traditions, the cauldron is seen as a representation of the womb of the Goddess. The cauldron is viewed as having symbolic powers of healing and creation. In Welsh mythology, the goddess Cerridwen possessed a cauldron whose potion—which takes a year and a day to brew—could give people healing, knowledge, and artistic inspiration. The cauldron also symbolizes renewal, rebirth, and hidden wisdom. In many ways, the symbolism of the vessel is aligned to the existence of the unconscious or subconscious mind.

Semantically, the *unconscious* is an ancient idea that assumes there is behind-the-scenes action going on behind everyone's usual perception. It's from the unconscious that we gain intuition, underlying beliefs and behavioral patterns, and dream symbolism. Many Freudian psychologists prefer the term *unconscious mind*, while many Jungians prefer *subconscious*. Some psychologists prefer to recognize the *sub*conscious mind as that which is just "beneath" one's usual consciousness; for example, forgetting and then remembering a person's name can be seen as a subconscious-to-conscious transmission of information. Following this definition, the *unconscious* mind is the portion of the psyche that represses and willfully forgets occurrences of trauma, hiding the pain deep within the mind. Its goal, then, is to never allow the conscious mind to recall the occurrence or emotions attached to it—this is an instinctual coping mechanism. Therapists, psychologists, and counselors work with both the conscious and unconscious minds.

Regardless of terms, it's essential to realize that part of human behavior is psychological suppression. Many personal experiences are buried deep within the mind. I would argue that all of our past-life experiences also exist on those deeper levels. I would also say that all of human experience exists deep within everyone's psyche, linking together all minds through time and space. The art you channel with this working may be blatantly part of your subconscious mind. On the other hand, it may appear to have no relation at all to your own psyche. Be open to any channelings you may receive!

Stepping Back & Further Application

Do you consider yourself an artist? Perhaps you wish to enrich your talents by purposefully tapping into unseen planes. Perhaps you feel as though you're not too artistically inclined at present, but wish to bring about artistic talents that are somewhere in your consciousness. Whatever the case, a working like this can bring artistic talents to the surface. Because so many art forms are connected to the unseen realms (of the mind or otherwise), a direct connection to these realms—coupled with the intention of creating art—can help hone creative powers. Everyone in the world has the power to create art; it's just a matter of honing that power, rigorously experimenting, and practicing without self-criticism. Art serves so many purposes: emotional expression, therapeutic release, political and social commentary, healing for others, and so on. What each artist does with their abilities is up to them alone.

Supplies

- a small amount of wormwood and rosemary
- 1 piece of citrine and 1 of orange calcite
- a stovetop cauldron, Dutch oven, or boiling pot
- about ½ gallon spring water
- appropriate art supplies (paints, water, pencils, etc.)
- a large canvas or sketchpad

Notes

- In this working, one can utilize written, drawn, painted, or sketched art. If your artistic medium is something different, you can draw what you receive while in circle and transfer it to the chosen medium afterward.

Procedure

Begin by casting a circle, calling the quarters, chanting, or raising energy as you normally would, performing protective exercises, and altering your consciousness. Clear your mind, bring focus to your breath, and meditate for at least a few minutes. When ready, begin the spell.

Place the wormwood, rosemary, and stones in the cauldron and put in enough water to make a brew. Bring it to the stove and, once it is simmering, chant:

> *Cauldron of creation, womb of life, Holy Mother who gives birth to all existence! I ask for your aid in channeling creations from the unseen layers of mind. I am an artist, and am thusly your humble servant. Reveal to me the messages I can deliver to this world!*

Quickly dip the ring finger of your nondominant hand into the brew (but don't let it burn you) and put it in your mouth, tasting the essence of wormwood. Smell the mixture and let its essence merge with your own.

Carefully bring the cauldron back to the ritual space. Put it nearby and grab the art supplies. Hold your nondominant hand over the steam rising from the cauldron and place your dominant hand on the canvas and art supplies. Clear your mind and erase the thoughts of the day. Say:

Art is sacred, art is pure.
From the depths, I summon you.
Rush upon me, ether and mind.
Reach through space, stretch through time.
From the watery depths of the psyche's abyss,
let me gaze into what exists.
Clear the blockages, render them transparent.
Now the unseen becomes apparent!

Take a number of very deep, swift breaths and see your mind going deeper and deeper down a dark tunnel. This is the tunnel of your mind. Draw whatever messages you receive as you go deeper and deeper. If it helps, visualize your perception spiraling down an infinite cauldron.

When your consciousness is palpably altered, don't struggle to get grounded: let yourself flow into the depths of the mind and the astral. Don't decipher or decode the messages, just get them down on paper. Whether you write notes about what you see or hear, or you actually start drawing or painting your visions, the important thing is to get it on paper to work with later. If you wish (and if it doesn't sever your trance), slightly open your eyes to see the images you're creating.

Continue the trance for as long as you'd like. Push your limits. When you feel like stopping, go deeper. If you start to slip out of the trance early (such as if you start thinking about the day, or the room, or your body), take a series of deep breaths and envision the depths increasing tenfold. Say "deeper" aloud if it helps you go down the mental tunnel.

When you've received a good amount of words, sounds, pictures, and so on, and have either made notes of them or have drawn them directly, slip out of the trance by first mentally bowing to the cauldron and then slingshotting out of the tunnel. See yourself rising, rising, rising, and simultaneously coming back to ordinary consciousness. When you've successfully returned, perform some grounding exercises and close the circle as you normally would.

Chapter 11

PLUTO

PLUTO

Zodiacal rulership: Scorpio
Color association: White, ineffable
Sephira: Kether
Number: 1
Day: None
Archetypes: Underworld God/dess
Themes: Death, rebirth, transformation, binding, destruction,
the subconscious, destiny, life cycle, intensity, triumph, absolute power

Last (Funerary) Rites: A Ritual Death

Many spiritual people say that suffering is a result of not following destiny. In an occult sense, it can be said that not aligning to spiritual Will causes a person to suffer. Other spiritual systems believe that suffering is a result of clinging to worldly experiences rather than being content that all things in reality are subject to change. Whatever the case, suffering exists. Suffering exists to be accepted, to be learned from, and to be released. A ritual death can help with this.

This working is, in a Plutonian sense, connected to the next working in this chapter—the rite of rebirth. As I discuss in the description of that ritual, a part of the self has to die in order to make room for new aspects to emerge. Holding on to the past can cause immense suffering.

In a ritual death, a person lets an old part of themselves die. After cultivating acceptance for past behavior, disposition, choices, and modes of thought, a person can work to release them.

——— • ———

When we realign to our Will—that is, our spiritual destiny—suffering can slip away much more easily. For this ritual, you must prepare by seriously meditating and contemplating what parts of your old self you wish to release. A ritual such as this could even mark a practitioner's instant of completely severing a physical, chemical, or emotional addiction (see the working on page 134 for another suggestion). What you release is up to you—just the same, you must do the work in real life in order for those things to actually and honestly be put to rest. The purpose of this working is to re-clarify one's life path so that blockages can slip to the wayside and be forever gone.

Keep in mind that once you ritually die, you must integrate new vibrations into your being that can replace the things you dismissed. Think about paradoxical (equal-opposite) things that can replace what is being put to rest. If, for example, you're releasing a habit of codependence, you could do work in your life to gather your own energy, rely on yourself, and stop moments of desperation when they start. If you're releasing tormenting fears, think of ways you can work to face them. This sort of "spiritual replacement" work can occur as you experience reality, seeping into your everyday experience. If the Universe is guiding you to lay down the tired body of your former self, analyze the reasons and intricacies, and work on ways of letting the new self emerge and shine in its place. On one hand, the old and new selves are still "you." On the other hand, the same "you" that you were yesterday no longer exists: all that exists is you Now. Reality is change, a process of continual rebirth—it's just a matter of intending those renewals. Once the nature of change is realized, you can willfully enter spirals of positive encouragement through everyday transformation.

Stepping Back & Further Application

Working to release issues of the past (behavior, thoughts, choices, or traumatic experiences) can be marked with a ritual death like the one outlined here. However, as I mentioned earlier, the work really carries over into your everyday experience. It's up to all of us to choose how we respond to our environment and our experiences. If we replay cycles of the past that no longer serve us, we are inviting pain into our lives and are allowing it to repeat in a perpetual loop of negativity. We must have the effort and humility to face and conquer our deepest issues.

If we consciously halt and change the things that no longer serve our path, we open ourselves up to learning new modes of behavior, thought, and being. We can choose consciously to integrate new vibrations into ourselves—this, too, reworks the neurotransmitter pathways in our brains, keeping us fresh and revitalized.

Supplies

- appropriate mourning clothing (see Notes)
- a black or white candle
- a stereo, headphones, or music device (optional, see Notes)
- a glass of organic apple juice
- a large semitransparent black veil (enough to cover your body)
- 2 large coins (Sacagawea dollars or Susan B. Anthony dollars work well)
- a glass of red wine or grape juice
- at least a handful of elderberries (fresh or dried)

Notes

- The mourning clothing used in this ritual can be up to you. You are dressing for your own funeral. Feel free to go all-out in black, veils, robes, a tuxedo, dress, tie, or whatever you'd like.

- If you'd like to play mournful music during this procedure, you may wish to select extremely depressing classical instrumentals (like Chopin's *Funeral March* on repeat), ambient (I recommend Aphex Twin's *Selected Ambient Works volume* II, disc 2), or other dark, atmospheric music. This can greatly help the practitioner "get in the mood to die." It's best that the music have no vocals.

Procedure

Begin by casting a circle, calling the quarters, chanting, or raising energy as you normally would, performing protective exercises, and altering your consciousness. Clear your mind, bring focus to your breath, and meditate for at least a few minutes. When ready, begin the spell.

Light the candle, turn off the lights, and turn on the music. Pick up the apple juice and, looking at the glass, declare:

Blessed is this fruit of the Earth. I declare and enchant this as holy poison.
As hemlock, as aconite, as nightshade, as belladonna.
As this enters my body and blood, I hereby sever my old self.
The person whom I used to be now dies with this drink.
[He/She] is no longer.
[He/She] is dead.

Drink the juice and cringe as if it has a bitter, fiery poisonous taste. Lie on the floor. Surround yourself with the elderberriesm then pull the veil over your body and close your eyes. Place one coin on each of your eyelids and cross your hands in an X formation across your chest. Relax every muscle in your body.

When you're comfortable, "feel" the "poison" coming on, entering your bloodstream, killing and destroying your former self. Your body enters small, quick fits of tremor and convulsion. The poison hurts, and then you relax. Cry, wince, briefly wail. Sense its destruction. You feel extreme pain, and then relax. Once more, and relax. Finally, you die.

Visualize your former self as a sticky astral body, slipping away from your physical self. Feel it separating from you, descending deep into the Earth, never to return again. (Simultaneously allow your mind to remain in your physical body, not descending with the former energy body.) Feel the effects of the "poison" as your former self ceases to be. It effortlessly slips away from your physical frame to merge with the Earth, its essence feeding the soil. Focus on this until you feel it fully released.

When the essence of your former self is securely and concretely dead and isolated in the Earth, take a series of extremely deep breaths. As you deeply inhale, your body convulses. You gather your strength. You realize that the poison doesn't affect this body, only the one that's now dead and buried. You lift yourself up. Immediately stand up and start jumping around. Quickly pick up the glass of wine or grape juice and declare:

Blessed is this fruit of the Earth!
I declare and enchant this as the blood of the gods.
As this enters my blood, I am revitalized. I am reinvigorated. I am reborn!
I declare that I am aligned to my Will! My former self is dead.
VANQUISHED! BURIED! DEAD AND GONE!

I enter the stream of my destiny. I am ready.
So mote it be!

Thank the spirits and close the circle as you normally would.

Self-Isolation: A Rite of Rebirth

The term *rebirth* is thrown around frequently in metaphysical and mystical circles. Quite simply, it refers to a second birth. Numerous religions worldwide utilize the force of a second birth—a spiritual birth—to signify one's coming into their tradition. Additionally, numerous cultures have coming of age ceremonies, which are rites of passage that secure a person's entrance into another phase of their life.

Rebirth happens constantly. Cells of the body are continually dying while new ones are being born. The nature of reality is birth, death, and rebirth; everything works cyclically. Nothing exists outside the dance of life and death. In a sense, we are "reborn" every millisecond. We are "reborn" every time we wake from sleep. We are "reborn" every birthday. These occurrences are natural. The real significance lies in the rebirth of the spirit. Because the spiritual planes are mirrors of the physical (and vice versa), it's only proper to assume that the spirit itself has its own cycles. This is also reflected in ideas of past lives and reincarnation.

Initiation ceremonies, whether in Pagan or occult systems or otherwise, quite frequently carry energies of rebirth. As a person enters into a new phase in life, their old self slips away to make room for the new. For every rebirth, a death must precede. This ritual assumes that one has experienced or is in the process of experiencing a spiritual death.

—— • ——

This ceremony of rebirth shouldn't be performed at any ol' time. It should significantly and acutely mark a transition phase in a person's life. No, the ceremony doesn't initiate a person into any particular rank or title. Instead, it fuels the fire of regeneration and renewal, helping the practitioner spring into new personal and spiritual ground. It may also be good to perform some time after the preceding ritual, "Last (Funerary) Rites: A Ritual Death."

If you are meant to perform this ceremony or something similar, you will simply have a sense of *knowingness*. At the same time, you may need to start planning a rebirthing ceremony days, weeks, or months prior to performing it. When life drastically changes directions, it's important to mark the significance of the shift. Whether your life has done this on its own, or whether you've recently entered a new social or spiritual role (father, mother, husband, wife, neophyte, initiate), ritually declaring your new placement in life can be empowering and motivating.

Rites of passage aren't frequent in the West. We have silly things like Sweet Sixteen parties and prom, but even these "initiatory participants" aren't given keys to the Mysteries of Life. America and the West could truly benefit by taking hints from other, more ancient cultures and their rites of passage. Perhaps if life changes were ritually marked (and in many cultures, the skin is literally and permanently "ritually marked"), there wouldn't be so many lost, aimless, and disenchanted souls wandering this Earth.

Stepping Back & Further Application

This ritual should be performed if you have recently experienced a type of spiritual death. Perhaps your old systems of belief have fallen. Perhaps those things you once held on to seem to be slipping away. Maybe you find yourself at a loss for what's next in your life.

Remember that this ceremony only *marks* a person's rebirth; this ceremony is not a rebirth in and of itself. The process of death and rebirth, in a spiritual sense, is just that: a process. A single ritual cannot contain keys for killing and resurrecting one's being. Even ceremonies that last days or weeks (like a shamanic death rite) can't contain all a person needs for the process. The ritual is a culmination of everyday experience.

In order to mark a person's rebirth, they must objectively realize that the Fates are pushing them into new paradigms of being. Like I said, this necessarily includes the death of the former self. Remember that this thing we call "self" or "I" is constantly changing; it is never one thing or another. Life's process pushes us into new phases of being, and sometimes ritually marking rebirth is the very rite of passage one needs to fully enter their unfolding destiny.

Supplies

- any combination of the herbs eyebright, High John the Conqueror root, lotus, mistletoe, mullein, Solomon's Seal root, and thyme
- a stovetop cauldron, Dutch oven, or boiling pot
- about ½ gallon spring water
- a small piece of amethyst
- athamé or knife
- 3 yards of inexpensive black or muslin fabric (cotton or another natural fiber)
- a Rose of Jericho (see Notes)
- a 1-inch-square piece of aluminum foil
- a small amount of salt
- a small amount of sulfur (brimstone)

Notes

- Roses of Jericho, also called "Resurrection Ferns," are the fern *Pleopeltis polypodioides,* and are native to the Southeastern United States. The ferns first appear to be completely dead, dried, and shriveled brown but "come to life" when placed in water. The reanimation of this curious plant carries vibrations of rebirth that are suitable to our purposes. These are available at some home and garden stores, witchy shops, and through various online retailers.
- As I mentioned earlier, please refer to the previous spell in this chapter for a ritual death. Some users may find it beneficial to perform a ritual death followed by a ritual rebirth such as this (depending on one's unique situation and reasons for doing the ritual).
- If you don't have powdered sulfur available, simply cut the heads off a few matches.

Procedure

Begin by casting a circle, calling the quarters, chanting, or raising energy as you normally would, performing protective exercises, and altering your consciousness. Clear your mind, bring focus to your breath, and meditate for at least a few minutes. When ready, begin the spell.

Put the herbs in the bottom of the empty cauldron, arranging them to look like the Pluto symbol. Staring at the symbol, start chanting:

> *Plutonian oceans, wash over me!*
> *I come as seeker, one on the threshold of this and that.*
> *My former self has been dying, and I mustn't feed it.*
> *I petition your aid, mighty and distant planetary satellite.*
> *Ignite my New Soul—give me New Life!*

Pour the water into the cauldron, drop in the amethyst, and put it on the stove. When it is simmering, stare into the mixture and repeat the chant a number of times. Bring the cauldron back to the ritual space to let the mixture cool.

Make sure that the cauldron is put in a safe spot and that no ritual tools (or anything else) are on the floor. Hold the athamé in your fist and stretch out the fabric.

Figure out a way to wrap yourself up tightly in the full length of fabric. Be sure to fully cover your head, arms, and full body. Be sure your hands (including the one gripping the blade) are fully covered. Mummify yourself. If you can manage it, try to make it so tight you can barely move. (But don't pile too much fabric on your face; let's avoid suffocation!) Be sure the end of the fabric is tucked in somewhere so it doesn't become unraveled in ritual.

Lay on the floor. Spend a long time in this vulnerable, restricted state of sensory deprivation. Though it's uncomfortable, you should be able to breathe just fine. During the time you're laying in this "cocoon," contemplate your old self. Think about those aspects of yourself that have been dying. Think about the old patterns that no longer serve you. Think about former modes of behavior, old systems of belief, and aspects of your old self that have slipped away with time. Don't cling to these. Instead, simply review them in your mind and recognize that you're transforming into a new level of being.

When the time is right, tightly grip the athamé and plunge it through the cloth as best you can. Put a lot of force, vigor, and energy into this. Scream and make noise if the mood takes you. (At the same time, be careful that the athamé doesn't hurt you.) Keep stabbing the fabric from the inside out, creating holes and rips. Force your way out, feeling the energy of rebirth. See yourself struggling to emerge from this cocoon-like shell. As your hands become more free to move, tear the fabric and eventually escape from the cocoon.

When you've undone the bind, throw the "shell" behind you. Immediately pick up the Rose of Jericho and, while staring at it, declare:

> *Plutonian oceans, you are washing over me!*
> *I have come as a seeker, and have discarded that for this!*
> *My former self is dead, and I can no longer feed it.*
> *I now invoke your aid, mighty and distant planetary satellite.*
> *Ignite my New Soul—I enter my New Life. NOW!*

Throw the Rose of Jericho into the cauldron. (It will be "bloomed" by the next day.) Pick up the aluminum sheet and place a pile of salt on top. On top of the salt, place a pile of sulfur. Look at the mixture and declare:

> MERCURY! SULFUR! SALT! *Holy Trinity of Life!*
> *I invoke your essence into my being!*
> *Create me anew. Assimilate my soul!*
> *By the three parts of creation, I align to my Great Work.*
> *I am reborn.* NOW! *So mote it be!*

Close the circle as you normally would. Keep the rose in the cauldron until the brew evaporates and it shrivels back up (don't worry, it won't diffuse the energy). Vow to concentrate on your New Self, and empower your path in new ways that nourish your soul.

Magickal Self-Defense: A Poppet for Binding

Although Pluto is technically a dwarf planet rather than a "real" planet, astrologers still recognize its influence and keep Scorpio (the sign with the most deep and secretive energies) assigned to its rulership. Because Pluto is the outermost celestial body, it carries associations of depth, the life cycle, and absolute power.

As an extremely potent influence aligned to Fate, Pluto's energy can be utilized in heavy spells that have influence on Fate—one's own or someone else's. For this reason, a binding spell is quite appropriate for the astrological influence. As always, doing magick on another person carries with it a necessity for exercising personal ethics.

When binding another person, the intention should be protective. If someone's causing harm and could use a metaphysical restraint, a binding is a great solution. Just the same, magick should only be performed after or alongside proper activity in the physical realm. All protective measures should be taken in mundane life.

As an interesting contrast, the term "binding spell" also covers a type of ancient Greco-Egyptian spell. As seen in the ancient PGM (*Papyri Græcæ Magicæ*) and PDM (*Papyri Demoticæ Magicæ*), binding was used in a more sinister light in antiquity, most notably for the purpose of binding a desired lover to the magician. The Neopagan form of binding certainly differs, as the intent is generally to manipulate someone's energy for the greater good instead of toying with destiny for selfish personal gain. While this book does include some cursing spells, parts of which are based on the ancient spells portrayed on papyrus documents, manipulating a love interest is not only karmically dangerous but ethically idiotic! There is never a legitimate need for such a "love" spell, hence the lack of its inclusion.

——— • ———

Binding magick was popularized in the 1996 film *The Craft*. In it, one of the characters binds another Witch from causing harm. Naturally, all sorts of teens and newbie Witches started trying to magickally bind each other when a problem arose.

Binding spells shouldn't be performed for fun—the situation should be serious and the intention should be for the betterment of others. Bindings aren't necessarily cursings, but they are spells of restriction and restraint. Because of this, the spell goes against a person's free will and can be considered an act of black magick. As I've mentioned before, black magick does have its time and place. Serious situations call for serious measures. Just the same, as with any magick, be prepared to accept full responsibility for anything the spell brings about.

Stepping Back & Further Application

What is your reason for wanting to perform a binding on someone? Is it your intention to protect (yourself or others negatively influenced by this person), or is it to dominate? Causing unnecessary injury is not only disrespectful to the energy of Pluto and the gods, but to the other person and yourself.

How can you "bind" this person in the physical realm? Have they broken any laws or engaged in damaging criminal behavior? What other actions can be taken? Do authorities need to be notified, or do the actions warrant a restraining order? If you don't work on the physical level, the metaphysical work won't align.

Binding spells are used to stop people who are causing harm. In that sense, it's positive magick. In another sense, it goes against a person's free will, so be sure that putting binding magick on someone really *is* the best solution. If they're not causing extreme harm to others, perhaps a different approach is needed. Have you tried talking to the person or solving the problem another way? Use a binding spell as a final effort.

Supplies

- a black candle
- the "essence" of the other person (see Notes)
- a black poppet (or an old black sock or piece of fabric that has been made into a doll)

- any combination of the herbs calamus, catsclaw, clove, and ivy (or poison ivy)
- a few yards of all-natural twine (like jute or hemp)
- a piece of black fabric or a black bag (to store the poppet when finished)
- a combination of black salt and white salt or black sand and white sand

Notes

- The "essence" of a person, also called *ousia*, is anything that carries their energy pattern, including DNA (such as hair, fingernail clippings, and excretions), or has come in contact with the person (this is the Law of Contagion, and can include a person's possession, footprint, handwriting, and so forth). A person's essence can also be tapped into by creating a picture of the person, or by simply writing their name and focusing on them.
- If you use poison ivy in this binding spell, be sure that you have genuinely good reasons to use this poison in ritual. As opposed to nontoxic ivy, poison ivy carries energies of destruction and toxicity, adding an element of curse to the binding.

Procedure

Begin by casting a circle, calling the quarters, chanting, or raising energy as you normally would, performing protective exercises, and altering your consciousness. Clear your mind, bring focus to your breath, and meditate for at least a few minutes. When ready, begin the spell.

Light the candle and place the essence of the person on the poppet, ideally in the face area. Beneath that, pile the mixture of herbs. Envision the poppet as a miniature "them" sitting there before you. Declare:

[Name]: *this is you.*
[Name]: *this is you.*
[Name]: *this is you.*

Envision the symbol of Pluto in your mind. Mentally superimpose this image on the poppet, seeing it sink and absorb into the doll. Say:

[Name]: *by the powers of Pluto, I bind you, I bind you.*
You can no longer cause harm to yourself or others.
You are restricted. You are restrained. You are bound. You are fixed.
In the name of the ancient ones and the depths of Pluto,
I bind you, [Name]! *I bind you,* [Name]!

Immediately start binding the loose herbs (aside from the salt or sand) to the poppet by using the twine. Though you're working with loose herbs, do your best to secure them to the doll. Try to get the herbs bound all around the figure so the energy touches every side. (You can also drip candle wax on the poppet and press the loose herbs onto the wet wax, adhering them to the doll.) While you are tying up the poppet, repeat the following a number of times. Chant it fast, chant it slow, and direct the energy right into the spell:

[Name]: *bound by Pluto,* [Name]: *bound by me!*
You can no longer inflict harm. So mote it be!

When finished, tuck in the end of the cord or tie the two end pieces together. Make it tight. Take the black candle and drip it all over the poppet. Next, place the poppet on the black fabric (or in the black bag) and liberally sprinkle the black and white salt or sand all over the doll. Tie up the fabric and close the circle as you normally would. Store the spell in a dark, untouched area of the house and only unbind it (releasing the spell) if the person changes their harmful ways.

Many Faces: A Past-Life Regression

One of the oldest views of the human soul is that of reincarnation. Being one of the most widely held views of the spiritual process, reincarnation holds that the essence of a person is reborn in a different "shell" after death. Some systems of belief see this as perpetual reincarnation in human forms, while others (notably Hinduism, Buddhism, and other

Eastern religions) believe that the soul can be born in plant form, animal form, or as a being in another realm. Many early Christians also believed in reincarnation, which may be a theological view in reincarnation (called *gilgul*) carried over from traditional Jewish Kabbalah.

Because past lives are not something that can be empirically proven by scientific study, there's no way of knowing how the process works—or if it's real to begin with. However, schools of science point out that energy and matter cannot be destroyed—only changed. Numerous religions and spiritual paths agree. One extension of this knowledge is the belief in past lives: consciousness must continue in a state of change. Nature tells us that everything works in cycles. Why would one's consciousness be any different?

——— • ———

Author, Pagan, and magician Donald Michael Kraig, in his lecture at 2009's PantheaCon (America's largest annual Pagan/occult convention—which *everyone* should attend!) reviewed some perceptions about how past lives operate. Indeed, the most obvious perception for those of us believers in the West is that "I" or "you" reincarnate over and over again into human bodies. This seems the most obvious way to view the issue. While this is a possibility, countless schools of thought teach that the "I" is ego (which has both positive and negative traits) and is therefore an illusion that is subject to change. In this way, the "I" that I am currently experiencing was not the same "I" that experienced "my" past lives. Confusing?

One example to clarify this line of thinking is to look at the concept called the Pool of Souls. Within this idea, it's believed that memory is mortal and thus separates from the soul after death—that is, memory (the mind) "goes" somewhere different than the soul. So what happens to the memories? According to this theory, the memory enters a Pool of Souls (like an akashic record database) where all memories in human history are stored. When a person remembers their past lives, then, they are tapping into the Pool of Souls, or the akashic records. Do those memories belong to the person performing the regression, then? Yes and no. Vibrationally, the past lives one perceives are linked to the regressor's soul in the moment. Like attracts like. At the same time, the "I" that I perceive now did not necessarily experience those memories precisely "in the flesh." Instead, the person who is "me" (which is actually a conglomeration of energy, flesh, and meta-forces) chose to recount those experiences as if they were my own.

Because countless people claim that they were Cleopatra, Napoleon, or Isis (seriously) in "past lives," could they really just be tapping into those former impersonal experiences and memories via this Pool of Souls? According to this theory, absolutely. But still, the idea of the Pool of Souls doesn't discount the notion that some people have serious psychological imbalances and feel a need to have been someone famous in order to compensate for suffering experienced in the current lifetime.

——— • ———

Other people believe that past lives are genetic. Because every cell in our body is constantly communicating, is it possible that memory is stored in the DNA? (I certainly believe so. Please see page 148 for more about the Mysteries of the Blood.) Could past-life memories actually be memories of our genetic ancestors? Possibly.

Some people even believe that everyone has a parallel life or lives. This is to believe that a number of people are linked on acute levels of consciousness and are having virtually identical experiences with different settings. According to this line of thinking, if I "remember" something about a past life, I may really be remembering an energetically parallel person's or peoples' memories.

Still other people believe that so-called "past-life memories" are actually more like dreams: a person is receiving arcane messages from the subconscious mind. At the same time, these symbolic transmissions are likely to have significance and relevance—just like nightly dreaming.

Regardless of the "real" nature of past lives—and, again, this is something that Donald Michael Kraig heavily emphasizes in his past-life and hypnosis work—the most important thing is that the "memories," whatever they are, carry immediate significance and relevance to this life's experience and are things that can advance the seeker's spiritual development. We must take the visions as they come and try not to over-analyze!

Stepping Back & Further Application

For this ritual, you will be entering a state of self-induced hypnosis. The method demonstrated here can be called *rapid hypnosis* or *fractionation*, and is greatly based on the work of hypnotherapist Dave Elman. It is believed that repeating hypnosis helps practitioners go deeper into a hypnotic or trancelike state, and that they are subsequently able to enter hypnosis more and more quickly. This is an invaluable skill to any meditator, mystic, Witch, magician, or spiritualist in general.

There's no telling what you'll experience during past-life regressions. It's good to keep an open mind about the experiences but not become attached to what you perceive.

There are numerous scientifically documented studies about past lives, most particularly involving children who come into the world knowing intricate details about the lives they had just lived. In many cases, they know acute, vivid details surrounding their former life, including their former name, their family's names, friends' names, residence, dates, the location of hidden items, cultural information, and other absolutely mind-blowing facts that they would otherwise have no way of knowing. While it's unlikely that you'll recount such incredibly detailed information about your past lives (whatever "past lives" truly are), it's good to know that there is documented and proven validity in regards to their reality.

Supplies

- a stick of sandalwood incense
- a blue candle
- 1 each of the stones bloodstone (or carnelian), a fossil of some type, petrified wood, and tiger's eye
- any elestial stone (see Notes)
- a bowl (preferably black) of water

- any combination of the herbs angelica, eucalyptus, gingko, marshmallow root, mugwort, sandalwood, and shavegrass (horsetail)
- a sterile lancet or pricking device to extract blood
- a notebook and pen

Notes

- It's a very good idea to make notes of your past-life regression experiences after you return from trance. These can be reviewed at a later time, and are likely to hold significant keys of information pertinent to your present lifetime.

- Elestial stones, also called "record keepers," are any stones with a number of terminations or jagged points along one side. If using an elestial stone, smoky quartz is a great option, as very few stones are capable of forming this design. For the purposes of past-life regression, these stones are beneficial because they capture moments of time in a series of jagged steps, thus mirroring the moments of time the regressor wishes to access.

Procedure

Begin by casting a circle, calling the quarters, chanting, or raising energy as you normally would, performing protective exercises, and altering your consciousness. Clear your mind, bring focus to your breath, and meditate for at least a few minutes. When ready, begin the spell.

To begin, turn off the lights, ignite the incense and candle, and put all the stones in the water. Place the herbs around the bowl and scatter some around your space. (An alternate option is to put them in an enchanted "past-life sachet" and wear it only when performing regression.)

Prick your finger with the lancet and allow a drop of blood to mix with the water. Stir it around and say:

By the pricking of my finger, I enter lifetimes once lived.
AKASHA! HOLY AKASHA! AKASHA!
Open your doors to me through the corridors of time.

Reveal my lives unseen. Show me what must be revealed.
With truth and clarity, I open the door to my soul's experience.

Close your eyes and enter a hypnotic state. Begin by envisioning yourself in a tunnel. At a very slow rate, you see numbers passing by you: 100 ... 99 ... 98 ... 97 ... These numbers begin to speed up faster and faster. After a couple minutes, you are seeing numbers fly by quickly: 40 ... 30 ... 20 ... When you approach 0, your consciousness sinks deep within itself. You are deeply inside your mind.

Next, envision a ruler vertically suspended in front of you. Perceive the number 100 at the top. You slowly bring your vision down this ruler: 99 ... 98 ... 97 ... When you reach 90, your consciousness sinks 10 times deeper within itself. Deeper. And deeper yet. As you slowly count down, reaching 80, you once again go 10 times deeper. This continues until you reach 0.

Establish your vision. See the scenery around you. Don't judge, just see what you see; don't rationalize the experience. Instead, get the visions as they come. Observe what you're wearing. Observe your age and gender. Observe your physical senses and how they interact with the environment. Where are you, what are you doing? Are you headed somewhere? Is there anyone else around you? Is it day or night?

By the force of your free will, project yourself further into that same life. See yourself aged in that life. Again, absorb what you're experiencing. Observe. Continue this for as long as you'd like. If you get any names, dates, locations, symbols, or scenarios, make a mental note. If you wish, allow yourself to slip into additional past-life experiences. Continue this for as long as you'd like without getting worn out.

When you've received at least some amount of information, see yourself rocketing back up that ruler, going from 0 to 100. As you ascend, your mind returns to your current and present experience. Your mind is returning ... returning ... coming back to the moment. Finally, you rocket backward through the tunnel of numbers by which you entered. Once you reach 100, open your eyes and find yourself back in your physical frame.

When you ground and center your energy, close the circle as you normally would. Then write notes of the experience in your notebook, and realize that you can come back to regress (either on those lives or others) any time you'd like.

Le Voyage dans la Pègre: An Underworld Descent & Exchange

The idea of the Underworld is present in cultures around the world. Religions far and wide hold varying notions of the afterlife and the land beyond this one. The term *Underworld* doesn't necessarily refer to Hell. Instead, it refers to the realms of the afterlife and the unseen. Allow me to give only a handful of perceptions.

The ancient Greek view of the Underworld included the belief that all souls of the dead would travel to this one place. Greeks understood the existence of various layers and levels of the Underworld, including the land of the dead ruled by Hades, the great pit of Tartarus (a home of the damned), the Elysian fields (for blessed and initiated souls), and the related Isles of the Blessed (or Elysian Islands), reserved for departed heroes. Five rivers were also seen as separating this world from the Underworld, on which souls of the dead were to travel. It should be noted that the Greek view of the afterlife varied considerably over time.

Annwyn (AH-noon) was the Welsh land of the dead. Ruled by Arawn (and later Gwynn ap Nudd), it can be seen as a type of heavenly realm. Wiccan views of the afterlife, or Summerland, are often somewhat similar to Celtic perceptions of Annwyn. The term *Summerland* is actually derived from the Spiritualist movement. The Spiritualist view of the Summerland is closer to a Christian view of Heaven than anything Pagan, which is why many Neopagans don't like the term (or simply use it as a synonym for "afterlife").

Ancient Egyptian mythology saw Duat as the afterlife's place of judgment. There, the deceased's heart carried the soul and was weighed on a scale next to the feather of Ma'at, which represented ultimate justice and truth. If the heart didn't weigh the same as the feather (and was thus polluted with sin), the soul was immediately sent to be devoured by

Ammut, the chimeric crocodile-lion-hippo goddess. If the soul weighed the same as Ma'at's holy feather, the soul was permitted to proceed to the heavenly realm of Aaru for all of eternity.

Divisions of the afterlife are seen across the globe and through all human history. The Christian mythology of Heaven and Hell is based on older ideologies and is not necessarily unique from other cultural views of the Great Beyond.

——— • ———

The Legend of the Descent of the Goddess is a metaphorical Pagan mythology known in a number of forms. The Descent, ideas of which we'll be using here, represents the death and rebirth of the seasons. Similarly, the Descent can be seen as a representation of the individual death/rebirth process that an initiate receives. Because existence itself is a process of life, death, and rebirth, the Descent has wide-ranging spiritual significance.

One of the myths surrounding the Sumerian fertility goddess Inanna is her descent to the Underworld (Irkalla). Ereshkigal, who was Inanna's sister and the queen of the Underworld, felt extreme hate toward her sister—the reasons for which are debatable. On Inanna's way to Ereshkigal's realm, gatekeepers instruct her to remove her elaborate clothing. After these are offered up piece by piece, she stands naked before her sister, who then kills her. After a series of events, Inanna is saved and revived (by the Food and Waters of Life), marking her rebirth.

Perhaps the other most well-known Descent of the Goddess legend is that of Persephone (Greek). When Persephone was picking flowers in a field, the Underworld god Hades burst through a crack in the Earth and abducted her. While Persephone was residing in the Underworld (which is *also* called Hades), her mother (Demeter) searched the land for her lost daughter. Demeter was later told of the incident by the all-seeing sun god Helios. As Persephone spent time in the terrain of Hades, the vegetation of the Earth died. Zeus forced Hades to release Persephone, but Hades managed to trick Persephone into eating pomegranate seeds. These seeds ensured that Persephone would return to the Underworld for a period of time every subsequent year.

These myths and others are stories of the Earth's vegetation cycle (origin myths for the seasons) and can additionally be seen as representing the psychological process of life/death/rebirth, such as that which is mirrored in the process of initiation.

Stepping Back & Further Application

The Underworld can be astrally accessed by the living for a number of purposes. In addition to various processes of initiation, a person can travel to other layers of reality to gain insight, heal others, detect curses, meet other aspects of self, and perform other "shamanic duties."

This working follows a sort of shamanic view of the Underworld and favors no mythological system over another. If you follow a particular pantheon and wish to incorporate specific gods or goddesses, go for it. Or you may prefer to journey to the Underworld in a fashion you're already familiar with. I encourage readers to incorporate their own mythologies into the working.

The goal of this working is to usher the ritualist into a psychological place where they are willing to offer up the unwanted in exchange for newness. Think about what you wish to give up in your life and what can take its place. This is not an exchange of power (in other words, you don't have to give up a positive ability), but it is an exchange of energy.

Think about opposites. The exchange should be of equal-opposites. Perhaps you wish to give up habits of self-destruction, either physical or psychological. Its opposite is self-healing, either physical or psychological. In this example, a door to extreme healing can open (perhaps the practitioner will discover physical or energetic healing arts) as the unwanted door to the past closes. Use this example to analyze your own situation and discover precisely the thing you wish to give up, simultaneously theorizing what its exchange may be. Be prepared for new and unknown doors to open while the thing you release begins its banishing cycle.

Supplies

- a fresh pomegranate
- 2 large, heavy rocks
- a black permanent marker

Notes

- Be sure to read the Stepping Back section and determine what it is you wish to exchange and what it is you seek in return.
- If a fresh pomegranate is unavailable for some reason, substitute pomegranate juice in a container.
- This working should be performed at nighttime, ideally an hour before sunrise.

Procedure

Begin by casting a circle, calling the quarters, chanting, or raising energy as you normally would, performing protective exercises, and altering your consciousness. Clear your mind, bring focus to your breath, and meditate for at least a few minutes. When ready, begin the spell.

On the pomegranate (or container of juice), draw a large symbol of Pluto. Turn off all lights and extinguish any flames so that you stand in total darkness. Close your eyes and resonate 6 times:

ZAZAS, ZAZAS, NASATANADA ZAZAS!

Set down the tools and start shedding all your clothing piece by piece. As you drop each item of clothing, say:

I shed this from my body to make way for the new.

Lay on the floor nude and set the pomegranate on your solar plexus (the upper belly beneath the sternum). Hold a rock in each hand and allow your hands to be weighed down. Feel the stones pressing down your hands, close your eyes, and listen to your heartbeat. Imagine this is a drumbeat, pulsing evenly and rhythmically. As you listen to this drum, you slip into a trance. Begin the visualization . . .

You find yourself walking along a path at night. You're walking very slowly. The crescent Moon and stars above you provide some amount of dim white light. You're naked and can feel the soft breeze and wet soil beneath your feet. You can smell the damp soil and the night-blooming flowers. You can hear the soft sounds of nocturnal creatures all around—the chirp of a bat, the hoot of an owl, and the call of a coyote or wolf in the distance. It seems as though the animals sense your presence and are welcoming you.

After walking along the path for a while, you see a massive tree silhouetted in the distance. It gets larger and larger as you approach it. Once you reach its base, you extend your hands and can feel the solid wood of the trunk. The trunk must be at least 10 feet across. You're not sure what kind of tree it is, and it's too dark to see the leaves, but its mighty presence speaks of raw power.

You notice a hole in the bottom of the trunk just large enough for you to fit in. Getting on your knees, you make your way in. You are instantly plummeted into the deep, dark Earth. In some way, you find yourself effortlessly passing through layers and levels of soil. You can feel the roots of the tree on your sides and can sense worms and other creatures around you. You descend deeper and the Earth gets darker.

Suddenly you stop. You find yourself suspended in a most deep, dark, condensed layer of Earth. In your mind, you declare what it is you wish to surrender. Envision the energy of the thing you wish to leave behind. See it sticking to your body, restricting your movement. Feel the pain and dissatisfaction associated with this energy. In the flash of a moment, you shake your energy body and the sticky matter falls away effortlessly. (At this moment, flip over your physical hands, freeing them. Place your palms on top of the stones.) The energy continues its decent into the Earth, no longer connected to you. In your mind, say:

You are banished, you are released, you are no longer, you are cast to the Earth.

Your intuition tells your energy body to extend its right hand. After doing so, you can feel a hollow space in the Earth. You can feel that there's a room of some sort just ahead of you. You forcefully kick yourself out of the spot you're stuck in. You enter the space and see that it's illuminated with a blinding white light. All you see is white; it's much too bright to even make out the walls. In your mind, say:

I have released [the released]*! In this chthonic place, I invoke* [the opposite] *into my being! I have offered up the old and replace it with the*

new! Oh ancient ones in the hollow Earth, hear my calls! I have exorcised the old—for this I must be blessed!

The white light becomes even brighter—more blinding than before. You close your eyes and feel the light entering your body, overwhelming you, filling you with the force you've invoked, the equal-opposite antithesis of what you released. This light is sending your energy body into convulsions; its extreme force is filling every cell in your being.

The light has now fully entered your body, imbuing you with the desired power. You suddenly find yourself weightless, floating upward at a great speed. You're ascending through the layers of the Earth—quickly, and then even faster!

You suddenly find yourself emerging from the hole in the tree trunk that you entered. It's daytime now. As you stand, you hear birds chirping around you and can see other animals darting in and out of the brush. The Sun illuminates the environment, showing you the trees and the Earth. You see the path on which you came, and you start to make your way back. You're mesmerized by the beauty of nature all around you as you walk.

The environment beings to blur—you see it slipping away before your eyes. You realize that you are returning to your physical body. Allow yourself to slowly slip back into your body and back into the room. When you've fully returned, declare:

Spirits of the Underworld, spirits of Old! I return renewed, endowed with the things I've sought! Close now the gates of the Underworld! I am blessed, and I bless you in return!

Clap your hands together 6 times. Bow to the directions, thank the chthonic gods, and close the circle as you normally would. Leave the pomegranate or juice at a tree trunk as an offering and continue to develop your newly given gifts on the physical plane.

Appendix I

FURTHER
READING &
BIBLIOGRAPHY

THE ELEMENTS IN MAGICK

Deborah Lipp—*The Way of Four*

Sorita d'Este & David Rankine—*Practical Elemental Magick*

ASTROLOGY

Julia & Derek Parker—*Parkers' Astrology*

Joanna M. Woolfolk—*The Only Astrology Book You'll Ever Need*

ASTROLOGY (BIRTHCHARTS)

Stephanie Jean Clement—*Mapping Your Birthchart*
 (modern astrology)

Kevin Burk—*Astrology: Understanding the Birth Chart*
 (classical astrology)

WITCHCRAFT (GENERAL)

Janet & Stewart Farrar—*A Witches' Bible*

Raymond Buckland—*Buckland's Complete Book of Witchcraft*

ESOTERIC QABALAH

Dion Fortune—*The Mystical Qabalah*

Israel Regardie—*The Tree of Life*

CEREMONIAL MAGICK & HERMETICISM (GENERAL)

John Michael Greer, et al.—*Learning Ritual Magic*

Franz Bardon—*Initiation into Hermetics*

HOODOO, VODOU, & SANTERÍA

Catherine Yronwode—*Hoodoo Herb & Root Magic*

Leah Gordon—*The Book of Vodou*

MAGICKAL HERBALISM

Scott Cunningham—*Cunningham's Encyclopedia of Magical Herbs*

Paul Beyerl—*The Master Book of Herbalism*

MAGICKAL STONE WORK

Scott Cunningham—*Cunningham's Encyclopedia of Crystal, Gem & Metal Magic*

Melody—*Love is in the Earth*

ALCHEMY

Mark Stavish—*The Path of Alchemy*

Jay Ramsay—*Alchemy: The Art of Transformation*

— · —

BIBLIOGRAPHY

Blake, Deborah. *Everyday Witch A to Z Spellbook: Wonderfully Witchy Blessings, Charms & Spells.* Woodbury, MN: Llewellyn, 2010

Illes, Judika. *Emergency Magic!: 150 Spells for Surviving the Worst-Case Scenario.* Gloucester, MA: Fair Winds Press, 2002.

———. *Encyclopedia of 5000 Spells: The Ultimate Reference Book for the Magical Arts.* New York: HarperOne, 2009

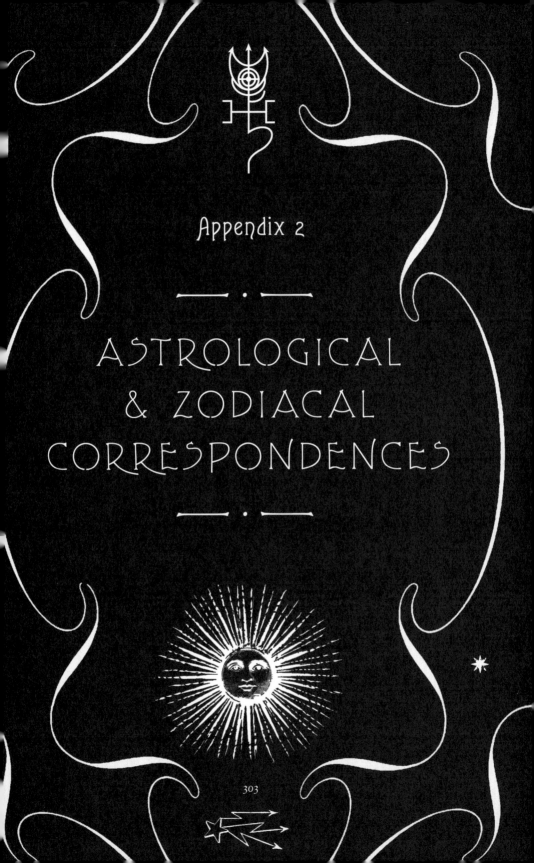

Appendix 2

ASTROLOGICAL
& ZODIACAL
CORRESPONDENCES

Rulerships

Sun: Leo

Moon: Cancer

Mercury: Gemini, Virgo

Venus: Taurus, Libra

Mars: Aries (and Scorpio, classical astrology)

Jupiter: Sagittarius (and Pisces, classical astrology)

Saturn: Capricorn (and Aquarius, classical astrology)

Uranus: Aquarius

Neptune: Pisces

Pluto: Scorpio

Zodiacal Qualities in Brief

Aries: newness, leadership, war, aggression, power, force, courage, confidence, rebirth

Taurus: abundance, luxury, beauty, love, lust, the physical plane, stability, preservation, aesthetics, practicality

Gemini: communication, duality, expression, knowledge, adaptability, commerce, the mental plane, study, the arts

Cancer: emotions, empathy, family, the home, protection, caregiving, psychic powers, intuition

Leo: creation, artistic expression, performance, glamour, rulership, dominance, luxury, confidence, optimism

Virgo: analysis, the mental plane, order, details, intellectualism, study, accomplishment, charity

Libra: balance, justice, diplomacy, partnership, beauty, romance, love

Scorpio: transformation, rebirth, the hidden, the extreme, morality, emotional depth, karma, vengeance

Sagittarius: abundance, goals, learning, philosophy, progression, luck, direction, optimism, fortune

Capricorn: work, goals, ambition, discipline, security, opportunity, the public

Aquarius: eccentricity, art, innovation, change, revolution, individuality, creativity

Pisces: emotions, empathy, psychic power, intuition, the dreaming, imagination, perception, renewal

Symbolism

Aries: Ram

Taurus: Bull

Gemini: The Twins

Cancer: Crab

Leo: Lion

Virgo: The Virgin

Libra: The Scales

Scorpio: Scorpion

Sagittarius: Centaur

Capricorn: Goat (or fish-goat)

Aquarius: Water-bearer

Pisces: Fishes

Days of the Week

Sunday: Sun

Monday: Moon

Tuesday: Mars

Wednesday: Mercury

Thursday: Jupiter

Friday: Venus

Saturday: Saturn

Elements

Earth: Taurus, Virgo, and Capricorn. Earth concerns all things to do with structure: stability, security, sustenance, materials, and physical reality (plant, animal, and mineral).

Air: Gemini, Libra, and Aquarius. Air concerns all things to do with the mind: perception, ideas, intellectuality, study, science, communication, society, and information.

Fire: Aries, Leo, and Sagittarius. Fire concerns all things to do with activity: motivation, invigoration, lust, sexuality, sensuality, passion, confidence, and transformation.

Water: Cancer, Scorpio, and Pisces. Water concerns all things to do with intuition: emotions, love, empathy, compassion, healing, psychic ability, astral travel, sleep, and dreaming.

Dualities

Masculine: Aries, Gemini, Leo, Libra, Sagittarius, Aquarius

Feminine: Taurus, Cancer, Virgo, Scorpio, Capricorn, Pisces

Qualities

Cardinal: Aries, Cancer, Libra, Capricorn

Fixed: Taurus, Leo, Scorpio, Aquarius

Mutable: Gemini, Virgo, Sagittarius, Pisces

Polarities

Aries/Libra

Taurus/Scorpio

Gemini/Sagittarius

Cancer/Capricorn

Leo/Aquarius

Virgo/Pisces

Approximate Solar Tides

Consult a yearly ephemeris for exact dates.

Aries: March 21–April 20

Taurus: April 21–May 21

Gemini: May 22–June 21

Cancer: June 22–July 22

Leo: July 23–August 23

Virgo: August 24–September 22

Libra: September 23–October 23

Scorpio: October 24–November 22

Sagittarius: November 23–December 21

Capricorn: December 22–January 20

Aquarius: January 21–February 18

Pisces: February 19–March 20

Body Part Rulerships

Aries: head

Taurus: neck, throat

Gemini: hands, arms, lungs

Cancer: chest, breasts, stomach

Leo: back, heart

Virgo: nervous system, intestines

Libra: lower back, butt, kidneys

Scorpio: genitals

Sagittarius: livers, thighs, hips

Capricorn: bones, knees, joints

Aquarius: circulatory system, ankles, shins

Pisces: feet

Planetary Qabalistic Sephiroth

Sun: Tiphareth (6)

Moon: Yesod (9)

Mercury: Hod (8)

Venus: Netzach (7)

Earth: Malkuth (10)

Mars: Geburah (5)

Jupiter: Chesed (4)

Saturn: Binah (3)

Uranus: Da'ath (11)

Neptune: Chokmah (2)

Pluto: Kether (1)

Colors

Sun: yellow

Moon: violet

Mercury: orange

Venus: green

Earth: gold, green-brown, ochre, olive, russet, black

Mars: red

Jupiter: blue

Saturn: black

Uranus: none (ineffable)

Neptune: gray

Pluto: white, ineffable

Planetary Hours

Day

	SUN	MON	TUE	WED	THU	FRI	SAT
Hour 1	☉	☽	♂	☿	♃	♀	♄
Hour 2	♀	♄	☉	☽	♂	☿	♃
Hour 3	☿	♃	♀	♄	☉	☽	♂
Hour 4	☽	♂	☿	♃	♀	♄	☉
Hour 5	♄	☉	☽	♂	☿	♃	♀
Hour 6	♃	♀	♄	☉	☽	♂	☿
Hour 7	♂	☿	♃	♀	♄	☉	☽
Hour 8	☉	☽	♂	☿	♃	♀	♄
Hour 9	♀	♄	☉	☽	♂	☿	♃
Hour 10	☿	♃	♀	♄	☉	☽	♂
Hour 11	☽	♂	☿	♃	♀	♄	☉
Hour 12	♄	☉	☽	♂	☿	♃	♀

Night

	SUN	MON	TUE	WED	THU	FRI	SAT
Hour 1	♃	♀	♄	☉	☽	♂	☿
Hour 2	♂	☿	♃	♀	♄	☉	☽
Hour 3	☉	☽	♂	☿	♃	♀	♄
Hour 4	♀	♄	☉	☽	♂	☿	♃
Hour 5	☿	♃	♀	♄	☉	☽	♂
Hour 6	☽	♂	☿	♃	♀	♄	☉
Hour 7	♄	☉	☽	♂	☿	♃	♀
Hour 8	♃	♀	♄	☉	☽	♂	☿
Hour 9	♂	☿	♃	♀	♄	☉	☽
Hour 10	☉	☽	♂	☿	♃	♀	♄
Hour 11	♀	♄	☉	☽	♂	☿	♃
Hour 12	☿	♃	♀	♄	☉	☽	♂

INDEX

311

Great gods of Darkness and Depth, I praise your name!
You are perceived in a hundred thousand faces,
And dictate your musings in a myriad of forms.
To your glory I dedicate this tome.
I do not fear thee—I walk with thee!
Dance with me in the gray fog,
For your names evoke all Mystery.
Have mercy on me, a humble servant who knows not his
deepest self.
Have mercy on me, for I seek your Wisdom preserved
through the ages.
Have mercy on me; for you are Great and I but a drifter.
I petition the blessings of the Old Ones:
Those who are both Creators and Soothsayers;
Those who are both Mighty and Terrible.
Hail, Slumbering and Watchful gods!
Praised be your name!
From your primordial depths, I summon thee.
Arise, Awaken! You are not forgotten.

~O.R.D.N.~

True, without error, certain and most true: that which is above is as that which is below, and that which is below is as that which is above, to perform the miracles of the One Thing. And as all things were from One, by the mediation of One, so from this One Thing come all things by adaptation. Its father is the Sun; its mother is the Moon; the wind carried it in his belly; the nurse thereof is the Earth. It is the father of all perfection and the consummation of the whole world. Its power is integral if it be turned to earth. Thou shalt separate the earth from the fire, the subtle from the gross, gently and with much ingenuity. It ascends from Earth to Heaven and descends again to Earth, and receives the power of the superiors and the inferiors. Thus thou hast the glory of the whole world; therefore let all obscurity flee before thee. This is the strong fortitude of all fortitude, overcoming every subtle thing and penetrating every solid thing. Hence are all wonderful adaptations, of which this is the manner. Therefore I am called Hermes Trismegistus, having the three parts of the philosophy of the whole world. That is finished which I have to say concerning the operation of the Sun.

—The Emerald Tablet of Hermes Trismegistus
(Standard English Translation)